LEFT: An illustration on the cover of Colliers *magazine in 1903 showing the resurrection of Sherlock Holmes at the Reichenbach Falls, where he supposedly died at the end of* The Memoirs.

PAGE 4: From A Study in Scarlet *in 1904: Sherlock Holmes crosses the laboratory to meet Dr Watson for the first time.*

METRO BOOKS
New York

An Imprint of Sterling Publishing
1166 Avenue of the Americas
New York, NY 10036

METRO BOOKS and the distinctive Metro Books logo are trademarks of Sterling Publishing Co., Inc.

Text © 2015 Martin Fido

ISBN 978-1-4351-6081-1

For information about custom editions, special sales, and premium and corporate purchases, please contact Sterling Special Sales at 800-805-5489 or specialsales@sterlingpublishing.com.

Manufactured in Dubai

2 4 6 8 10 9 7 5 3 1

www.sterlingpublishing.com

SHERLOCK

The facts and fiction behind
the world's most famous detective

Martin Fido

METRO BOOKS

New York

CONTENTS

INTRODUCTION

In 1951 a pavilion at the Festival of Britain was called "The Lion and the Unicorn". Its exhibits demonstrated the two supposed sides of the British character: the masterful, unimaginative, industrial and colonial empire-building lion, and the fey, whimsical, romantic, artistic unicorn. Rudyard Kipling and Lewis Carroll. Gladstone and Disraeli. Landseer and Richard Dadd. "Land of Hope and Glory" and the "Enigma Variations".

As the examples show, the paradoxes work well for the late nineteenth century, the period when Arthur Conan Doyle created one of the finest of all Lion and Unicorn combinations: brave, plodding, down-to-earth Dr John H. Watson, the sleepy leonine; and brilliant, nervous, outlandish Sherlock Holmes, the fabulous monster. It is a complementary friendship with useful literary precedents. The eccentric visionary and the all-too-plain man: Don Quixote and Sancho Panza. The difficult tormented soul and his reassuringly decent companion: Hamlet and Horatio. The man we might not really like, and his closest friend who is so amiable that we accept him on trust: Mr Pip and Mr Pocket.

Leonine and unicorn-like qualities co-existed incongruously in individuals of late Victorian and early twentieth-century England. Unprecious anti-aesthete Kipling collected two beautiful little art nouveau mirrors that still hang on the wall of his dining-room in Bateman's, and drew some striking illustrations in Beardsley's manner. The Reverend Charles Lutwidge Dodgson wrote turgid mathematical treatises and even more turgid pamphlets on dull points of Oxford University internal politics and priggish churchy morality. Except in those off-moments when he wrote about the Mock Turtle or the Jabberwock or the White Knight, or more tweely about Bruno and Sylvie and the fairies.

And Sir Arthur Conan Doyle combined in himself characteristics of both Sherlock Holmes and Dr Watson. Like Holmes, he was willing to challenge conventional opinion. And challenge it very eccentrically, becoming the best known proponent of Christian spiritualism: the only educated "intellectual" willing to believe that two adolescent Yorkshire girls lured real fairies into a real wood to take real, unfaked photographs of them. Like a Watson, on the other hand, he saw through medical quackery with blunt common sense, and denounced both an over-touted cure for tuberculosis and supposed rejuvenation treatments with animal glands. Like Holmes he was generally unaffected by vulgar prejudices. He recognised that Sir Roger Casement was honourably entitled to negotiate with Germany for a neutral Ireland during World War I, and that this supposed "treason" was not worsened because Casement's private life happened to be homosexual. Like a Watson, however, Doyle himself was far from neutral, and supported the war fervently once it had started, as he had previously supported the imperial expansionist Boer War. Holmes-like, he tried to refuse the knighthood he was offered for writing an effective response to propaganda atrocity stories put about by continental pro-Boers. Watson-like, he yielded to the argument that stubborn refusal would embarrass the king. And so Conan Doyle became Sir Arthur. (Interestingly Kipling resisted similar pressure, and steadfastly refused to become Sir Rudyard.)

One other great characteristic linked Conan Doyle with his creations. Not in itself either lion-like or unicorn-like, it is simple decency. Not great or sophisticated moral awareness, let alone sanctity. Just a plain ability to tell right from wrong in most situations and act appropriately. Holmes and Watson and Conan Doyle all stood up for right in unpredictable situations. I don't suppose reading a Holmes story has ever made anyone imagine a mean or base act to be clever or "street-smart". Which cannot be claimed with confidence for his hard-boiled thriller successors (James Bond, say, or Mike Hammer), or, indeed, some of his Gothic horror fiction predecessors.

Within the fictions, Conan Doyle created a perfect symbol for the core of Holmesian and Watsonian decency at the heart of a wicked world: 221B Baker Street. Outside that cosy, untidy, Bohemian bachelors' nest the streets are dangerous. Outside the snug lamplit room with its blazing fire the weather is foul. Fog almost hides the other side of Baker Street. Snow turns to slush and freezes, making the pavements treacherous. Inside, the tea-cups rattle reassuringly as Mrs Hudson brings up refreshment. The gazogene and spirit-case stand by if stronger waters are required. In 221B Baker Street we enjoy the safety of childhood with a motherly figure producing endless good breakfasts. We enjoy secure middle-class Victorian prosperity, when two young men of limited means could club together for jolly good digs, and never suffer a day's anxiety about paying their bills as their careers settled down smoothly. The comfort which made the smug world of the Forsytes appealing to harried mid-twentieth-century television viewers is present with a simplified legendary gloss. Holmes and Watson in their snuggery represent good in a world which may be evil. Yet they reduce those two epic absolutes to the common morality to which we can all aspire. And their world holds labelled and recognisable features of the day-to-day world still around us. Oxford Street. The Wigmore Street Post Office. Paddington and Kensington. By contrast, sinister figures lurk south of the river, where an empty house in Brixton hides a corpse; the territory east of London Bridge has its opium den. The placid country is still more sinister than the town. Dartmoor is a place of "black" granite and terrible

CHAPTER OPENER: Benedict Cumberbatch as Sherlock Holmes and Martin Freeman as Dr Watson from the hit BBC television series Sherlock.

bogs; America a land of salt deserts and desolate miners' valleys. The far east yields treasures and murders. Sherlock Holmes ventures out from Baker Street into Adventure Stories and returns victorious to the haven of home.

Recognisable reality framing romance: it was a heady combination which Buchan would imitate as Richard Hannay's adventures took him from familiar London pavements and railings to a remote harbour with thirty-nine steps. James Bond would shift from the daily world of efficient secretaries and West End clubs to mysterious locations dominated by exotic villains. And intellectual superman Holmes supplied romance in himself, anchored to reality by workaday Watson.

It was a formula for success, and deservedly won it.

LEFT: Arthur Conan Doyle, the creator of Sherlock Holmes.

Some Facts and Figures

- There are **56 short stories** and **4 novellas** about Sherlock Holmes.
- **27 murder or homicide cases** are effectively solved, though in **2** there was no murder, only an attack by an animal, and **1** other proved an accidental death.
- Holmes loses **2 clients** he should have protected against murder – **3** if he assumed any responsibility for John Douglas *aka* Birdy Edwards. He himself (it transpired) escaped from "The Final Problem" wherein he was an apparent murder victim.
- The **murderer** or would-be murderer **escapes**, or dies naturally in **4 cases**, is **killed by his own device or his intended victim in 2**, commits **suicide in 1**. Holmes traces **4 murderers he does not hand over to justice** and he and Watson witness **1 homicide they do not report**.
- **10 missing or mysterious persons** are traced or otherwise explained. In **2 of these**, as also in "The Speckled Band", the villain's motive is preventing a daughter or stepdaughter from claiming her **rightful inheritance**.
- **7 cases of theft of valuables or planned robberies fall to Holmes**; also **5 cases centre on blackmail** in one form or another.
- **4 attempts to acquire important state secrets are foiled.**
- **2 unacceptable marriages** are prevented by Holmes's intervention: **one an enforced abduction**, the other an **engagement** to a murderous fortune-hunting cad.
- **1 illicit inspection of a university examination paper** is cleared up.
- **1 break-in** aimed at recovering counterfeiting equipment and counterfeit money is intercepted.
- **1 academic's simian behaviour** is explained.
- In **32 cases** Holmes works (or competes) **with the police**. From Scotland Yard men, there are:
  - **11 cases with Lestrade**, **4 with Gregson** (who collaborates with colleagues in three of his cases: 1 with Lestrade, **1 with Baynes of Surrey**, and **1 with Leverton of Pinkertons**), **4 with Hopkins**, **2 with Bradstreet**, and **2 with Jones** (if Athelney and Peter Jones are the same), **1 apiece** with **Forbes**, **Lanner**, **Morton**, **MacDonald**, **McKinnon** and an **Unnamed Inspector** ("The Three Gables").
  - From other forces there are **Gregory** of Devonshire, **Forrester** of Surrey, **Martin** of Norwich, **White Mason** of Sussex (who collaborates with MacDonald), **Sgt Coventry** of Hants, and **PC Anderson** of Sussex.
- **Mycroft Holmes assists in 3 cases.**
- **Wiggins and the Baker Street Irregulars assist in 2. Simpson, a solo Irregular in 1. Former criminal Shinwell Johnson in 1. Newspaper gossip stringer Langdale Pike in 1.**
- Holmes's "friend and rival" **private detective Mr Barker of the Surrey Shore assists in 1.**

OPPOSITE: Peter Cushing as Sherlock Holmes in the 1968 television series.

CHRONOLOGY

SHERLOCK HOLMES's LIFE (and Watson's)

c.1852 Birth of Watson

1854 Birth of Holmes

c.1870 Watson starts medical studies at London University

c.1873 Holmes goes to University, spending two years in residence and coming down without taking his degree

c.1874 Watson a houseman at St Bartholomew's Hospital, with Stamford as dresser

c.1875 Holmes lodges in Montague St, continuing his studies in the British Museum Library and (without crossing Watson's path) at St Bartholomew's. He takes occasional cases from former Oxonians

1878 Watson graduates MD, University of London, and proceeds to Netley to train as Army Surgeon

c.1879 Holmes takes the case of Musgrave's missing servants and finds the lost crown of Charles I. Also publishes *Upon the Distinction between the Ashes of the Various Tobaccos* (with coloured plates)

1879 Watson joins 5th Northumberland Fusiliers, posted to India to join regiment at the front in Afghanistan

1880 Watson wounded at Battle of Maiwand and invalided out. Holmes starts fulltime practice

1881 Holmes & Watson meet and take 221B Baker Street. Holmes publishes "The Book of Life"

1886 Holmes publishes *On Variations in the Human Ear*

1887 Holmes ill from overwork: probably in consequence of perceiving Moriarty's hand behind so much crime

1888 Watson marries Mary Morstan

1889 Watson in practice in Paddington

1890 Watson in practice in Kensington

1891 Moriarty dies at Reichenbach
Holmes travels the world as Sigerson for the next three years
Mycroft retains 221B

c.1893 Mrs Watson dies

1894 Holmes return to London

c.1895 Dr Verner buys Watson's practice with money secretly advanced by Holmes
Watson returns to 221B

1895 *(Nov or Dec)* Queen Victoria privately bestows an emerald tiepin on Holmes for recovering submarine plans

1896 Homes publishes *On the Polyphonic Motets of Lassus*

1897 Holmes ill again; recuperates in Cornwall

1903 Holmes retires to Sussex to keep and study bees
Watson rumored to be remarried and in practice in Queen Anne St

1907 Holmes identifies deadly *Cyanea capalata* in a deep pool on the Sussex shore

1912–14 Asquith and Grey prevail on Holmes to infiltrate American Fenian movement. Holmes, as Altamont, proceeds to Chicago, Buffalo and Skibereen before becoming enrolled in Von Bork's spy ring

1914 Holmes publishes *Practical Handbook of Bee Culture with some Observations upon the Segregation of the Queen*
In August Holmes summons Watson to help with the capture of Von Bork, one week before war breaks out. Watson rejoins Fusiliers
Undated Publications of Sherlock Holmes: *On the influence of a Trade upon the Form of the Hand, On Tattoo Marks, On Secret Writings* and *On the Dating of Documents*

ARTHUR CONAN DOYLE's LIFE

1859 Birth of Arthur Ignatius Conan Doyle in Edinburgh, son of Charles Altamont Doyle, artist and clerk

1866 Attends Newington Academy, and stays briefly with Mary Burton, sister of Scottish historiographer-royal

1868 Enters Hodder, preparatory school to Stonyhurst

1870 Enters Stonyhurst

1875 Stays with Jesuit community in Feldkirch, Austrian Tyrol. B. C. Waller lodges with Doyles

1876 Starts medical studies at Edinburgh University

1877 Charles Altamount Doyle loses clerkship. Doyle family move to house in Waller's name

1879 ACD's 1st short story "The Mystery of Sassassa Valley" published in *Chambers's Journal*

1880 Cruises the Arctic on the whaler and sealer *Hope*

1881 Graduates MB and cruises West African coast on steamship *Mayumba*. Charles Altamont Doyle begins alcoholism treatments. Mary Foley Doyle and youngest children move to B. C. Waller's estate at Masongill

1882 George Turnavine Budd engages and sacks ACD in Plymouth. ACD starts general practice in Portsmouth

1885 Marries Louise ("Touie") Hawkins

1887 *A Study in Scarlet*

1889 *The Sign of Four*
      Mary Louise Conan Doyle born

1890 Condemns Koch's tuberculin

1891 Moves to London as eye specialist. "A Scandal in Bohemia" starts Holmes "Adventures" in *The Strand*. Abandons medicine for fulltime writing

1892 Alleyne Kingsley Doyle born

1893 Doyles visit Switzerland and see Reichenbach Falls. Louise declared consumptive. Charles Altamont Doyle dies
      ACD joins Society for Psychical Research

1894 Lecture tour in America

1895 Visits Egypt

1896 Falls in love with Jean Leckie

1897 Moves to Hindhead

1900 Joins Langman's Hospital in S. African War. William Gillette plays Holmes on London stage

1901 Writes "The War in South Africa, Its Cause and Conduct"

1902 *The Hound of the Baskervilles*. ACD knighted for Boer War pamphlet

1902 "The Empty House" brings Holmes to life again in *The Strand*

1906 Death of Louise Doyle. ACD takes up Edalji case

1907 Marriage to Jean Leckie

1912 Campaigns over Congo, submarine threat and Slater. *The Lost World*

1914 Organises local volunteer force and embarks on *History of the British Campaign in France and Flanders*

1915 *The Valley*

1918 Kingsely and Innes (ACD's brother) die. *The New Revelation* published, starting ACD's Spiritualist campaign

1920 Friendship with Houdini. Australian lecture tour. Cottingley fairies incident publicised

1922 Spirtualist propagandising in America

1927 *The Casebook of Sherlock Holmes*

1930 Death of Conan Doyle

1
THE LIFE OF SHERLOCK HOLMES

The biographer faces a problem. The essential primary source lies in the case histories published by Watson. But Watson was extravagantly careless about dates. His claim that a case happened in a given year can rarely be relied upon. In one notorious instance he remarks that a client reported the mystery as starting eight weeks previously, and then places that starting date a good seven months too early!

He doesn't even remember the year of his own marriage correctly. There is no doubt at all that he first met Miss Mary Morstan when she consulted Holmes in the late summer or early autumn of 1888 – "nearly ten years" after 3 December 1878 in her own words, though typically, Watson specifies two different months. Yet Watson places another case in the spring of that year while recalling it as taking place after he had wooed and wed Miss Morstan and left Baker Street. And in yet another he describes visiting Baker Street during his wife's absence, though the client placed the events a full year before Watson had actually met her!

Astonishingly, Holmes proved an even worse chronologist when in retirement he wrote up two of his own cases. For in complaining about the period when Watson deserted him for a wife, he inadvertently dated it to 1903, a decade after the doctor had been bereaved! These lapses have led some scholars to postulate speculatively that Watson married three times!

Clearly both men were impressionistic in their dating. This is confirmed by Watson's tendency to recollect slangy dialogue and approve illustrators' sets and costumes which reflect his dates of composition and publication rather than the dates when cases actually occurred. Holmes retired in 1903, which makes it quite implausible that he ever uttered a professional threat in the words, "It won't be funny for you, Steve, if I get after you". Watson, recalling "The Three Gables" case in 1927, was remembering the *impression* of up-to-date forcefulness made by the more pedantic language Holmes would have used in 1902.

Lamentably, there are no objective documents against which to check inaccuracies. The registers have been purged of papers relating to Sherlock Holmes. Officialdom has tampered with the birth certificate held at the Sherlock Holmes Museum in Baker Street. Every detail except the name is erroneous. The hand of Mycroft Holmes and the Secret Service is apparent. The unofficial agent who captured Von Bork deserved no less concealment than the beneficiary of a Witness Protection Programme or a covert officer in Her Majesty's Military Intelligence. And so the powerful arm of bureaucracy has swept away the paper-trail that would have given us unquestioned facts about Sherlock Holmes.

Brilliant researchers have examined almanacs and weather reports and emerged with detailed chronologies of Holmes's cases. I cannot compete with their learning, and they do not always support one another's conclusions. I am sure they and their successors will correct me on many points of detail. But apologetically, impressionistically, I offer a life of Sherlock Holmes sketched in around the few certain dates ...

Education and early years

Sherlock Holmes was born in 1854, in a small country squire's family. He never tells us where, but since he thought of the Peak district as the North of England – and he did not, like Arnold Bennett, exaggerate his own provincialism – we may deduce that he was a southerner. He was unfamiliar with Dartmoor and once loosely described Herefordshire as "the West country". So it is safe to assume he was not a west countryman. This becomes especially evident when he describes Sussex as "the south west" at the outset of "The Five Orange Pips" case. No one from west of Hampshire would ever do so.

In fact, there seems little doubt that Holmes hailed from Sussex. He instantly recognised Sussex clay and chalk on John Openshaw's toe-caps. In all other cases where muddy boots gave him a clue it came from newly turned earth in his immediate vicinity, like that in the roadworks outside the Wigmore Street Post Office whence he deduced that Watson had just sent a telegram. Moreover his retirement to Sussex suggests a return to his home county.

The Holmes family were not dully conventional: they did not name their boys James and John or George and Charles, but Mycroft and Sherlock. Presumably family names, these also possibly lay on the Holmes side. Sherlock's grandmother was sister to one of the Vernets (three French painters, fl. 1689–1863), and her connections who settled in England changed their name to Verner. Other than that, we know nothing about his forbears.

The Holmes boys were both tall, with fine retentive memories and remarkable powers of observation and deduction. But in other ways they were very different. Mycroft, inclined to corpulence, was pathologically lethargic. Sherlock was thin, febrile and active. Mycroft had a gift for figures, and never went out for entertainment. Sherlock learned the violin and enjoyed nothing more than a concert or the opera. Yet the brothers were very close. In adult life, Mycroft restricted his movements almost entirely to perambulation from his lodgings to work nearby in Whitehall, and thence to the equally close-at-hand Diogenes Club, where he was guaranteed a social life rather less effusive than a Trappist's. But he broke this pattern willingly at his younger brother's need. Once he actually took a hansom cab to reach Baker Street before Sherlock could walk there. Still more amazing, at Sherlock's request he once muffled himself up in the guise of a cabman and drove Watson from the Lowther Arcade to Victoria. He was the only person allowed to know that Sherlock survived his wrestling match at Reichenbach in 1891. And he kept up his brother's rooms at 221B Baker Street for the next three years.

Two such individualist lads would have done better with private tutors than at public school. We have no idea which educated them. We know that Sherlock's geography was neglected, since he had to send for a map to confirm that Ballarat is in Australia, and swallowed his *Gazetteer's* misinformation that Andaman Islanders are hideous, indigenous cannibal pygmies. Notoriously he boasted of not knowing the solar system.

His Latin was up to Responsions (Oxford and Cambridge admissions), since he attended university. Watson does not record which, and since Holmes used the Oxford term "quadrangle" and the Cambridge term "court" almost indiscriminately, there has been debate ever since. The strong likelihood of Oxford rests on his describing Cambridge as "inhospitable", though Dorothy L. Sayers adduced a complicated argument to prove him a Cambridge man. On his way to chapel one morning he was bitten by his friend Trevor's bull terrier, and Miss Sayers argued that since dogs

ABOVE: A view of the entrance of St Bartholomew's Hospital where Dr Watson and Holmes met.

OPPOSITE: From Conan Doyle's Adventures of Sherlock Holmes: *Mycroft Holmes sitting in his brother Sherlock's house as Holmes and Dr John Watson enter.*

are forbidden in college, Holmes and Trevor must have been in digs, which would apply to first year Cambridge but not Oxford men. Miss Sayers's argument, alas, may be vitiated by the application of twentieth-century experience. Surely in 1870 most colleges housed all their undergraduates, so that Trevor's dog was illegally kept? The phrase "down to chapel", too, suggests rooms on a college staircase, and not across town. Holmes, we conclude, was an Oxford man.

Which college? Well, a man of his intellectual rigour would have preferred Lincoln, whose Rector, Mark Pattison, was trying to drag Oxford up to the scholarly level of the German universities. But Sherlock's acquaintance with aristocratic Reginald Musgrave as a contemporary undergraduate slightly militates against Lincoln, which has never been very posh. In fact, since Holmes is above all else "effortlessly superior" he may have been a Balliol man. Whichever of the two was his college, he was an oddball, and in his second year his curious deductive methods attracted attention across the university.

A vacation visit to the Trevor family where he saw a case of blackmail and interpreted a coded letter showed him his *métier*. And then he went down after two years without completing his degree. Oxford was still "a trade union for classics". Science, which Holmes favoured, made pathetically little headway. And so he took his interest in inorganic chemistry to London. At St Bartholomew's Hospital's chemistry laboratory he made (organic) experiments to find a test for bloodstains, and in its mortuary he improved upon the experiments undertaken (on rabbits) at Edinburgh after the Burke and Hare case in 1829, and thwacked dead bodies with a stick to see whether they bruised. He probably paid for his education out of his patrimony; we never hear of his parents' being alive. He pursued branches of knowledge like anatomy and the properties of poisons which would be useful to a consulting detective. He made no attempt to graduate and become a doctor, and he never met a houseman called Watson whose years might just have overlapped his.

He lodged in Montague Street, and doubtless spent time in the British Museum Library opposite. He studied criminal history, but paid little attention to the private lives of his subjects. He thought the poisoners Palmer and Pritchard were "at the heads of their profession", when in fact they were very mediocre GPs. He thought Charlie Peace the murderous cat-burglar was a violin "virtuoso", which he wasn't, and the forging and poisoning dilettante hack Thomas Griffith Wainewright "was no mean artist", which he was.

OPPOSITE: The British Museum in London, which was near enough to Holmes's lodgings for him to study in its library.

LEFT: Reginald Musgrave, a college friend of Holmes.

DR JOHN H. WATSON

By the end of 1880 Holmes was ready to leave Montague Street and embark on his 23 years of active professional life. He had written the monograph on tobacco ash which would grow famous alongside him. He had undertaken detective work for three former undergraduates and had been down from Oxford four years when the old Lincoln or Balliol man Reginald Musgrave MP engaged him to trace his philandering butler and jilted maid. Finding King Charles I's lost crown during this investigation brought Holmes rapid professional standing. By the time he was 28 years old, his clients included the ablest of Scotland Yard's CID, Gregson and Lestrade. A decent-sized consulting room was now more important than easy access to the British Museum. And Holmes learned that ideal digs were available in Baker Street, with a large sitting-room and at least two bedrooms.

There was one drawback. Neither Holmes's private resources nor his income from detective consultancy would stretch to the higher rental. He was as prudent financially as he was daring in the face of physical danger. So he looked about for a possible room-mate to take the second bedroom and share the rent.

Thus it was that a young doctor or medical student called Stamford came into the chemistry lab at Bart's on the memorable morning when Holmes completed his search for a reliable precipitant blood test, and introduced a possible solution.

RIGHT: Holmes and Watson travelling to Devon.

OPPOSITE: A painting by the American artist Richard Caton Woodville Jr featuring the British Royal Horse Artillery saving their guns from the Afghans at the Battle of Maiwand during the Second Afghan War. This is where Dr Watson was injured.

Dr John H. Watson, late assistant surgeon to the Fifth Northumberland Fusiliers, had a wound pension which was not covering his living expenses, so that he needed to retrench by finding reasonably priced accommodation. Stamford had been Watson's dresser at Bart's, where Watson had evidently served his term as house-surgeon.

Though by no means intellectual, Watson had gone so far as to take his London University MD in 1878, thus giving himself a qualification which in England – unlike Scotland or America – suggested an ambition to rise higher than general practice. The humble MRCS sufficed for Sir Henry Baskerville's friend Dr Mortimer. Wisely, Watson did not in the end strain his brain as a consultant or an academic. Instead he went to the training school at Netley and took the army surgeon's course. He was well fitted for an overseas military career, having already visited three continents and learned the ways of their women. (He would always have an eye for a pretty girl or a lovely lady.) He had seen the gold diggings at Ballarat, where, in the year of Holmes's birth, rebellious Australian miners erected and defended the Eureka Stockade in protest against a colonial governor's extortionate taxation. Watson was two in 1854, so he did not see that birth pang of Antipodean democracy. But it seems probable that, like his friend and subsequent literary agent Dr Conan Doyle, he passed his student vacations adventurously, signing on as a ship's doctor to travel the world.

From Netley he was posted to India in 1879, and when he reached Bombay it was to find the Second Afghan War already raging. He joined his regiment at the front and was wounded in the Battle of Maiwand, where he would have been killed had not his loyal orderly brought him away on a packhorse. The jezail bullet in his shoulder which grazed an artery and left a stiff arm that Sherlock Holmes instantly detected, subsequently caused mysterious trouble in his leg, afflicting him with a temporary limp and the delusion that he was wounded in the lower limb. Happily he recovered fully in due course, returning to his natural fitness and athleticism.

But by 1881 he was invalided out of the army, believing himself permanently handicapped. He returned to London with a pension. Not till the very end of his life, in the last Holmes case he was to memorialise, could Watson bring himself to admit why he failed to live on the government's generous 11/6d (57p) a day. 5/9d of it (28p) was going straight into the hands of the bookmakers. Watson was addicted to backing the nags!

It was his only moral weakness. He was a burly giant who always perceived the 5ft 10in Metropolitan Police Inspector Lestrade as "a little man", whether "rat-faced" or "a wiry bulldog". It would seem that Lestrade's jowls and nose spread sideways as he aged. Holmes, standing over 6ft, always seemed taller still to Watson by virtue of his lean build. Watson himself had a rugby player's muscularity and had played for Blackheath before going abroad.

He was an officer and a gentleman. Queen's regulations made him grow a full moustache in the army. All commissioned officers had to. He had been to a public school, and showed its high moral influence, for Holmes once remarked that he was incapable of dissimulation. He never tells us his school, but it certainly was not Arnold's reformed Rugby, since it was still so undisciplined that Watson joined a mob of little boys in chivying "Tadpole" Phelps – two years his senior – all round the quad with a cricket stump. The bullying scene is painful, but Watson's presence at the heart of the crowd was prophetic – the immature boy in the quad who was to become the mature man in the street. Phelps's meekly forgiving nature when he sought Watson's – or Holmes's – help in later life showed exemplary good public school manners, though it is impossible to believe that Watson had the mental ability demanded by Winchester, the "Manners Makyth Man" school par excellence.

Though bullying was prevalent at Eton, it, too, is unlikely to have been Watson's alma mater. It spawned the master criminals John Crew and Colonel Sebastian Moran during his lifetime, and Holmes would surely have twitted him on his fellow Old Boys had Watson worn the blue striped tie.

Holmes was far too excited by his discovery of the new blood test to pay proper attention to his new companion. Though Watson claimed to keep a bull-pup, Holmes never asked the searching questions that mysterious animal's instant and absolute disappearance warranted. He had no suspicion that the slightly formal doctor would become his chronicler and a bestseller by virtue of that. Certainly neither man imagined that they would become such close friends that they would forever be remembered as a couple like Laurel and Hardy or prunes and custard.

221B BAKER STREET

Surely 221B Baker Street was the most famous bachelor lodgings in the world? Yet letters so addressed when Holmes and Watson moved in would not have arrived. As learned historical topographers have demonstrated, the section of road named Baker Street has doubled in length since 1881, when it ran only from Portman Square to Paddington Street and the house numbers did not stretch beyond the 80s. The same topographers are sure that the reiterated number 221B was not created by Watson's shaky memory or the illegible handwriting to which his errors of dating are commonly attributed. They believe that he wished to conceal the actual address, no doubt wishing to spare Mrs Hudson, the landlady, the hordes of Japanese tourists and raucous-voiced walking tour guides who infest the district today. The easy accessibility of Wigmore Street and Oxford Street, the presence of a plane tree in the back yard, and the proximity of an empty house reached through back alleys and courts on the other side of the road have led to general agreement that the original "221B" was toward the lower – southern – end of the street and on the western side. Different numbers have been proposed by different scholars, but on one point there is unanimity. It is the only house in flat-fronted Baker Street that has ever been described as having a bow window in the first floor. Which will make it instantly identifiable if anybody ever comes across it again.

BELOW: Sherlock Holmes's sitting room at 221B Baker Street.

Seventeen stairs opposite the street door led up to the floor with the large and comfortable sitting-room that attracted Holmes. This had markedly large windows fronting the street, one of them that unique bay, which had an entrance somehow connecting to Holmes's bedroom on the same floor. Watson's bedroom and at least two lumber-rooms were up another floor.

In the wall opposite the sitting-room door was the fireplace on whose mantelpiece Holmes secured his correspondence with a jack-knife. The friends' armchairs faced each other across the fire. They had a breakfast table and an upright basket chair noticed by Sidney Paget, their approved portraitist, which Watson may have removed later to his marital home. There was a large table in the corner which Holmes covered with flasks and retorts for his chemistry experiments. There were shelves for reference books. And shelves for the ever-expanding encyclopaedia of Holmes's own selection of cuttings. These found **Adler, Irene**, nestling between **Adler, Rabbi**, indeed, the *Chief* Rabbi in the 1880s, who may or may not have been friendly to Holmes, as he was definitely a personal friend of Dr Robert Anderson, head of that Scotland Yard CID about which Holmes was prone to be so rude; and an unnamed staff-commander whose precise identity and monograph on deep sea fishes have escaped the most scrupulous research since the unfortunate loss of Holmes's invaluable index.

That untidy accumulation of cuttings, building up over months until Holmes had a clear-out and pasted some in albums and stuffed others in a trunk in the lumber-room, rather annoyed Watson. Still more off-putting was the way that

Holmes, when in one of his queer humours, would sit in an arm-chair, with his hair-trigger and a hundred Boxer cartridges, and proceed to adorn the opposite wall with a patriotic V.R. done in bullet-pocks.

That verb "would sit", conveying that the offence happened frequently, speaks volumes for Watson's tolerance of his friend's eccentricities!

But then, Watson rather plumed himself that he and Holmes were "Bohemian" — a word which suggested trendy artistic rebellion against dull social proprieties. And so, like "beatnik", or "hippie" or "alternative society", it could be used to justify indolent scruffiness as a revolt against boring bourgeois taste. Watson, whose reading was as likely as not to be a yellow-backed pulp novel designed to pass the railway traveller's time, read Henri Murger's *Vie de Bohême* in Baker Street — some forty years after it was *le dernier cri*, though a decade before Puccini gave it new fame as an opera. Probably the rather innocent free-love practised by the young intellectuals was the main attraction for Watson, who found Holmes's habits of keeping cigars in the coal scuttle and tobacco in the toe of an old Persian slipper too raffish for his taste. And as a doctor he simply disapproved of the 7%

OPPOSITE: Holmes and Watson, elegantly attired for the city, stroll along Oxford Street.

solution of cocaine Holmes injected – legally, if unconventionally in the 1880s – as a cure for *ennui*. For Watson, at heart, was conventional. His amusement was billiards, played with a scion of the Thurston family, who manufactured billiard tables, whereas Holmes's was classical music or various forms of amateur scholarship. Sherlock Holmes's untidiness contrasted with personal fastidiousness. He was clean as a cat, and except when knocking about Baker Street in dressing-gowns – grey, mouse-coloured, or resplendent purple as Watson observed – or travelling to the country in an overcoat as full and sweeping as a lady's ballgown, which Sidney Paget sketched a couple of times, he was, as Paget also observed, almost as perfectly tailored as the elegant and cynical lawyer-politician F. E. Smith. "Chumming" with Watson – the word was the old India hand's term for sharing digs – matured Holmes from the polite companion who called Watson "Doctor" and was slow to reveal his unusual occupation, through the

genially patronising friend who addressed the doctor as "My boy" after Watson had married, to the phase of teasing the good doctor habitually and pretending that his down-to-earth common sense represented some unusual obtuseness. As one might expect of a fellow-countryman of Beatrice and Benedick's creator – far more convincing lovers than Romeo and Juliet – Holmes's jocularity masked ever-deepening affection for his friend: a love which might truly have led him to murder "Killer" Evans in "The Three Garridebs" case, had that villain's bullet done more than graze Watson's thigh. And the progression, as often happens in Watson's historiography, is more precisely marked in his order of publication than his dating of events.

And so the cosy bachelor-life was set up in the years before Watson's marriage, and re-established after he was widowed.

SETTLING DOWN

In 1881, Holmes's article "The Book of Life" appeared, unsigned, in a journal Watson read at Baker Street. When he remarked that it seemed twaddle, Holmes admitted his authorship, and although he never explained just how a man might deduce the existence of Niagara or the Atlantic from a single drop of water, he did for the first time acknowledge his occupation, and gave his room-mate a demonstration of "the science of deduction". This was a skill he shared with Mycroft. Both brothers observed minute details of a man's or woman's appearance or possessions, and were often able to reach a handful of telling conclusions about their occupations, recent travels, or situation in life. Watson was immensely impressed, though the trick rarely played any important part in solving a case for Holmes, and in the end, if we are allowed to select our objects, most of us can recognise such tell-tale features as British Legion lapel badges, a few Old School or regimental ties, odd socks, shoes with lifts or unfashionably comfortable uppers, white poppies around Remembrance Day, or the pallid, untanned line round a finger from which a wedding ring has been removed. And these are the kinds of clues on which Sherlock based his skill.

Detective consultancy explained the curiously spotty nature of Holmes's education. Watson remarked that his knowledge of anatomy was "Accurate but Unsystematic". This was perhaps generous. In later years, noting the (psychosomatic?) limp mysteriously induced by the bullet in Watson's shoulder, Holmes commiserated with him on his damaged Achilles tendon! But Holmes gave excellent justification for neither knowing nor caring whether Ptolemy or Copernicus described the movement of the earth and stars aright. And he was probably pulling Watson's leg when he pretended not to care about philosophy or know who Carlyle was. For not only did he misquote and improve upon the sage's definition of genius as "transcendent capacity of taking trouble", but seven years later he would refer Watson to the Swiss philosopher Richter as Carlyle's source, and recommend him to read Winwood Reade's magisterial defence of scientific theistic agnosticism.

Once Watson knew Sherlock was a detective, he was allowed to see him detecting. First in the Eugene Drebber or Jefferson Hope case. Watson was understandably impressed to learn that his friend

BELOW: An illustration from the story "The Adventure of the Norwood Builder" in The Return of Sherlock Holmes, *showing police Inspector Lestrade with Sherlock Holmes and Dr Watson.*

had published a monograph on cigar ash and could distinguish any known brand at a glance. He was not to know how famous this rare illustrated pamphlet would become and how avidly sought by collectors. He noted that Holmes's knowledge of London was such that he could identify the route a cab took through darkened streets. He discovered that detailed examination of the crime scene as early as possible was crucial to Holmes's methods, and learned that a man's height could be calculated from his stride between footprints. He met the "Baker Street Irregulars", the band of street urchins Holmes kept in his pay to trace and follow vehicles or vessels he wanted to find in London. Later in his, career, Holmes could people a street with a well-rehearsed crowd if he needed one, rather as a director would a stage.

Holmes rather despised the police, Watson learned. He accused Scotland Yard Inspectors Lestrade and Gregson of forming theories and acting on them without

assessing the evidence, though he thought of them the best of that rather poor bunch, the Metropolitan CID. Of course, by modern standards Holmes was equally at fault in rapidly concluding that the body in Lauriston Gardens had been poisoned by the cab-driver who drove the man there, and that the motive had to do with the woman's wedding ring lying on the body. Gregson was right to follow up Drebber's hatmaker and learn from him the dead man's London address. Lestrade carried out a vital task in finding the whereabouts of Drebber's secretary Stangerson. Both discovered pieces of the puzzle that confirmed Jefferson Hope's subsequent confession. But Holmes's methods put an occupation and a name to the murderer, and correctly identified the means he used. It was a little hard on a man starting out in independent practice that the Scotland Yard men got all the credit. Several years later, Watson published an account of this first case he had observed. And in an arty-Bohemian imitation of James McNeill Whistler's practice of naming obvious portraits "Arrangement in [this or that colour]", he called it *A Study in Scarlet*.

In 1883 Holmes prevented the terrifying Dr Grimesby Roylott from murdering his surviving stepdaughter as he had already killed her sister. Watson's incompetent dating has obscured the strong probability that another case with a similar motive came before Holmes in this period, when Miss Violet Hunter was employed, nominally as a governess, but actually to impersonate the incarcerated Alice Rucastle whose father was determined to retain control of her inheritance. No wonder Holmes regarded Miss Mary Sutherland's case as "a trite one" when that stepdaughter asked him to trace her lost fiancé Hosmer Angel in 1888!

ABOVE: Colin Jeavons as Inspector Lestrade in the 1980s television series.

OPPOSITE: Professor James Moriarty, the "Napoleon of crime".

Two other important cases taking place before Watson married and left Baker Street in 1888 were like the Jefferson Hope case in that they involved secret societies in America. Both took place toward the end of the period. In both of them Holmes had the misfortune to lose his client.

The 1887 case of "The Five Orange Pips" brought him up against survivors of the Ku Klux Klan, which had been disbanded in 1871 and was almost forgotten until its revival as a xenophobic, anti-Catholic, white supremacist society in 1915. Few people knew much about it, and Holmes's *Encyclopaedia* proved as fine a mine of misinformation as his *Gazetteer* when it told him the name derived from the click of a rifle being cocked. It was actually an illiterate mispronunciation of the Greek "kuklos", meaning circle. How and why Colonel Elias Openshaw betrayed the KKK was never made clear, but punishment for his personal sin of aggressive racism was visited on two more generations, despite Holmes's accurate calculation of the ship on which the racist avengers sailed.

Soon after that he proved that "murdered" John Douglas had survived after killing the assassin sent after him by the lawless terrorist Scowrers of Pennsylvania, whose destruction he had encompassed twenty years earlier when he worked for Pinkerton's Detective Agency. But Holmes's earnest advice to Douglas to leave England at once could not save him. For a still more sinister hand than that of the Scowrers had become involved: Professor Moriarty's.

MORIARTY AND MARY MORSTAN

In later years, Watson would remember wrongly that he heard of Moriarty only after his marriage. In fact Holmes told him about the "Napoleon of crime" when he was summoned to Birlstone Manor to investigate the murder of John Douglas. The petty criminal using the alias Porlock had warned of the threat to Douglas, and Holmes explained that he suborned Porlock to keep him informed of his master's doings.

James Moriarty was precocious. His treatise on the Binomial Theorem, published when he was twenty-one, won him immediate appointment to the Chair of Mathematics at one of the smaller universities; at that time probably Birmingham, Bristol, Durham or Southampton. His book *The Dynamics of an Asteroid* was so difficult that scholarly journals were hard put to find competent reviewers. He seemed set for a brilliant career, though he modestly made no attempt to move his European reputation to Oxbridge, the continent, or the Scottish universities. Holmes warned the abler men at Scotland Yard that Moriarty was behind some of the most baffling crimes confronting them, but they dismissed this as a bee in the detective's bonnet. Only young Inspector MacDonald paid attention when Holmes told him the picture he had once seen in Moriarty's study was a Greuze with a possible value of £40,000. The Moriarty family was respectable but not rich. One of the professor's brothers was a west country railway stationmaster. And the professor himself drew a salary of just £700 a year from his post. Herein lay Moriarty's genius: keeping himself out of sight and apparently living within the means of a relatively poor provincial professor, while hiding money in six different British bank accounts, and doubtless huge deposits in Switzerland. He paid the big-game hunter and card-sharp Colonel Moran a higher salary than the Prime Minister's to serve as his criminal chief of staff.

It has been speculated, probably rightly, that it was the stress of working against the only crook with a mind to match his own that made Holmes ill in 1887, when the Netherland-Sumatra Company case and the schemes of Baron Maupertin

(fronting for Moriarty, no doubt) left him ill on the continent, and he went to recuperate with Watson's friend Colonel Hayter in Reigate. Some time after this, however, Holmes struck his first successful blow against Moriarty, because disquieting rumours led to his resigning his chair and moving to London as a humble coach for would-be army officers. And we know of no one but Holmes, Watson and MacDonald who had the faintest suspicion of the professor's true nature.

But before Holmes and Moriarty confronted each other overtly, the bachelor domesticity of 221B Baker street was shattered. In the summer of 1888 Miss Mary Morstan came to Holmes with the problem of her father's disappearance ten years' previously; the six pearls sent to her anonymously over the past six years, and the anonymous note of the morning asking her to be at the third pillar of the Lyceum Theatre that night. Watson was instantly smitten by that simply but elegantly dressed little lady, with her blonde head in its plain grey turban. On the night he met her he found himself babbling about his adventures in Afghanistan and telling her how a musket looked into his tent and he fired a double-barrelled tiger-cub at it, for all the world like *Martin Chuzzlewit's* John Westlock smitten with Ruth Pinch as he watches her cook, and solemnly telling her brother that a pudding came into his office and took a chair.

By the end of the adventure Watson and Miss Morstan were both relieved that the ill-gotten Agra treasure had sunk in the Thames, for both knew a man of his honour would never marry a woman rich enough to keep him. Holmes's distaste at his friend's yielding to emotion was unconcealed, even though he admired Miss Morstan's ready detective instincts in retaining just the right papers of her father's to solve the Agra treasure mystery. We may be more impressed by her wit on 10 June 1889, when speaking to her friend Kate Whitney in Watson's presence she called him James. Although Miss Dorothy Sayers speculated that this was because his middle name was Hamish, and he preferred its Anglicised form to his baptismal John, I think we can be sure that so old a friend as Mrs Whitney was being invited to share a private (if rather untimely) jest. With a husband who could never remember just when they had married, or which limb of his own carried an Afghan bullet, surely Mrs Watson had said merrily to her friend, "He'll forget his own name, next! I'll show you!" And, indeed, wool-gathering Watson didn't turn a hair when referred to by a name that was not his.

Still, Mary was the perfect wife. She not only tolerated the "Captain Vague" aspect of Watson, she never objected when Sherlock Holmes summoned him away

at a moment's notice for some adventure. And what an excellent husband he was! He was quite imperturbable when required to go down to the East End in the middle of the night and collect Elias Whitney from the noisome opium den, which was equipped with an oubliette into the Thames, where he made his second discovery of Holmes's truly amazing skill in make-up and disguise. The first had come during Miss Morstan's case, when neither he nor Athelney Jones detected Holmes in the guise of an old seaman. In the opium den Holmes exhibited the astounding ability to create and erase wrinkles all over his face with a simple alteration of his muscles. But as he had told Watson when discarding his previous disguise, this was necessary as his steady work during the 1880s meant that some of the criminal classes were beginning to recognise him.

Actually he was making useful friends in low places. Not only was Moriarty's underling "Porlock" in his pay, but Holmes was the associate of low-life boxers, fighting three rounds with the bruiser McMurdo (who subsequently became Bartholomew Sholto's bodyguard) on the occasion of his benefit night at Alison's rooms in 1884. And, in the year that Scotland Yard was ridiculed for unsuccessfully hunting Jack the Ripper with champion bloodhounds, Holmes knew just where to borrow a mutt that had the skill they lacked and which could follow a trail over city pavements. Though Toby did have the advantage of a quarry who trod in creosote.

TO REICHENBACH AND BACK

As bohemianism over-ripened into *fin-de-siècle* decadence, Holmes seemed a more conservative, establishment figure. A famous man. Important to the state. His first case with constitutional ramifications was recovering the missing corner of "The Beryl Coronet". A national – nay, an *imperial*, treasure. It was mutilated in an attempted theft after the second largest private bank in London accepted it from the Prince of Wales as security for a £50,000 loan. Mr Holder, the banker, was too discreet to ask why his client needed this sum. But we may guess that either the Prince backed himself imprudently in a game of baccarat, or his son and heir, Prince Albert Victor, was being blackmailed over the homosexual brothel that he frequented. Royalty gave Holmes no mark of recognition for keeping the scandal out of the papers; the Prince may never have known how nearly he lost the state trinket he pawned.

The royal family should have been even more grateful that Holmes never revealed the descent of the Old Etonian and Oxonian master-criminal John Crew, illegitimate grandson of one of George III's squalid offspring. Crew's small, white hand betokened royal blood; his misplaced lordly superiority was reminiscent of Edward VII's sudden retreats to lofty heights of frozen dignity.

The king of Bohemia was grateful when Holmes told him that there was no longer any danger of his former mistress releasing a compromising photograph of the two of them. After refusing an emerald snake-ring, Holmes accepted a gold

OPPOSITE: Holmes and Moriarty wrestle on the path beside the Reichenbach Falls.

and amethyst snuff-box as a reward. A "compromising" photograph in 1888 was unlikely to be lubricious, any more than the politician who subsequently tried to steal Watson's notes on his misdeeds with a lighthouse and a trained cormorant would have been "sleazy" by the standards of today.

Another royal client was the king of Scandinavia. And the reigning family of Holland gave Holmes a ring for handling yet another delicate matter. Holmes boasted discreetly of his important clients, though he didn't much like aristocrats or foreign royalty.

It was Watson's schooldays friendship with "Tadpole" Phelps that brought Sherlock his first cabinet client: Phelps's uncle Lord Holdhurst, the Foreign Secretary. Contrary to wild speculation and fiction-writers' suppositions, the Home Office did not ask Holmes to catch Jack the Ripper at the end of 1888, and he did not soil his hands with pursuing that sordid sex-maniac. Instead, his dramatic visit to Baskerville Hall on Dartmoor at this period became one of his best-known exploits, thanks to Watson's masterly re-telling of the story.

But in 1891 Sherlock Holmes disappeared. When Colonel James Moriarty tried to rescue his brother's good name – which also happened to be James! – the world quickly learned from Watson that Sherlock Holmes finally persuaded Scotland Yard to arrest the Moriarty gang that April. They knew that Holmes and Watson went to the Continent to evade the professor's assassination attempt, hiding behind luggage on Canterbury East station so as not to be spotted by Moriarty's pursuing special train.

In May, Moriarty tracked Holmes to Switzerland and lured Watson away with a false appeal for medical help. For several years, the world believed that Sherlock Holmes and Professor Moriarty met on the path overhanging the Reichenbach Falls, wrestled together and tumbled to their death. The public mourned the loss of the greatest detective the world had known. Many wore crepe bands in his memory. Only Mycroft knew that Holmes's "final" note, abandoned stick and cigarette case were a blind to cast other Moriartians off the scent.

For Holmes's mastery of Japanese baritsu wrestling enabled him to elude the professor's grasp and leave the master criminal to die alone. Yet he instantly found that Moriarty was not the only survivor of Scotland Yard's round-up. The gang's second-in-command, Colonel Moran, had accompanied his boss to Reichenbach, and started pelting rocks down at Holmes as soon as it was safe to do so. Sherlock had to go deeper to ground for a longer period than he had anticipated.

Mycroft remitted money to him and kept the rent paid on the rooms in Baker Street. Sherlock adopted the name Sigerson and went to Tibet, a country closed to the outside world since 1791. The Dalai Lama being a child in 1891, "Sigerson" visited the regent, whom he loosely described and misspelled as "the head Llama", and anticipated Heinrich Harrer in giving better accounts of the land than Mme Blavatsky's theosophical fantasies.

From Tibet, "Sigerson" crossed Meso-potamia and, as daring as Sir Richard Burton, followed his visit to the forbidden city of Lhasa with an even more dangerous visit (for an infidel) to holy Mecca. While in the House of Islam, the agnostic Hajji went to the Sudan and visited the ruins of Khartoum, abandoned and destroyed after General Gordon was killed there in 1885. The alcoholic, imperialist and evangelical Gordon was a hero to Watson, who owned pictures of him and the almost equally scandal-tainted evangelical American anti-slavery preacher Henry Ward Beecher. So it may have been loyalty to his friend that prompted Holmes to make pilgrimage to the place where relief came too late for Gordon. It was here that Holmes met the Mahdi's successor, Khalifa Abdullah el Taashi, who apparently slipped out of his new capital, Omdurman, to confer secretly in the remains of the old one. The meeting hardly benefited him. Holmes sent a full report to Whitehall, something of obvious value to Kitchener in preparing the war that overthrew Abdullah in 1898.

Holmes next visited Montpellier, where his chemist's mind turned to practical research on coal tar derivatives – so he may have invented that disinfectant-smelling soap. But in France he learned that Colonel Moran was now the only surviving senior Moriartian at liberty. Holmes returned unannounced to London, throwing Mrs Hudson into happy hysterics, and causing Watson to faint for the only time in his life. He masterminded the arrest of Moran. He commiserated with Watson on the loss of his perfect wife during the previous three years. But he took the chance to finance his distant cousin Dr Verner to buy out Watson's practice. And the bachelor establishment of 221B Baker Street was perfectly restored with Watson at liberty to do nothing but help Holmes.

THE FINAL YEARS

Life in Baker Street after 1894 continued as it had done prior to Holmes's disappearance. A page-boy was added to the establishment, so that it was no longer necessary for the landlady to announce such visitors as did not admit themselves to the upstairs flat. Mrs Hudson never again took a short holiday as she had done in 1888 or '89, leaving her friend Mrs Turner in charge of Number 221.

The naughty nineties' propensity for scandals gave Holmes a good deal of work. He and Watson destroyed the blackmailer Milverton's lucrative files after watching one of his high-born victims assassinate him. Holmes felt no real regret that the adventuress Isadora Klein burned the *roman-à-clef* which would have exposed young Maberley's suffering as one of her lovers. But then he always had a soft spot for rather naughty ladies, even those with no pretensions to class like Lord Robert St Simon's discarded mistress, the dancer Flora Millar, or the fallen Kitty Winter, whose vitriolic revenge on the man who ruined her seemed no more than the well-deserved wages of sin.

"The Illustrious Client" of that case was Edward VII, formerly Albert Edward Prince of Wales, enjoying Holmes's services again; this time at his own covert instigation. Holmes's monarchist loyalty blinded him strangely to some rather obvious facts. "A loyal friend and a chivalrous gentleman" was his comment: a description few others would have applied to the King! Watson, too, thought this

OPPOSITE: From "The Adventure of Charles Augustus Milverton", one of the 56 short stories written by Conan Doyle, first published in 1904.

the supreme moment of his companion's career. And so neither asked why the king troubled himself to rescue Violet De Merville from the clutches of a lustful and murderous foreigner. The lady was far too strait-laced to have been a royal popsy, and it would be unlike Edward to go out of his way to save an obstinate and exasperating prude from her own folly. One has to ask what lurked behind this affair. The king, Holmes was told, had taken a *paternal* interest in Violet since she was a little girl in short frocks. Surely the courtier Sir James Damery spoke more truly than he knew? Surely General de Merville's wife must have taken advantage of her husband's absence at the Khyber or some other far-flung danger-spot to cultivate an intimate friendship with royalty, and Violet was the offspring of that unhallowed union? Such heredity would explain the outrageous imperiousness with which she treated Holmes and Kitty Winter when they tried to open her eyes to her fiancé's true character.

The recovery of the Bruce-Partington submarine plans might more truly be called the supreme moment of Holmes's career. That it won him a private interview with Queen Victoria and her gift of an emerald tiepin is perhaps less evidence of its importance than Mycroft's appearance in Baker Street to engage him on the case. Watson had always understood Mycroft to be a mere auditor whose prodigious arithmetical skills served one department in Whitehall. He now learned that Sherlock's brother was the unique and indispensable civil servant whose great brain encompassed all affairs of state in all departments, and whose conclusions were always required when affairs spanning several different spheres were under consideration. Repeatedly, Mycroft's fiat determined British government policy, whether Liberals or Conservatives were the ruling party. That this keystone of the kingdom thought only Sherlock could intercept the plans was, perhaps, a higher compliment even than the Prime Minister and (Under) Secretary of

State for European Affairs paid when they engaged Holmes personally in "The Second Stain" affair.

Lesser patriots might have felt that the two cases Sherlock handled for Pope Leo XIII were the high points of his career. But the agnostic Englishman probably disliked the pontiff's denunciation of Anglican orders and would have mocked at the idea that one unprovable claim to "apostolic succession" was better than another. Both Holmes brothers modestly declined public honours, Sherlock refusing a knighthood in 1902. More prized was the emerald tiepin, his gift from "a certain gracious lady" who had acutely detected his pleasure in jewels.

He made more money, of course, in winning the £5,000 reward somewhat fraudulently offered by the Duke of Holdernesse for the recovery of his son. And he did not expose to the world the scandal of the boy's illegitimate brother. But as was so often the case, he was disappointed by the aristocracy; only British royalty never let him down.

Though he described himself as a poor man to the Duke, he was prosperous enough to retire at the age of forty-nine, and retreat to the little farm near the Sussex coast where he devoted himself to apiculture and the writing of his *Practical Handbook* on the topic. He also wrote up two of his own cases, and it must be confessed that for all Watson's inaccuracies, he was a far better narrator. The embarrassing fame Watson's writings brought Holmes, and the dramatisation of some of his exploits in 1898 by American actor William Gillette and the literary doctor Arthur Conan Doyle probably hastened his retirement, as did his illness of 1897, aggravated by some secret vice euphemised by Watson as "indiscretions" – perhaps a furtive return to cocaine. After retiring he shunned publicity. His professional place was probably (inadequately) filled by his south bank rival, Barker, whose distinctive tinted spectacles Watson spotted at a crime scene while Holmes's return from Reichenbach was unsuspected.

In 1912 the peace of the bee-farm was broken by Prime Minister Asquith and Foreign Secretary Grey. They decided that German espionage must be foiled, and Holmes should do the job. Responding to his country's call, Holmes grew a hideous goatee, adopted the name Altamont and a vile American accent, and went to Chicago to masquerade as an Anglophobe Irish-American.

"Altamont" was busy for the next three years, joining the Fenians in Buffalo and returning as a subversive to Skibbereen, where Von Bork's network, as anticipated, recruited him. The happy result was that just before war broke out, Von Bork's agents were all rounded up, and Holmes and Watson destroyed his indexes and engineered his deportation.

Retiring and secretive at the last, Sherlock Holmes died without leaving anyone to report the date, the cause, the place, or the site of his grave.

OPPOSITE: A cartoon from Vanity Fair *showing the American actor William Gillette as Sherlock Holmes.*

HATS, COATS AND TOBACCO

The silhouette greets the underground traveller at Baker Street. Wear a deerstalker hat, and suck on a drop-stem pipe, and it doesn't matter whether you're Jeremy Brett or Lucille Ball or Fifi the Wonder Dog: you're impersonating Sherlock Holmes.

The word "deerstalker" never occurs in the annals. The "earflapped travelling cap" was mentioned in "Silver Blaze". In "The Boscombe Valley Mystery" Holmes's "long grey travelling cloak" was twinned with his "close-fitting cloth cap", which Sidney Paget's illustration revealed as the deerstalker. In *The Hound of the Baskervilles* Holmes was in "his tweed suit and cloth cap ... like any other tourist upon the moor" when he turned up in the hut circle. Paget got it wrong here: his illustration of Holmes's shadow showed the soft Homburg the detective evidently preferred for town and suburban wear. It is a pity to find Paget in error, for we generally need the illustrations to know about Holmes's attire. He wore cap and tweeds on the heath behind "The Priory School", on the road frequented by "The Solitary Cyclist". And in "Black Peter's" cabin, he travelled to Norfolk in ulster and cap to investigate "The Dancing Men". He seems to have worn the deerstalker in town on one occasion only: when he came back from his travels after the catastrophe at the Reichenbach Falls. In his "Return" he may have felt it necessary to ensure that even Watson made no mistake when he dropped his disguise as the grumpy old book-collector. Not only was he depicted wearing country tweeds and deerstalker in town, but he and his dummy in the window at 221B Baker Street wore the mouse-coloured dressing-gown. The returned Holmes's appearance was that popularised by the actor William Gillette during his absence from *The Strand Magazine*, while Watson and Paget still believed his bones to be lying below the waters at Reichenbach.

OPPOSITE: Rathbone was most widely recognised for his many portrayals of Sherlock Holmes.

LEFT: The essential elements of Holmes – hat, pipe and magnifying glass.

Holmes's tweed suit, by the way was always trousered and never knickerbockered. And his immense, flowing ulster (never so named by Watson) did not bear the familiar shoulder cape. It had a hood like a duffle-coat. The elegant caped ulster worn with a bowler in "The Speckled Band" was twinned with the deerstalker as a glamorising improvement by Gillette and his successors.

In fact Holmes's most consistent sartorial habit was tucking his bow tie under soft turned-down shirt collars. It was a big spotted bow when Watson met him in Bart's. It was a plain bow, still in the same mildly Bohemian fashion, in his retirement in "The Adventure of the Lion's Mane", even though the style was by then dated, and the elderly Holmes was wearing a very youthful lounge suit and a sort of porkpie hat, to accompany the extraordinary rejuvenation which made him at nearly 60 look decades younger and fitter than his ex-rowing-Blue companion. Holmes's tie was still the Bohemian tucked-in bow in one of his smartest moments, when he shadowed Sir Henry Baskerville and Dr Mortimer along Oxford Street and Regent Street. For this he wore a frock coat and Watson a cutaway, and the two of them were resplendent in shiny toppers. Watson, as was normal even when he and Holmes both wore bowlers, sported a stiff upright collar like most other respectable gentlemen.

The bachelor eccentricities of Sherlock Holmes were most fully listed in "The Musgrave Ritual": "his cigars are in the coal-scuttle, his tobacco in the toe-end of a Persian slipper, and his unanswered correspondence transfixed by a jack-knife into the very centre of his wooden mantelpiece." The jack-knifed letters, like the patriotic V.R.s pistol-shot into the wall, were never mentioned again. But the sitting-room chemical experiments continued and in the new century were supported by "scientific charts upon the wall" ("The Mazarin Stone"). The documents and cuttings saved and pasted into scrap-books grew over the years into the vital indexes to which Holmes turned for information on anything from old cases to vampires. The phases of lethargy between cases when "he filed his cuttings were also the occasion of his shooting cocaine or morphine until, round about 1898, Watson felt he had definitely weaned him off the habit. There was a hint of a return to it in 1903, when Watson referred to "the violin, the shag tobacco, the old black pipe, the index hooks", as Holmes's "institutions", with "others perhaps less excusable" ("The Adventure of the Creeping Man").

For the new Puritans of today Holmes's and Watson's tobacco addiction must be an inexcusable habit. That Watson would not object to Holmes's "strong tobacco" was one of the first points settled between them. Holmes's usual was shag: in "The Crooked Man" he shared Watson's Arcadia mixture. In "Silver Blaze" he smoked "the strongest black tobacco": tarred, rope-like twist, perhaps? Certainly his smoking habits were wet and disgusting in 1889, when he made his early morning pipe from the previous day's dottles and plugs saved on the mantelpiece! Well might Watson mention "the oldest and foulest" of his pipes in "Shoscombe Old Place", or Holmes describe his "filthy habit" in "The Veiled Lodger" and a "course of tobacco-poisoning" that Watson "so often and so justly condemned" ("The Devil's

Foot"). Smoking could take the place of eating when Holmes wanted to think, and in "The Copper Beeches" he smoked a clay pipe for meditation and a cherrywood for disputation. Briar served for meditation at other times; and for Charles Augustus Milverton's housemaid's benefit, a clay was part of the plumber "Escott's" disguise. The drop stem was adopted by Gillette as more convenient when acting. It has no place in annals or illustrations.

In addition to the indispensable pipe, Holmes always seemed to carry a cigar-case, and often, especially when travelling, a cigarette case. He blew smoke rings from his cigarettes on the train to Dartmoor in *The Hound of the Baskervilles*. He appreciated the professor's hand-made Egyptian cigarettes in "The Golden Pince-Nez", and the unexpectedly unpoisonous cigars at Coldoni's Italian Restaurant in Gloucester Road. Tobacco is the worst deprivation he suffered when pretending to be "The Dying Detective", and "John Douglas" was desperate for a cigar after two days' hiding in *The Valley of Fear*.

Nicotine seemed indispensable to Holmesian thought. But Mycroft didn't smoke; he snuffed.

HOBBIES AND TASTE

Holmes was a scientist. He met Watson in Bart's when he had just perfected a test for the presence of blood, finding a reagent which could only be precipitated by haemoglobin. In Baker Street he returned to his Oxford love, inorganic chemistry. Watson grew familiar with the smell of hydrochloric acid in the flat, and was unsurprised when Holmes proved a substance to be bisulphate of baryta. Had he been a member of the Faraday Society, Watson might have been hugely impressed, for chemists are familiar with sulphate of baryta – the heavy spar used in permanent white paint – but only Sherlock had ever come across the bisulphate.

Holmes's reading was another badge of membership in the intelligentsia. Apart from Winwood Reade's *The Martyrdom of Man*, he rarely ever read a book in English unless it was several hundred years old. *The Martyrdom* proposes a rational agnosticism based on the coherence of evolving nature. Dogmatic religion is rejected. The concept of some unifying "force" within and behind all things is proposed in place of traditional notions of God. The book made shockwaves in 1872, but won increasing acceptance after Reade's death

BELOW: The Lowther Arcade, where Holmes bought the cheap fiddle, which turned out to be a Stradivarius.

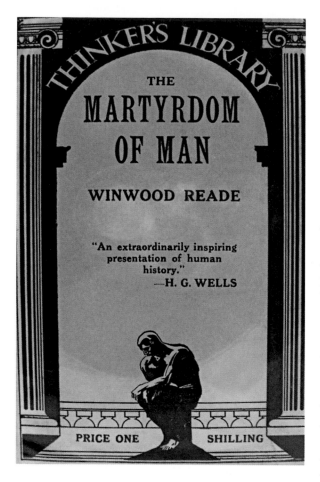

three years later, and passed through 18 editions by 1910. Its ideas are almost clichés today. Holmes's unique critical genius is perceptible, however, in his assessing this work as "one of the most remarkable ever penned", and full of "daring speculations".

Reade and the newspapers aside, Holmes's reading in modern English was confined to the *Encyclopaedia* or *Gazetteer*, and with unaccustomed modesty failing to observe that if he didn't know a fact, his reference books were likely to get it wrong. He also knew the layout of the Bible and the stylistics of *Whitaker's Almanack* and Bradshaw's *Railway Time Tables*. The first book Watson ever saw him buy was Philippe de Croy's *De Juris Inter Gentes* (On The Law Among Peoples), published in Liège in 1642, and once owned by William Whyte, who wrote his name (as well as reading his books) in Latin. Later Watson saw Holmes reading an old black-letter (Gothic print) volume, which must have been published at least a century earlier than de Croy's book, unless it was in German.

Holmes loved examining mediaeval documents with a view to scholarly research. Thus he was studying early English charters in a university library when "The Three Students" came to his attention. And when Inspector Hopkins drew him into the business at Yoxley Old Place, Holmes was examining a palimpsest – an old manuscript on parchment or sheepskin with the writing erased to allow re-use. Rather to Holmes's disappointment, the text he recovered was only fifteenth-century Abbey accounts.

But amateur scholarship always delighted him. In Cornwall he propounded the theory that the old Cornish language was related to Chaldean and had been imported by Phoenician tin-traders (at the same time, no doubt, as they took Chaldean to Brittany, Ireland, Wales and Scotland, where related Celtic tongues were spoken). Ancient times were much on his mind in that Cornish holiday. He chatted to Watson about "Celts, arrowheads and shards", the context making it impossible to know whether the Celts were iron-age implements dug up with the arrowheads and shards, or the ancient people who wielded them.

For light reading Holmes preferred a classic text in a foreign language. He quoted Goethe on occasion (once approving his pithiness). He recognised a quotation from Balzac in "Hosmer Angel's" letters. And on the train to Boscombe valley, while Watson struggled to read a yellow-back novel, the arch-misogynist Holmes was enjoying Petrarch's love poetry!

But then, his passion for classical music proved his romantic (if highbrow) taste. When not performing the strange feat of laying his violin across his knees and improvising chords, he was likely to be playing Mendelssohn's lieder. (Presumably arrangements of some of the pianoforte *Songs Without Words*, since Mendelssohn wrote no lieder for voice or violin.) He enjoyed the recitals of the Spanish virtuoso Pablo de Sarasate and the attack and bowing of Mme Norman-Neruda, performing under the baton of Sir Charles Hallé, who later became her husband. Again, Holmes admired arrangements, since he praised her playing of something by Chopin (who wrote no violin solos) that went "la la la lira lira lay". It may have been the Valse in C# Minor, if the second "la" was stressed and drawn out. And as has been observed, he must have annoyed other concertgoers mightily by his habit of conducting languidly from his seat! Watson at least had something on stage to watch when Holmes dragged him off to the Wagner night at the opera or to hear the De Reszke brothers in *The Huguenots*.

Holmes's love of early music was essentially scholarly, and it is a tragedy that his definitive monograph "On the Polyphonic Motets of Lassus" was never followed by an account of the composer's otherwise unknown *non*-Polyphonic music, which the title implies Holmes had found.

Music lured Holmes into one of the only two mean actions ever recorded against him: snapping up the Stradivarius he found in Lowther Arcade without hinting to the Jewish dealer that it was worth far more than the 55 shillings (£2.25p) he paid. The other meanness was trifling with the affections of Charles Augustus Milverton's housemaid.

Finally the visual arts. The bespectacled and moustached gentleman above the bed of "The Dying Detective" is no oil painting in any sense. Perhaps it is a family photograph of Dr Verner. It certainly isn't Mycroft.

Watson found his friend's artistic ideas crude when they visited an exhibition of modern Belgian Masters in Bond Street before pushing on with the Baskerville case. But who were these mysterious late 1880s masters? Surely Watson must mean Van Gogh, the Brabantian and sometime resident of Brussels. Holmes's geography would not have been up to explaining that Vincent's birthplace was in the part of Brabant in modern-day Holland and not Belgium. One can well believe that "The Potato Eaters" (1885) looked "crude" to Watson, who blandly transferred the epithet to the great and perceptive mind that was trying to open his eyes to the future direction of painting.

OPPOSITE: The Martyrdom of Man – one of the few English books that Holmes read and enjoyed.

BELOW: Mme Norman-Neruda (1839–1911), later known as Lady Hallé, one of Holmes's favourite violinists.

2
ARTHUR CONAN DOYLE'S LIFE

Charles Altamont Doyle, clerk in the Scottish Office of works, was the youngest and least successful son of John Doyle, the cartoonist who, as "HB", transformed British political caricature from the grotesque and savage style of Gillray to the politely humorous portraiture of John Tenniel and Bernard Partridge.

Charles's three brothers were respectively a successful portrait painter and book illustrator, the director of the National Gallery of Ireland, and the brilliant Dicky Doyle, who designed the famous cover of *Punch* which graced that journal for 107 years. Charles's draftsmanship was much inferior to his father's and brothers'. His preferred subjects were fey or phantasmagoric, without the delicate definition of Dicky's flying vignettes surrounding Mr Punch and Toby. His career stuck obstinately at the level of clerk in the civil service.

The family were devout Irish Catholics. Charles, segregated from their fashionable London life by his employment in Edinburgh, married his landlady's Irish Catholic daughter, Mary Foley. She was a prodigious snob, who traced the genealogy and heraldry of her Protestant maternal family, and persuaded herself that she was descended from a cadet branch of the Percys, and Plantagenet blood ran in her veins. Her husband's family was of better standing than the Foleys, and she alleged that they were no mere Irish Doyles but were descended from the old Anglo-Norman D'Oils, and connected to the poet and baronet Sir Francis Hastings Doyle, once famous for "The Drunken Private of the Buffs", and numbered among Oxford's variously distinguished Professors of Poetry. Mary left no report on the lineage of the Foleys, so it must be assumed that no amount of ingenuity could dress them in robes of greater distinction than the rest of mortality.

Her son, who achieved real distinction, was always attached to his unquestionably loving and supportive mother. According to family tradition her children called her "the Ma'am", and so addressed her, as though she were Queen Victoria. It is persuasively suggested by Owen Dudley Edwards that they actually called her "Mam", as quite simple Foley children might call their Irish parents "me mam and dad". Arthur Conan Doyle always treated his mother's hifalutin claims respectfully in print, but the aside that Sherlock Holmes's odiously proud client "The Noble Bachelor" Lord Robert St Simon had Plantagenet blood on one side and Tudor on the other shows that he did not value them as she did, and his creation of a comic character who found that his descent was not from the Dodds but the "D'Odds" suggests that he knew just how much the "D'Oil" genealogy was worth!

Arthur Conan Doyle was born on 22 May, 1859, his parents' third child and first son. He was named Conan for his grand-uncle and godfather Michael Conan, a journalist living in Paris. He was given the baptismal name Ignatius, which he never used. He believed he carried the middle name Charles, which was never recorded. Unlike Shaw, he never complained, but like GBS he was to have "the devil of a childhood".

CHILDHOOD AND SCHOOLING

CHAPTER OPENER: Sir Arthur Conan Doyle in the guise of his most famous creation, Sherlock Holmes, from The Crown Magazine *in 1907.*

Like Shaw's, the dark shadow overhanging Conan Doyle's childhood was his father's drunkenness. The family was discreet about this failing – the more understandably because it finally led to his incarceration and death in an asylum. We don't know exactly when his sense of failure drove this gentle, soft-bearded man to spend more and more time out drinking with rough companions from louche Edinburgh society.

We don't know how many, if any, of Conan Doyle's fictional descriptions of violent drunks were based on traumatic boyhood experience. We can see that the family lived in genteel poverty which might not be far removed from Mary Foley's background as a landlady's daughter, but which was a far cry from the fashionable life in a Nash Terrace off Regent's Park that John Doyle sustained by borrowing. Some of the London Doyles and their intellectual society friends paid rare visits to the Edinburgh Doyles if in Scotland – Little Arthur once sat on Thackeray's knee. Charles Altamont Doyle could not afford to take his family south to visit their relatives.

When Arthur was about seven, he was sent to stay with one of his mother's posher friends: Miss Burton, sister of the Scottish historiographer royal. She lived at Libberton Brae, two miles out of the smelly centre of "Auld Reekie", and Arthur was to attend the nearby school, Newington Academy, ruled by a pock-marked, tawse-wielding, one-eyed simulacrum of Wackford Squeers. It has been speculated that Mary Doyle wished to spare him scenes of drunkenness in the home, though this seems the less likely as the Doyle family soon moved to a house in Newington, and Arthur returned to their care.

At this period he remembered scrapping with a boy called Eddie Tulloch who lived on the prosperous side of their road, Sciennes Hill Place. Arthur described himself as champion of the boys from the poorer side: he may equally have been fighting as a "Pape" against a "Proddy", since Tulloch's father was a Baptist minister. Anyway, manly fisticuffs would become one of his great delights. The battler exchanging black eyes with another child in the roadway grew into the young man who kept boxing gloves in his gear and was always ready for a sporting round.

When he was nine Arthur went south to boarding school. Hodder was the preparatory school attached to Stonyhurst, the famous Jesuit school which had been founded at St Omer in the bad old days when English Catholics were persecuted, and transferred to Lancashire in 1794. At Hodder he was taught by young Father Cassidy, one of those absolutely inspiring teachers whose pure love for children makes their pupils love their classes. At Hodder, Arthur made the one school friend who was to remain a friend in adult life. James Ryan, one year younger than himself; a fellow Irishman by descent and Scot by birth. Arthur Conan Doyle retained a pleasing Scottish accent all his life.

Stonyhurst was less delightful. There was no teacher with the warmth and understanding of Cassidy. Discipline was maintained by a rubber ferula rather like a gym shoe sole, which the boys called "the tolley". Its blows on the hand caused instant swelling, and Conan Doyle believed he was beaten unusually often. He was accustomed to being controlled by loving reason in the home, and Cassidy had used the same means of discipline at Hodder. By contrast, Stonyhurst, like most large schools, just didn't have time to give such individual attention. So, faced with unreasoning authority and directives to "Do this because I say so", Conan

OPPOSITE: Charles Altamont Doyle with his son Arthur.

ABOVE: Stonyhurst School in Lancashire, where Conan Doyle went as a child and which later was the inspiration for Baskerville Hall.

Doyle, like many another boy before and since, simply refused to comply – and was beaten accordingly. His account of reasoned discipline at home, and the fact that Charles Altamont Doyle was responsible for categorically – and wisely – refusing the Jesuits' offer of free education if Arthur were to be dedicated to joining the order, leads one to doubt the suggestion that he was kept at school, never returning even for Christmas vacations, because Charles's drunkenness now made the home intolerable. But whatever the reason, he certainly did not return home until he was seventeen; indeed, a Christmas spent with his Uncle Dicky in London when he was sixteen was his first Christmas away from school after he started at Hodder. And with Uncle Dicky he visited the Tower and Madame Tussaud's Chamber of Horrors and saw Irving play Hamlet.

He was a big lad and good at games. Like many other nineteenth-century public schools, Stonyhurst played cricket and football with its own variations, like the right to punch a soccer ball with a closed fist. But Conan Doyle was a natural athlete, and able to train his muscles and eye without forming habits to detract from his excellent sportsmanship in later life. He also became a great yarn-spinner. His mother had always encouraged his avid reading. He loved romantic adventure writers like Mayne Reid and Captain Marryatt and Sir Walter Scott, to whom his mother also claimed some remote kinship. At school he found other boys would pay him with tuck to listen to his stories. He learned the serial-writer's trick of breaking off at a critical moment, and demanding another jam tart before revealing what happened to the heroine with the scimitar descending over her trembling head.

He was serious but not pious. While still at school, he realised he no longer believed that Eucharistic bread and wine turned into flesh and blood. Instead of receiving communion hypocritically, he accepted a wise Jesuit's arrangement that he serve mass so that his abstinence would not be noted. He was able without being over-intellectual. Nobody contemplated his pursuing classics or pure mathematics – the academic staples of the universities. Nor was there money for him to go to Oxford or Cambridge. But practical training as a doctor could be acquired from home. Arthur would study medicine at Edinburgh.

First, though, the Jesuits sent him to their house at Feldkirch in Austria for a year. He would have fretted, working out time at Stonyhurst. He gained immensely from his time in the Tyrol, improving his German and acquiring an affection for the German romantic poets. Acquiring, too, a cosmopolitan enjoyment of the continent which would preserve him from bone-headed British blimpishness, even when he exulted in the myths of High Imperialism.

BRYAN CHARLES WALLER

While in Feldkirch, Arthur received correspondence from a young man, just six years his senior, who had taken lodgings with the Doyles in Edinburgh. Bryan Charles Waller was on the verge of completing his MB and taking an important

role in the Doyle family's life. Just how important was not recognised until Owen Dudley Edwards's study of the young Conan Doyle in the 1980s. But when it is observed that Arthur's youngest sister "Dodo", born in 1877, was christened Bryan Mary; that the family moved to a larger house with more lodgers that year, where young Waller rather than Charles Doyle became the official tenant; and that Mary Foley Doyle spent the last 40 years of her life living on Waller's estate in Yorkshire, we must feel that, willy-nilly, Arthur had an elder brother foisted upon him.

And quite a striking elder brother. Already, before the age of 25, he was the author of a published volume of poetry: something which gives real kudos to an undergraduate. A pedigree and heraldry snob after Mary Doyle's own heart, boasting his descent from a knight who (perhaps) captured the French king's cousin at the Battle of Agincourt. On which very shaky grounds the Wallers quartered the royal arms of France with their own! They also claimed connection with Sir William Waller, the Civil War general; Edmund Waller, the poet of "Go, lovely Rose" fame; Hardress Waller, the markedly inferior poet who was one of the signatories of Charles I's death warrant; and some Wallers who could interest only genealogically besotted descendants.

More immediately, Bryan Charles was the nephew of Bryan Waller Procter, a man of letters who knew everyone from Leigh Hunt and Charles Lamb to Dickens

ABOVE: Edinburgh University, where Conan Doyle studied medicine between 1876 and 1881.

and Thackeray, and is better remembered today for being known to them than for the verse he wrote under the name "Barry Cornwall".

Tears — amidst thy laughter seen,
Pity — mingling with thy joy
This is all we ask from thee,
Hermione, Hermione!

His daughter Adelaide Anne Procter, another friend of all the literary world, did marginally better with "The Lost Chord" as her main claim to fame. Bryan Charles Waller might have been forgiven for feeling that he improved on his uncle and cousin rather than deriving glory from them.

Glory seems to have been much in his mind. He wrote to Arthur in Feldkirch urging him to abandon all outworn theology and put his trust in himself. This rather Nietzchean teaching may have led Conan Doyle to that enthusiasm for Winwood

Reade which he made Holmes lay egregiously before Watson. Certainly at this time, and probably with Waller's encouragement, Conan Doyle finally abandoned all faith in orthodox Catholicism. He had been offended by a sermon at Downside in which the preacher consigned all non-Catholics to Hell. This was a direct challenge to someone with Arthur's robust common sense, especially as Pope Pius IX had already pronounced *ex cathedra* that the idea of the Immaculate Conception of the Blessed Virgin was a truth to be accepted reverently by all Catholics. In his late teens Arthur abandoned all faith in dogmatic religion forever, and, indeed, was a philosophical materialist for several years.

Waller remained at the university while Arthur was an undergraduate. With his MB granted, he put up his plate in Edinburgh, and continued to work for his MD and strive to win a university lectureship. He inherited the family estate at Masongill in Yorkshire in 1877. He came to be regarded by his tenants as unpleasantly "stuck-up". But in Arthur's eyes he was surely, like Sherlock, and unlike any Doyle or Foley, the son of a line of country squires.

Charles Doyle's clerkship was swept away by a new broom in the Office of Works that year. He was reduced to that book illustration at which he had already almost failed. His alcoholism no doubt contributed, for he embarked upon courses of treatment that achieved little. He began having epileptic fits. He dreaded being interned, but certification and incarceration in an asylum in Fife proved the only answer to his problems. Arthur and Waller almost certainly coped with this sad situation together over the next few years. As Charles and the London uncles were all shocked by Arthur's lapse from Catholicism, while the forward-looking, pro-vivisectionist, theist and nominal Anglican Waller approved, the surrogate elder brother's influence was probably very strong at this time, and most likely inspired that sense of admiration in the presence of a choice and master spirit which informs Watson's early relations with Holmes. And Waller's intellectual arrogance became part of the more famous fictional character, as in some of the earlier stories did his habit of interspersing his speech with "ha!" and "hum!".

Somehow Arthur kept up his medical studies while his family seemed to crumble around him. In 1879 his older sister Annie went to Portugal as a governess. By 1882 his younger sisters Lottie and Connie had followed her. In that year Mary Doyle was invited to take up residence in a cottage at Masongill. She took Arthur's youngest siblings, Innes and Dodo with her. And as far as is known, she never again lived with Charles Altamont Doyle.

Perhaps it is fortunate that Edinburgh University was starkly utilitarian in those days. It enjoyed neither the dreaming spires nor the silly social life of Oxford and Cambridge. Raw students were licked into the shape of lawyers or doctors. Professors were cheered or jeered according to the value of their teaching. Class and accent counted for little or nothing. Contacts might. Arthur's school friend James Ryan followed him to the university, and Waller made him his class assistant.

Meanwhile, Arthur's surgery classes brought him in contact with the other great source for the world's most famous detective. Dr Joseph Bell, an extracurricular demonstrator, took a fancy to the admiring young student, and appointed him as a clerical assistant. Neither he nor young Conan Doyle had any inkling that this association would inspire one of the world's best-known literary conjuring tricks.

UNIVERSITY ARCHETYPES

Arthur was Joe Bell's out-patients' clerk. Like a receptionist today, he took the names of arrivals and ushered them in to the presence of the doctor. He had time to study their appearance before Bell saw them, and he was hugely impressed by Bell's occasional habit of making instant observations about the personality, habits and complaints of complete strangers. These could be extremely simple, like telling

OPPOSITE: Leigh Hunt, who was a friend of Waller's uncle, "Barry Cornwall".

ABOVE: Arthur Conan Doyle graduating in 1881.

a man he had a drink problem because he carried a flask in his pocket. They could be given a more complicated explanation than they deserved, like the case of the highland soldier Conan Doyle recounted, whom Bell declared to have been in Barbados recently on the deductive grounds that he was sunburned. He suffered from elephantiasis, which was commoner in the West Indies than in England, and the Highland regiments were currently stationed on the island he thus astutely pinpointed. Yet the conclusion might have been reached far more quickly with the observation that elephantiasis was so closely associated with Barbados as to be nicknamed "Bajey leg".

Never carried over to Holmes was Bell's frank acknowledgement that he could make gross errors. His original intention was to enforce on his students the need for detailed observation in diagnosis and to show that it could be practised as a habit before the patient was formally examined. He believed, too, that when the trick came off it put the patient a little in awe of the doctor which, in itself, would assist in the cure. Confidence in one's physician or surgeon having a definite placebo effect. Conan Doyle at first felt the awe, and even after he had learned to play the deductive parlour trick himself, impressing his children immensely by his ability to identify facts about unknown diners in restaurants, he knew that awe was something that could be usefully passed on to readers. So he held Watson in a state of naïve amazement and let him get things wrong when he tried to make his own observations and deductions. And for truly whopping failure in the parlour trick, he created another doctor based on himself in his novel *The Stark Munro Letters*. The doctor confidently tells a man he is a drinker come to have his bronchitic lungs treated, only to learn that he is the gas company's man with a smoker's cough come to collect an outstanding bill! The incident may well have happened to Conan Doyle.

Conan Doyle repeatedly acknowledged Bell and his parlour trick as the "original" of Sherlock Holmes. Somehow he apparently learned of Bell's private interest in true crime, and so by linking an encyclopaedic knowledge of "sensational" case histories with the amazing ability to deduce character from observed appearance, he came up with the detective to end all detectives. In *A Study in Scarlet* he gave Holmes Bell's notion that the memory should not be cluttered with unnecessary facts: irrelevant material belonged in the "lumber room" of the library, to be looked up as needed. In *The Sign of Four* he tacitly dropped this notion, realising that a great universal genius was better identified by the breadth of his knowledge. But Holmes's slightly inhuman detachment from warmth and feeling – effectively and touchingly highlighting the moments when he expresses his true affection for Watson – owed something to the lofty and unsociable eminence from which Edinburgh professors stooped to their pupils. Shambling, athletic Conan Doyle was amazed to come across Bell on the Isle of Arran once, and discover that this Great Detached Brain ever did anything so ordinary as to go on holiday.

He made early efforts to give Holmes Bell's appearance. The "hawklike nose" is clearly Bell's big beak. The small clear grey eyes rather close on either side are Bell's too, and the general appearance of a silent and brooding Red Indian. Paget's better looking detective with hair elegantly receding at the temples in place of Bell's wiry grey brush was a happy improvement, and fortunately did not seem incompatible with Conan Doyle's words.

If Bell and Waller both contributed aloof superiority to Holmes, Bell's colleague William Rutherford, Professor of Physiology, was equally superior but totally

un-Holmesian in his vehemence and noisiness. He had a barrel chest and a big, black, spade beard and his voice boomed ahead of him in ways he sometimes used for showing off. Students waiting for him to come and give them a lecture might hear him start to deliver it while still in the corridor outside, so that the first piece of information was received while the lectern was empty, and the professor would stride in, still orating, to take up his place without a break in the flow. This was a man who succumbed to the professorial temptation to play the eccentric for generations of students to enjoy remembering. Conan Doyle used him – he said so – in creating his most popular character outside the Holmes books: Professor Challenger, discoverer of *The Lost World*.

Intellectual ruthlessness was something Edinburgh University cherished. Conan Doyle noted it in the aggressive vivisectionism of Waller and Rutherford. He himself regarded vivisection as a deeply regrettable necessity to be used as sparingly as possible. He was, however, impressed by the violence with which Rutherford would tear into an unfortunate amphibian imported from the continent for dissection, shouting in his affected accent, "Ach! These Jarman frags!" Conan Doyle was always a bit of a sucker for the determined charlatan: it is part of his Watsonian charm. And it certainly seems to be the most superficial and least professional attributes of Rutherford, and to a lesser extent Bell, that attracted him. To this extent his "brilliant" creations, Holmes and Challenger, are always open to the amused mockery of those who have a sound grasp of topics they purport to have mastered.

In an older fellow-student, however, Conan Doyle met the true charlatan who would temporarily enthral him; attempt to ruin him; and show him the blustering manic and paranoid personality which makes Professor Challenger so entertaining on the page, and would make him such a figure to shun in reality. George Turnavine Budd was the son of a genuinely great doctor who made important contributions to the understanding and treatment of cholera, typhoid and scarlet fever. He was the nephew of the Professor of Medicine at King's College, London. In his own estimation he was a greater man than either. In Conan Doyle's opinion, there was something of genius about George Turnavine Budd. It was an opinion that led him into trouble when he graduated.

WORK AND PLAY

But before Arthur Conan Doyle put his whole career and reputation at risk by ignoring good advice, and attempting to go into partnership with George Turnavine Budd, he gained a great deal of experience that he would turn to equally good literary use. It was essential that he earn something to contribute to the family finances. Pride would hardly let them all depend on Waller's charity while Charles gently dissolved in alcohol. Arthur combined his elementary medical training with the need to acquire medical experience. In the vacations, he offered himself as a doctor's assistant.

His first attempt was a humiliating failure. Hoping to learn about the city poor, he joined a Dr Richardson in Sheffield. They parted in three weeks, and Arthur drifted down to London, where the successful Doyles (now living in Maida Vale) found him "too Bohemian", or so he said. And he was tempted to take the Queen's shilling from a recruiting sergeant. Four months working for Dr Elliott at Ruyton-of-the-eleven-towns in Shropshire was more satisfactory. He gained confidence when he was the only doctor available to attend a man who had been injured by an exploding cannon at a celebration. Arthur extracted the jagged iron from his head and closed up the wound and felt he was going to make a doctor after all.

His best assistantship was with Dr Hoare in Birmingham. This time he managed to learn about the city poor. He mastered midwifery. He worked with Hoare in

1878 and 1879; possibly in 1880–81 as well. He could have had a permanent assistantship with Hoare had he wanted it after graduating MB in 1882. Mrs Hoare was maternally fond of him.

But he had acquired a taste for adventure and signed on as a ship's doctor as soon as he was qualified. It was his second long cruise.

The first, and more important, had come before he entered his final year. A fellow-student was going to spend seven months in the Arctic on the whaler *Hope*. At the last minute he was unable to go and asked Conan Doyle if he would take his place. The pay was ten shillings a month and three shillings share in every ton of blubber taken. Assured that he could have his friend's Arctic kit, Arthur jumped at the chance and never regretted it.

The cold clear light and pellucid waters of the midnight sun fascinated every explorer who went to the Arctic. Arthur felt that the air off Greenland was the healthiest he had ever breathed. The crisp chill cleared away the rheumaticky taint of smelly Edinburgh and drizzly Lancashire and foggy London. The company of hardy seamen was good for a lad who celebrated his twenty-first birthday on this cruise. The steward saw his boxing gloves and challenged him to a bout the first

BELOW: The icebergs of Greenland, where Conan Doyle enjoyed the purest air he ever breathed.

day out, telling the mess later that he was the finest surgeon they'd ever had because Arthur had blacked his eye!

At the same time the brutality of clubbing seals; the fascination of hunting whales and identifying the huge warts on the flukes of one that always got away; the sudden deaths of men whipped overboard by the harpoon lines; the sight of polar bears and Arctic foxes on the ice floes: all these things and the ever-present absence of women stimulated a romantic yearning that Conan Doyle never forgot. He would write adventure stories capitalising on his seamanship. But he would also write strange, fascinating romances of men loving spectres or were-wolves and going willingly to love and death in the embrace of their ghostly mistresses.

The *Hope's* captain was so impressed with Arthur that he offered him extra money to sign on for another cruise as harpooner as well as surgeon. (From which we deduce that the young man was, unthinkingly, stronger than his creation Holmes, who could not transfix a pig with a harpoon.) And he had made the money he needed: £50 was sent to his mother in Masongill, and a small balance bought him books for his final year.

Before taking his first qualified post he went to Bristol, where his friend Budd had set up in general practice, expecting to do as well as his father had done. The South West, from Somerset to Plymouth, was full of Budds practising medicine. At least one other practitioner grumbled that it was virtually impossible to break into their territory. Young George Turnavine decided to start at the top. He might not earn as much as his father, but he could spend as much. Working on the principle that people would only be persuaded to throw large quantities of money into a really thriving concern, he set up a luxurious establishment on credit and ignored every warning that a smash was bound to follow extravagant living without concomitant earning. Conan Doyle was amused and prudent enough to refuse every invitation to come in with his friend, who found it necessary to call a meeting of his creditors and put on a fine act of beseeching them to let him make a fresh start before he paid them.

So when Dr Conan Doyle was entitled to put the letters MB after his name and invited to hang up his brass plate below Dr Budd's or Dr Hoare's, he chose instead to sign on as surgeon on another vessel. The *S. S. Mayumba* was taking a handful of passengers and various packages of freight to West Africa. Had the voyage proved a success, Conan Doyle might have become a Merchant Naval doctor, or even a colonial. But it was far less enjoyable than Arctic whaling. He was seasick in the Bay of Biscay and almost died of fever off the Guinea Coast. He was not impressed by the *Mayumba's* habit of tossing its freight into the sea near dropping-off points that lacked good anchorage, and trusting the currents to deliver goods to their owners. He would have liked to do more for the disconsolate white man they couldn't help when he signalled them from a sandbank that he had retreated to from his ranch because "his kaffirs" had revolted. Arthur, believed by some admirers to be a model of racial egalitarianism way ahead of his time, never even considered that the

man's use of an opprobrious term from another part of Africa might suggest a rather provocative attitude on his part. Although he was impressed by the black American Minister to Liberia he met off Monrovia, he did not much care for West Africa itself or its muddy snake-ridden rivers and "savage" people.

Back in England he made no fresh attempt to find an adventurous post abroad or on the ocean wave. Instead he listened to the siren voice of George Turnavine Budd, who offered him a position in a growing concern in Plymouth.

GEORGE TURNAVINE BUDD

Budd was unstable. Cursed with get-rich-quick ambitions, he was incapable of settling down to work steadily and sensibly. His Bristol relatives had probably paid off the most importunate of his creditors; Budd himself had no intention of paying anyone.

In Plymouth he had devised a characteristically eccentric form of practice. There was to be no repetition of the expensive carriage which had not driven him to the expected rich patients' houses in Bristol. Here he set up a surgery, and invited the world to come for free consultations. Naturally his waiting-room was packed, which led to the first possibility of charging. The average wait to see Dr Budd would be three or four hours, unless a patient wanted to pay a stiff fee for queue-jumping. As Budd calculated, the penniless crowds wanting free advice were an advertisement drawing people who could afford to pay. And by making them pay for a time-slot rather than a consultation, he kept up the sham of being a doctor who treated people without charging.

Sham it was if treatment entailed prescription. All medicines had to be purchased from the practice. They were prepared by Budd's wife: a quiet little woman, quite overshadowed by her violent and voluble partner. As she had no pharmaceutical training whatsoever, this was potentially risky. But risk was not something that ever deterred George Turnavine Budd. Advertisement was obviously important for this doctor who was more interested in money than medicine. And direct advertisement was professionally prohibited. But Dr Budd could get himself talked about. He bellowed at the patients as they waited. He stamped about and pushed people out of his way and refused to treat some people at all and carried the role of the overbearing medic to such a pitch that all those patients who were ready to be impressed by a bullying doctor rejoiced in one who suffered fools with such a complete abnegation of gladness. And those who wondered about the touch of mania in Budd's goings-on consoled themselves (like Conan Doyle) with the reflection that "Great wits are sure to madness near akin".

Some of Budd's medical precepts would have been dismissed as madness with no wit at all by any competent doctor. The preposterous claim that "tea is pure poison" could not easily be substantiated. Making old ladies swear never to drink it again might have had little effect on them. But in those days there was little in the pharmacopoeia that went beyond purgatives and emetics. A comforting bedside manner was often the only thing the best of doctors could offer as "treatment". And if a patient was finding that Tender Loving Care really had no effect, the shock of Dr Budd's Untender Unloving Bullying might have proved an invigorating placebo.

Conan Doyle's place in this madhouse was to carry out any surgery or midwifery that came the practice's way. Budd was far too busy over-acting the Mad Scientist to do any real work. He assured Conan Doyle that they would become rich beyond the dreams of avarice. He fuelled his own pipe-dreams further with the hope of inventing some great weapon that would assure victory to the power that possessed it. He tried

G Budd

to design impregnable body-armour for infantrymen, and may have speculated on the possibility of electromagnets deflecting shells and bullets from their targets. He was enraged when his letters to the War Office were treated with the contempt they deserved.

His temper was uncertain. Conan Doyle was uneasy when Budd, like Mr Lamb, the steward on the *Hope*, proposed a boxing match. Conan Doyle had a substantial weight and reach advantage. But he started sparring, lightly, until Budd lost his temper at being unable to establish supremacy, and started hitting out wildly. Conan Doyle warned him that this was supposed to be a light bout with pulled punches. Budd only made renewed attempts to hurt him. So Conan Doyle knocked him down. Budd sulked, and then pretended his whole attack had been a joke.

Naturally Arthur's friends were concerned that he was associated with this manifest charlatan. The Hoares would have welcomed him back to Birmingham. Mary Doyle, probably influenced by Bryan Waller, wrote to her son urging him to leave this disreputable debtor. Arthur wrote back defending his partner, and the correspondence grew a little heated.

And then Budd resolved the problem himself. He and his wife grew increasingly reserved and distant to Conan Doyle, until at last Budd suggested that there really was not room for the two of them in the practice, whereupon Conan Doyle immediately offered to leave. But Budd wouldn't hear of his going without being bought out. He had, after all, taken a risk and made an investment of time in coming to Plymouth. Budd offered to pay him £1 a week while he settled in to a new practice in a new town. The money would enable him to buy furniture and equipment on credit.

Conan Doyle accepted the proposal, though he would take the money only as a loan. And he hit upon Portsmouth as a suitable new home.

No sooner had he taken a house and prepared to start in practice there, than a letter came from Budd cancelling the agreement and withdrawing all offers of finance. Budd had found the torn-up remains of one of Mary Doyle's letters, he said, and discovered that she had called him "the unscrupulous Budd", "a bankrupt swindler". He was certainly not going to assist a man who allowed such correspondence to continue while in partnership with him. Conan Doyle was very surprised, it not being his habit to tear up letters and throw them away; and, indeed, a search of his pockets revealed that he still had the very letter Budd purported to have found! That could only mean Budd had been surreptitiously reading his correspondence and arranged the dissolution of partnership with every intention of leaving Conan Doyle high and dry as soon as he had committed himself to purchases he might be unable to pay for without the weekly pound. The result would be that Conan Doyle, too, would look "a bankrupt swindler".

Arthur had a very even temper. He thanked Budd for having ended the only disagreement he had ever had with his mother, and doing so in a way which showed she had been right all along. And he set his mind to the difficult task of building up a practice from nothing with no private means to support him.

OPPOSITE: George Budd, the capricious "friend" of Conan Doyle.

SOUTHSEA AND MARRIAGE

Fortunately, Arthur had a small secondary source of income. Pushed to the maximum, it seemed to bring in £50 a year. But that was near enough to Budd's offer. And so, while he lived in a house with a simply furnished consulting-room, a cabin trunk serving as cupboard and table in the second parlour, and a bare truckle bed in his bedroom, he wrote more earnestly than he ever had before.

He was still a student when he received his first fee for a published story. *Chambers's Journal* printed "The Mystery of Sassassa Valley" in 1879. Arthur did not see his name in type: fiction in weekly and monthly journals was usually anonymous. And while the measly fees were welcome at the time, he soon realised that recognition was even more important. It might be flattering to have his work mistaken for that of R. L. Stevenson in 1884: it would have been more useful to have editors asking for work from Conan Doyle.

As the title suggests, the young author aimed for a popular readership, not the arty intelligentsia. The "mystery" is a gleaming red eye which terrifies natives who believe it to be a monster. The solution is that it is a jewel, revealing the whereabouts of a treasure. The inspiration is Poe's "The Gold Bug", and the author of *Tales of Mystery and Imagination* would always be a great exemplar for Conan Doyle, whose predecessor at Edinburgh University (and Rutherford's Bar), Robert Louis Stevenson, also gave credence to the view that romances and horror stories were not just for children.

From the time he was 20, Arthur Conan Doyle was a professional writer, working to help support himself. He contributed to *Pearson's*, to *Temple Bar*, to *The Cornhill* in the years when it was trying to recover readers by shedding its highbrow material, to the *Boy's Own Paper* which supplied a respectable evangelically biassed outlet for the racy adventure stories lads loved but which were deemed irredeemably vulgar and almost immoral when printed separately in the cheap and smudgily illustrated "penny bloods". He learned his trade as he went along. His first story with a touch of real originality appeared in 1881 in *London Society*. "That Little Square Box" is narrated by a timid fool on a passenger boat, who believes that Fenians have brought an infernal machine aboard. (The section of the Irish Nationalist movement was engaged in one of its counter-productive terror campaigns at the time.) In fact the box is a pigeon-fancier's coop.

In 1883 *Temple Bar* printed "The Captain of the 'Pole-Star'" in which Conan Doyle's gift for economical but evocative description conjured up the Arctic ice-floes and a neurotic, obsessed seaman running across them to his death at the ghostly summons of his former lover. The young writer was impressed by the greatest of all whaling writers, Herman Melville.

Melville's influence was apparent again the following year, when "J. Habakuk Jephson's Statement" appeared in *The Cornhill*. This took up the true mystery of the *Mary Celeste*, found undamaged but abandoned in the Atlantic with its log missing and no apparent reason why the captain should have sacrificed his crew, his wife and his infant daughter to the deep. Conan Doyle proposed that the occupants of the ship had been massacred by former black slaves, obsessed with race hatred. The idea was clearly indebted to Melville's "Benito Cerino", a tale of slaves overpowering and controlling their European ship's officers. It also seemed so convincing that the British consul in Gibraltar issued a straight-faced declaration that it was not true! This was the work that was mistaken for Stevenson's, and Conan Doyle's characteristic carelessness in fully Gallicising the ship's name to *Marie Celeste* was inadvertently followed by many subsequent writers.

With his earnings from writing reaching that princely sum of about £50 a year, Conan Doyle's tax returns incurred the suspicion of the inspectors. "This is very unsatisfactory," reproved the Inland Revenue. "I quite agree," Conan Doyle scrawled on the letter before returning it.

LEFT: The American writer Edgar Allan Poe.

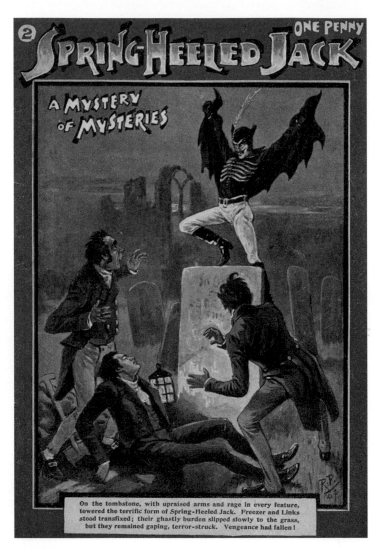

SPRING-HEELED JACK

ONE PENNY

A MYSTERY OF MYSTERIES

On the tombstone, with upraised arms and rage in every feature, towered the terrific form of Spring-Heeled Jack. Freezer and Links stood transfixed; their ghastly burden slipped slowly to the grass, but they remained gaping, terror-struck. Vengeance had fallen!

ABOVE: Spring-heeled Jack, a "penny dreadful". Conan Doyle's early work aimed just a little higher.

He was not doing too badly in medicine, however. The London Doyles, noting that there was no Catholic doctor in Portsmouth, offered him introductions to the local Catholic community. But Arthur Conan Doyle was always a man of outstanding integrity. He point-blank refused to profit by the religion he had abandoned. Instead he took himself out into the community at large. He was a sportsman, and played football and cricket with local clubs. His cricket ultimately reached first-class standards, and he once took the wicket of Dr W. G. Grace, the greatest sportsman of the age. He was a writer of adventure stories and ghost stories, and he took an interest in the serious efforts emanating from the Cambridge intelligentsia to find out what real, scientifically observable basis might lie behind sightings of ghosts. This led him to local seances and table-turning sessions: occasions which initially evoked nothing but scepticism in him.

He was earning enough to make his contribution to the family finances at last. Sister Annie had died. Lottie and Connie had entered the servitude of being governesses. And young Innes was sent down to live with his elder brother. The two became good friends, and Arthur dressed the lad up in a page's uniform to announce patients and give the consultations a touch of class.

In 1895 he accepted as a resident patient a boy with cerebral meningitis. There was no cure for this, and the harrowing medical "treatment" consisted of nursing young Jack Hawkins until he died. Jack's sister Louise (nicknamed "Touie") saw a lot of the young doctor. They fell in love. With Louise's small private income of £100 a year added to his practice, there was sufficient money to justify marriage. And Louise was introduced to "the Ma'am", who sensibly (and volubly) approved. The wedding took place at Masongill parish church, and Dr Conan Doyle was blessed with a helpmeet who would prove a perfect, obedient and supportive Victorian wife: detached from his work and his sporting and intellectual life, but ready with his pipe and slippers and whisky and soda when he was ready to relax.

TAKING GHOSTS SERIOUSLY

The practice flourished when the doctor was married. Soon he had completed his MD, and was earning £300 a year: quite a comfortable income for a young professional couple. The modestly successful short-story writer experimentally extended his range to the novel. A work called *The Narrative of John Smith* was lost in the post between author and publisher, never to be seen again. But in the first years of his marriage Conan Doyle completed *The Firm of Girdlestone*, a Trollopean tale of murky business and marrying heiresses with useful pictures of the medical world as Conan Doyle knew it. By the time it found a publisher the author would have embarked on the detective tales which made him world-famous and the historical novels which he believed marked him down for more lasting literary laurels.

Young Conan Doyle was good at losing manuscripts. Probably the very first story he ever tried to publish was "The Haunted Grange of Goresthorpe", whose manuscript, apparently delivered without a return address, lay undetected in the files of *Blackwood's Magazine* until long after its author's death. The subject – the ghosts of an alcoholic murderer and his victims – reveals the appeal of the occult. And this was probably one of the interests Louise shared with him at first. For he went with her to seances run by her friends in Portsmouth. And in the President of the Portsmouth Literary and Scientific Society, Conan Doyle met a man who persuaded him not to throw up table-rapping in disgust.

Major-General Alfred Drayson was an amateur mathematician and astronomer of some distinction. His theory that the earth wobbles in its rotation was at first dismissed, and then accepted; likewise his observation that the satellites of Uranus did not move from east to west. He was a fine whist player who had written books about the game. And, like Conan Doyle, he contributed to the *Boys' Own Paper*. He was a far more suitable friend for a scientifically minded doctor than his spiritualist

BELOW: Spiritualist séances struck most people as silly, as can be seen in this cartoon from Punch.

predecessor in Portsmouth: a medium called Horstead who delivered messages sent from "Behind the Veil" by John Wesley and assorted politicians. In fact, Conan Doyle's propensity for Watsonian intellectual hero-worship emerged again. Drayson, he decided, was of the same stature as Copernicus, and he listened when Drayson produced a down-to-earth yet still mystical explanation for the mundane absurdity of most seances.

The Fox sisters of Hydesville, New York, set off the great spiritualist activity of the mid-nineteenth century. Like the eighteenth-century fraudsters of the Cock Lane Ghost, they sat among "manifestations" largely consisting of mysterious knocks and raps which answered questions in a simple code – one knock for yes; two knocks for no. Laborious recitations of the alphabet were used to obtain longer messages, and little groups in the western world started meeting together to contact the spirits. The Cambridge-originating Society for Psychical Research collected and verified data, and invented some pseudo-scientific terms: telepathy for thought transference; apporting for the mysterious movement of objects. People who believed spirits spoke or wrote directly with or through them called themselves "mediums" (of communication): it sounded more scientific than "shamans" or "necromancers"!

But as Conan Doyle quickly discovered, most spirit messages were trite, trivial or frankly stupid. The physical manifestations reported sounded like the work of third-rate conjurors: tables and chairs lifting themselves momentarily; tambourines and guitars flying around the room and producing a few ghostly notes. Louise might enjoy such stuff, but he was on the verge of giving it up. Drayson's level-headed interest gave Conan Doyle pause. He did not at first accept Drayson's explanation of spiritualist triviality: that spirits, like people, included the silly and the immature and the waggish among their number, and seances inspired by vulgar curiosity would receive the attention only of silly spirits. But in time he came to accept it wholeheartedly. For the moment, he kept up a general interest, and started subscribing to the major spiritualist journals.

In 1887 he was convinced that some genuine insights from another world were being revealed at some seances. A professional medium, issuing personal messages in "automatic writing" to all present at a seance, gave Conan Doyle a note which read, "This gentleman is a healer. Tell him from me not to read Hunt's book." Conan Doyle was convinced that no one present could have known he was at that time wondering whether to read Leigh Hunt's *Comic Dramatists of the Restoration* in preparation for the historical novel that would become *Micah Clarke*. After that, as Conan Doyle told the spiritualist journal *Light*, "I could no more doubt the existence of the phenomena than I could doubt

the existence of lions in Africa, though I have been to that continent and have never chanced to see one." The belief was not yet a central part of his life, let alone an element of his public persona. But it would come to determine the course of his last ten years on earth, and ultimately prevent him from being offered a peerage.

His doubts about Leigh Hunt's book cast an interesting sidelight on his character. He had just completed an MD thesis which dealt coolly and scientifically with syphilis. He was honest and undisturbed about the deprivation he felt on the whaler *Hope* with no feminine company for seven months. He was to tell the world that fictional Dr Watson knew the women of three continents, and the factual watchfulness of Stonyhurst's Jesuits reduced the boys' sexual experimentation compared with other public schools. Yet he was daunted by the possible "pollution" of reading about bawdy Restoration playwrights. In fact, as all his writings showed, he enjoyed perfectly normal sexual health. He expected men and women to enjoy satisfying sex lives. He did not condemn those who broke the bounds of convention. But he saw no need to challenge that convention for the sake of challenging it. He disliked schoolmasterly spying, but quietly approved of the Jesuits' suppression of sodomy. Although the son of an alcoholic, he never yielded to either drunkenness or teetotalism. He normally maintained admirable moderation and harmony with his age's ethos.

OPPOSITE: The Cock Lane ghost house, where Elizabeth Parsons faked spooky rappings in 1762 to blackmail her father's lodger.

ABOVE: The home of the Fox family at Hydesville, New York, which was reputedly haunted by the spirit of a man who was murdered there.

FROM DOCTOR TO DETECTIVE WRITER

The third to be written, *A Study in Scarlet* was the first of Conan Doyle's novels to be published. He returned to the "adventure" mode which predominated in his short stories, seeing the "detective" as a man who enjoyed an adventurous life in the mundane surroundings of modern city life. His models (as Holmes dismissively indicated in the books) were Poe's Dupin and Gaboriau's Lecoq – Frenchmen from the nation which pioneered policing and gave it a bad name for political spying. Conan Doyle took logical deduction from Dupin and expertise in reading footprints from Lecoq. He added promising features from Bell; intellectual arrogance from Waller; selective polymathic knowledge from Drayson. And he sent Sherlock Holmes off on the dispiriting manuscript journey around publishers.

James Payn, popularising editor of *The Cornhill*, liked it but rejected it because "shilling shockers" were a glut on the market. How close Conan Doyle had come to the "penny dreadfuls" which the *Boy's Own Paper* high-mindedly sought to replace! Arrowsmith's returned it without bothering to unroll it from the cardboard cylinder in which Conan Doyle always packaged manuscript. Ward, Lock accepted it grudgingly. Like Payn, they thought shilling shockers abounded: they had published several themselves. But for a once-for-all payment of £24 they would take it. It would do for a *Christmas Annual*. In a year's time.

Conan Doyle accepted the money and turned to a project dearer to his heart. He had always loved Sir Walter Scott's historical romances. Nobody called them shilling shockers. And he loved Macaulay's character-filled history. His rejection of Catholic bigotry blinded him to the equal narrowness of Calvinism. Indeed, as a scientifically trained man of his time he was sufficiently impressed by the inexorability of cause and effect to find Calvinist predestination akin to scientific determinism. Of course, his rejection of dogma encompassed a generous rejection of any notion of eternal punishment. And since he found Macaulay and his Whig view of history sympathetic, he took it that the Puritans Macaulay favoured were benign. And so he prepared to write on Monmouth's rising of 1683 from the standpoint of a Protestant rebel.

Blackwood's rejected *Micah Clarke* because Conan Doyle's attempts at seventh-century speech were little better than Godwottery. (He always had a poor ear for archaisms and dialects.) Bentley's returned the manuscript with the damning irony that, "The novel's principal defect is that there is a complete absence of interest." Cassell's didn't think historical novels were commercial. Conan Doyle, who had just sold *A Study in Scarlet* for £24, began to wonder whether he would accept £2 for *Micah Clarke*. And then learned Andrew Lang grabbed it for Longman's, Green. He was enthusiastic. He would himself write an excellent historical romance in eight years time, showing Joan of Arc's career as seen by *A Monk of Fife*.

Conan Doyle was thrilled. It seemed far more important than the appearance of *A Study in Scarlet* in *Beeton's Christmas Annual*. The Holmes book had required only a little imagination and some recollections of articles attacking Mormons for terrorising

other settlers. *Micah* represented real work, and he buckled down to even more earnest research in preparation for an even greater historical novel, this time set in the reign of Edward III.

1888 was a good year. *A Study in Scarlet* was reprinted in volume form, and though it earned Arthur no more money, he was able to win his distressed and hospitalised father the commission to illustrate it. *Micah Clarke* was generally received favourably. Joseph Marshall Stoddart came across the Atlantic talent-hunting for *Lippincott's Magazine* and invited Conan Doyle to dinner at the Langham Hotel. Also present were Oscar Wilde and MP T. P. Gill. Conan Doyle was amazed and inclined not to believe that Wilde had read and enjoyed *Micah Clarke*. Had he been familiar with Wilde's reviewing, he would have known that Wilde read new work voraciously, and his besetting weakness, surprisingly, was undue generosity to other writers. But Watsonian modesty was again to the fore as Conan Doyle felt that Wilde towered over them all, while still seeming to think all his companions interesting and worth listening to.

The results of that gathering were commissions for Conan Doyle to produce a new Sherlock Holmes novella, and Wilde to write the book that became *The Picture of Dorian Gray*. Yet with his first child, Mary Louise, born within the year, and his mediaeval novel *The White Company* snapped up by Payn for publication in early 1891, Conan Doyle was still restless, and his attention swung back to medicine. In 1883 he had published an article mentioning Robert Koch, the German bacteriologist. In 1890, Koch was an international sensation as the press declared that his new discovery, "tuberculin", meant the end of that devastating Victorian

ABOVE: The Langham Hotel, where Conan Doyle agreed to write a second Sherlock Holmes novel. It subsequently featured in several of his stories.

OPPOSITE: An early cover of The Strand Magazine.

killer, consumption. Conan Doyle wangled a commission from the *Daily Telegraph* to go to Berlin and report Professor von Bergmann's demonstration at the University. Alas, all seats were taken when he arrived, and von Bergmann snubbed him badly. But working from an American student's notes, Conan Doyle acutely spotted that the cure had not been proved – as Koch had been warning all along. The *Telegraph* published Conan Doyle's sensible caveat, and was under no necessity to eat its words a few weeks later when tuberculin proved useless and the irresponsible gutter-press which had hyped Koch against his will turned and rent him.

In the train returning from Germany, Conan Doyle chatted to another doctor who advised him to leave general practice and specialise. Conan Doyle thereupon behaved very rashly. He hurried his family off to Vienna, intending to take a course in ophthalmology. But his German was not up to it. He spent most of his time skating with Louise, which didn't prevent him from returning to England, moving to an apartment in Montague Place facing the back entrance to the British Museum, and opening a surgery in Devonshire Place.

By his account, nobody came. A specialist practice in London was not like a general practice in Hampshire. He could not go to sports clubs and literary societies and drum up patients. His books sold just well enough to maintain his modest standard of living. But it was a time of depression and failure. And then George Newnes launched a new magazine with a new idea, and the name Conan Doyle suddenly became famous.

TRIUMPH AND DISASTER

The journal was the brainchild of editor Greenhough Smith. Why not start a popular (middlebrow) magazine with adventure fiction, celebrity interviews and features, instructive essays on science and nature, and a picture on almost every page? Illustrate the fiction by the photogravure process, so that the half-toned shading matched the photographs accompanying the features. Give away an artistic print with every number. Write everything in clear, clean prose, avoiding the mannered overwrought style fashionable among the intelligentsia. Keep the artwork plain and manly, or romantic and mistily mediaeval, but never decadent. None of the unentertaining, over-cerebral, pretentious, incomprehensible piffle of the deeply revered George Meredith. None of the beautiful flowing indecency of Aubrey Beardsley. A family magazine that an ordinary

SIR NIGEL
is the hero of Sir A. Conan Doyle's stirring new serial which commences in the December Xmas Double Number of the " Strand Magazine." The above picture illustrates a thrilling incident in the first instalment.
STRAND MAGAZINE

golfing solicitor or accountant could understand and appreciate and leave unashamedly around the house without shocking his wife and daughters.

Newnes jumped at the idea. *The Strand Magazine* was born to instant success. And word went round that the editor would welcome a series of self-contained short adventure stories featuring recurrent characters. This would have the appeal of familiarity, like a serial novel. But there would be no impatient feeling that the narrative had broken off at an exciting point; no loss of interest if a number was missed.

Conan Doyle, who had a comic story accepted in an early number, wondered whether his detective character would fill the slot. Holmes and Watson had been fully imagined and created in the two novels, and he could economically allow the reader to assume a knowledge of them and pick up their salient characteristics as the stories rolled on. No need to stop and describe them at length. Scandal seemed a basis for adventure in 1891. It was the year when nonconformists reeled from the revelation that the "Prince of Wales Played Baccarat for Money", and High Society was devastated to learn that "Sir William Gordon-Cumming Cheated at Cards". Conan Doyle depicted Holmes rescuing a "Rather Ruritanian Royal from Scandal" involving a most un-Beardsleyesque mistress: no "Slinky Southern Sexiness" or "Lascivious Languor in the Boudoir"; all cleverness and wit and dressing up in boy's clothes and rushing precipitously into marriage with an "Honourable Man She Truly Loved". As a second sample, Conan Doyle sent in what would remain one of Holmes's most delightful pieces of pure detection, "The Red-Headed League" in which the extravagant idea of a huge bequest to be shared among the most flaming-haired applicants, proves to have a rational but far from workaday explanation. The great detective starts by showing off Professor Bell's observation and deduction trick, and finishes by making dear, mundane Dr Watson carry a pistol to the familiar neighbourhood of Aldersgate for the capture of an Old Etonian master-criminal with royal blood.

Smith and Newnes accepted them on the spot, calling them the best short stories since Poe. They commissioned four more for a series of six. They commissioned Sidney Paget, whose print of Lancelot and Elaine had been the "free gift" with the first *Strand*, to draw the detective. Conan Doyle was paid 30 guineas (£31.50p) for the series and Paget 20 (£21.00). The success was instantaneous. The Strand's circulation

leaped to half a million. Readers' letters showed that this was due to Sherlock Holmes. Paget's illustrations (which Conan Doyle didn't really care for) brought him to life. The detective's genius, exhibited in the text, was attached to a handsome face and superbly dressed frame. Many people refused to believe that this righter of wrongs was merely a fiction. The creation took on greater reality than the creator.

But the regular byline "Conan Doyle" was good advertisement. The heroic Irish name was sufficiently out of the ordinary (like the forename Sherlock) to suggest someone impressive. It all attracted attention to Arthur's other books, and to his delight *The White Company* and *Micah Clarke* started selling almost as successfully as Sherlock Holmes.

Before Holmes had completed his first six *Adventures* in *The Strand*, Arthur was overworked. He found Greenhough Smith's deadlines tough, and fell victim to flu. As the fever receded, it dawned on him that he was financing an unremunerative medical practice by writing. He had never really been a scientist by temperament. And he tossed his handkerchief to the ceiling as he realised that he could give up doctoring and be a full-time writer.

The unbelievable offer of £1,000 for another Sherlock Holmes series confirmed the wisdom of his decision. The Doyles left Montague Place and bought a large house in Upper Norwood. Mr Dunlop's invention of the pneumatic tyre had

OPPOSITE: Sir George Newness, who launched The Strand Magazine, *after which the name of Conan Doyle became famous.*

ABOVE: Baccarat at Tranby Croft: the scandal that hurt the Prince of Wales.

ushered in the cycling mania. The Doyles bought a tricycle tandem and went for long healthy spins through the Surrey countryside. Arthur was completely happy as his powerful legs pumped the wheels round, and his smiling, pretty little wife steered them through good fresh air. The birth of their son, Alleyne Kingsley, in 1892 slowed her down considerably. But Arthur wasn't worried.

He was accepted into literary society. Jerome K. Jerome, whose *Three Men in a Boat* and *On the Bummel* were almost as fresh-air-fanatical as Arthur himself, became a particular friend. Like Arthur, he was an unpretentious entertainer with a good-humoured acceptance of things as they are, and a simple and sentimental moral optimism. J. M. Barrie was another friend. The men were both proud Anglo-Celts from Scotland; both quietly interested in things fey; both keen cricketers. Arthur played for Barrie's literary team the "Allakhbarries". He played for the MCC while that was still a local London club. He once represented England on a team that went to Holland.

Holmes went from strength to strength, and when Arthur fretted about the deadlines and the strain of making up plots, his mother invented "The Copper Beeches" for him. Still, he wanted to devote more time to historical fiction, and more time to Louise, who seemed to be slow in recovering from Kingsley's birth.

They could afford a recuperative holiday in Switzerland, but it didn't seem to help. And on their return in January 1893, Arthur suddenly saw his wife coughing blood. It was, he knew, a death sentence.

TREATING THOSE TWO IMPOSTERS

The nineteenth century knew no cure for consumption once blood was coughed up in sputum. Before that it was just possible that the right climate, precaution against over-exertion, and tender loving care might arrest the tubercle's progress. But bloodspots in the handkerchief made prognosis certain. Increased coughing, weakness and death. It might take weeks, months or years. But premature death was certain. It had come to Keats, and successively to Anne, Emily and Charlotte Brontë. Victorians feared consumption as post moderns fear cancer.

Arthur had cause to feel guilt as well as distress. He was a doctor. He should have recognised the symptoms during Louise's second pregnancy. He might just have done something effective at that point.

As it was, he set about urgently bolting the stable door with the horse in full flight. He arranged to spend more time in Davos, Swiss air being supposed to be good for consumptives. He arranged for the children to be cared for by their maternal grandparents and aunts while he and Louise went abroad for her health. And he decided to end the time-consuming distraction of devising Holmes plots and meeting Smith's deadlines. To end the series he killed his hero. This was really extraordinarily unprofessional. He should have had the strength to refuse more Holmes stories without putting his publishers in the dreadful position of suggesting that their most popular product was finished with no possibility of revival. Twenty-thousand readers cancelled their subscriptions on reading "The Final Problem"! Thousands more wrote furious letters to the editor. The Prince of Wales let it be known that he disapproved.

Conan Doyle was in Davos and didn't turn a hair at the fuss. While Louise lay on her back and coughed, he was introducing Norwegian cross-country skiing to Switzerland. And turning his mind more and more to psychic matters.

Charles Altamont Doyle died in October, having swallowed his tongue in a fit. Three weeks later Arthur took out a subscription to the *Proceedings of the Society for Psychical Research*. Its president was the stylish intellectual Conservative politician Arthur Balfour, who had been devastated by the loss of his fiancée, and started a lifelong bachelor search for a medium to put him in touch with her. He recognised the fraudulence or self-delusion of every seance he attended, but he went on hoping. The society's vice-presidents included Alfred Russel Wallace, who shared with Darwin the honour of propounding a rational theory of evolution: Balfour's brother-in-law, the Cambridge don Henry Sidgwick; George Eliot's protégé, F. W. H. Myers; the physicist Oliver Lodge; and the inventor of the radiometer and isolator of thallium, William Crookes. The array of distinguished scientists brought out all Conan Doyle's unscientific Watsonian naïvety. Such men could not be dishonest and could not be mistaken. Crookes, especially, had carried out a long series of experiments with a pretty young medium named Florrie Cook between 1870 and 1874. He had concluded that a spirit called Katie King really did materialise when Florrie was motionless in a trance inside a lath and cloth "cabinet": that Katie was the spirit daughter of another emanation, bearded ghost "John King" who was really Sir Henry Morgan, the piratical ruler of seventeenth-century Jamaica! Katie was quite a sexy emanation, whose phosphorescent curves could be detected under translucent muslin robes, and who revealed, unusually, that there was marriage and remaining in marriage and continuing to consummate marriage in the next world.

Conan Doyle ignored the fact that the other SPR chiefs privately thought Crookes was too severely myopic to detect Florrie Cook's conjuring skills in darkened seance rooms, and anyway the great chemist (to the distress of his wife and daughters) was so enamoured of the medium that he would never expose her

OPPOSITE: Arthur and his first wife "Touie" Conan Doyle, tricycling in the early 1890s.

cheating as others had done. Conan Doyle believed that Crookes's experiments almost certainly proved that there was life after death. And this mattered to him with Charles dead and Louise gradually dying.

Katie King's unspiritual sexiness was also appealing. Louise's illness meant that Arthur's sex life was passing into the realm of memory. It was good to think it might be revived after death! Some of his short stories at this time reverted to the linked themes of sex, death and yearning which had figured in his premarital writing. And his novella *The Parasite* created his most effective vampirish femme fatale: a passionate white West Indian who hypnotises the young man she desires into attempting the murder of his fiancée. In 1894 Arthur went to America on a lecture tour, accompanied by Innes. He was overworked, as visiting English lecturers often were in the nineteenth century. But he was a success. And unlike many of his predecessors, he loved America. He would long harbour the hope that a United Anglo-American Empire might one day dominate the world.

In Vermont he visited Kipling, who expected to reside forever in New England with his American wife and had not yet quarrelled disruptively with her brother. Conan Doyle taught Kipling golf, which the latter would play with red balls on the snow. And although worry about Louise and the tension of enforced celibacy could make Conan Doyle short-tempered and insomniac, he still seemed a genial sporting giant (6ft 4in in his socks), exulting in billiards and backgammon, fishing and cricket, and playing soccer when past the age of 40. He had remained modest and unaffected by the onrush of wealth and success in 1891. He stayed benign and generous to the world when suffering real distress in his private life. He, of all men, seemed to live up to the balanced temperament Kipling praised:

If you can meet with triumph
and disaster and treat those
two imposters just the same ...

After returning from America, Arthur took Louise back to Switzerland, and then to Egypt to avoid the harsh winter. While in England, he built a house at Hindhead, which some people believed to be as good for TB as residence abroad. And it was at Hindhead that he met Jean Leckie.

A VERRAY PARFAIT GENTIL KNIGHT

Jean was a quietly vivacious, attractive young woman in her twenties. An athletic rider who loved hunting. A far more intelligent and outgoing personality than Louise. She and Arthur fell in love immediately.

This was unsurprising. Through no fault of Louise's, but quite unavoidably, Arthur was suffering from sexual malnutrition and depressed self-esteem. The

OPPOSITE: Dr Conan Doyle tending to the injured in the Langman Hospital in South Africa.

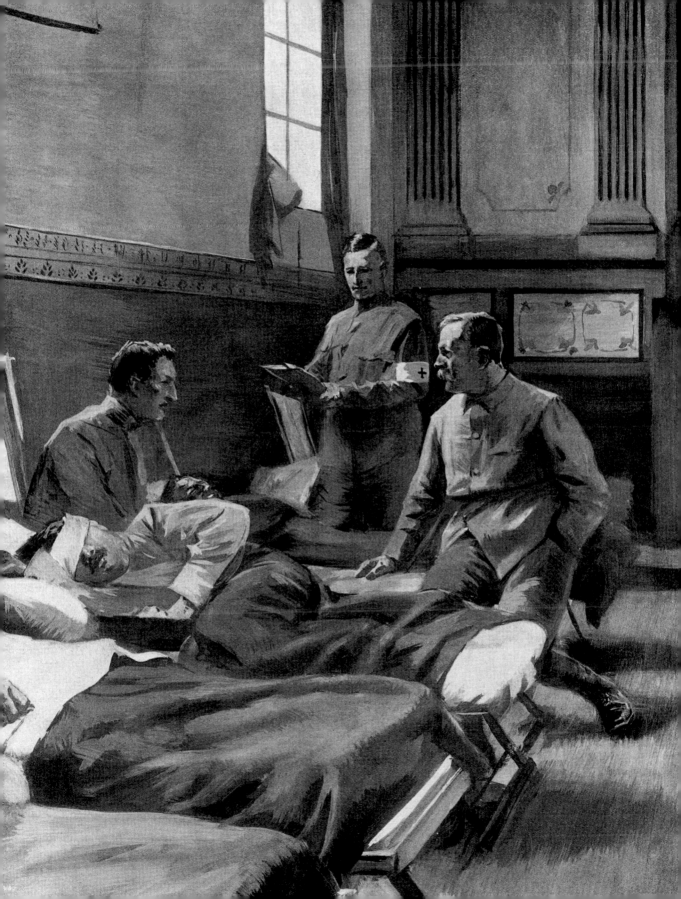

strenuous activities he and Louise enjoyed together – skating and tricycling – could never be revived. He had failed to diagnose her illness. The public insisted on seeing him as the creator of Sherlock Holmes, when he wanted to be thought the best historical novelist since Scott. His winter in Egypt had not produced the journalism he anticipated: describing warfare in the Sudan. His new house in Hindhead had taken ages to complete, and still wasn't satisfactory. A sportsman approaching 40, he knew his athletic days were numbered. Everything conspired to make him ready to accept and return the compensation of an attractive young woman's devotion.

But it was his conduct on finding himself in love that marked him as noble. Louise, he decided, must never know. Nor would he secretly betray her sexually behind her back. Her death at some premature moment was certain. Jean and he would simply have to contain themselves in silent frustration until the event occurred. And there was to be no hideous hoping for Louise to die quickly, no unseemly rejoicing when her time came.

His sister Connie, after a flirtation with Arthur's friend Jerome K. Jerome, had married another young writer, E. W. Hornung. Both were appalled by Arthur's decision, and urged him to consummate his love with Jean. He refused, and was strongly supported by "the Ma'am". He had been typically frank in telling his family he had fallen extramaritally in love. His mother gave him well-deserved backing, uncritically accepting both the rightness of Jean for him and the rightness of his decision that, whatever the cost to themselves, they must do nothing for which they might reproach themselves. We do not know whether the attempt to conceal the affair from Louise worked. We must honour Arthur for attempting concealment which (as his openness with his family showed) was genuinely for her sake and not his own "reputation". And we may honour that staunch fidelity which still left him headachy and insomniac, even though the adoring support of Jean gave him some quiet contentment. The lovers deserved the outstandingly happy marriage they contracted in 1907.

Much of Conan Doyle's writing at this time drew attention to the idea of the warrior. Nigel Loring, knightly hero of *The White Company* (for all his name sounds more like a public schoolboy in a merchant bank), stayed in his mind, and Conan Doyle's pedantic recreation of fourteenth-century chivalry would be given a "prequel" in Sir Nigel (1903). Another pedantic study, this time of Napoleon, had produced no great novel in *The Great Shadow* of 1892. But the remembered Napoleonic facts were put to brilliant use in the "Brigadier Gerard" stories which tumbled into *The Strand* at the turn of the century. Napoleonic Baron de Marbot's swanking memoirs had amused English readers immensely. Conan Doyle now took Marbot as the model for a genuinely brave, genuinely soldierly Frenchman, whose fine horsemanship and loyalty are persistently let down by his stupidity. Yet he is too obtuse to see this, and thinks his bungling is a tribute to his élan. Few English writers would have resisted the temptation to make Gerard fancy himself as a lady's man – very French! Probably none but Conan Doyle could have approved Gerard's amatory successes without leering or sneering. In the background the emperor's ambiguous presence as the object of Gerard's loyalty is totally effective. Conan Doyle eschewed the habits he derived from Scott's intrusive footnotes and Charles Reade's crapulous *The Cloister and the Hearth* – which he believed to be the best historical novel ever written! – and wore his learning lightly and artistically. He always had a nice sense of humour when he chose to use it, and the best of the Gerard stories are certainly among the best things he ever wrote.

The same years saw the dramatisation of Holmes. Conan Doyle wrote a draft. American actor William Gillette, who wanted to play the role, wrote a draft. The two were combined. The manuscript was lost. Gillette rewrote it more or less from memory with a new ending. And the play took the stage from 1899 with resounding international success.

A real war caught Conan Doyle's attention in 1897. He had never been a warrior and was too old for the yeomanry to accept him to take up arms against the Boers. But he urged that Britons should be fighting this war for themselves and not relying on colonials from Canada and Australia to do it for them. In 1901 his friend Archie Langman organised a medical unit financed by his wealthy father, and Dr Conan Doyle put on uniform and went to run a temporary hospital at Bloemfontein.

The experience proved vile. Lord Roberts, in lifting the siege of Bloemfontein and marching on, had omitted to leave a guard over the water supply. The Boers destroyed the outlying waterworks, and the town was dependent on ancient polluted wells. First typhoid, then cholera spread through the town and the hospital. Conan Doyle's work entailed more cleaning faeces than closing wounds. The hospital stank. Catching a mild bout of fever himself, Conan Doyle convalesced by riding toward the front with a reconnaissance unit, and thoroughly enjoyed the experience. Like Kipling, who was in the same war, he tended to write about gunfire and explosions as though they were romantic and jolly attributes of the landscape or weather.

After he had served for three months, it was clear that the war was now running in England's favour. Conan Doyle was sent home, where he wrote 5,000 words a day to race out a pamphlet defending the British authorities against atrocity charges in the continental press. Much to his embarrassment, this patriotic effort earned him a knighthood when Edward VII came to the throne in 1902. And although his mother thoroughly disapproved of the war, she loved having a real chivalric title in the family at last, and joined those who impressed on him that he must accept the honour.

ABOVE: Jean Elizabeth Leckie, Conan Doyle's second wife.

IN SHINING ARMOUR

Conan Doyle's fame was at its peak in 1902. *The Hound of the Baskervilles*, timed to appear as Gillette's play opened in London, had revived Sherlock the previous year. Eight years' absence had made the public's heart grow fonder: Sherlock Holmes might never have been the overwhelming model for all other detectives had he not been sorely missed, and had he not returned in a triumphant adventure rather than a series of stories demanding strenuous plotting to a monthly deadline.

Such stories were to come, however. American magazine proprietor S. S. McClure had been Conan Doyle's first syndicating publisher, and the only American willing to take up *The White Company*. Conan Doyle had once helped McClure out of a cash-flow crisis by "investing" $5,000 in his new magazine. Now *McClure's Magazine* was thriving, and the proprietor sent Conan Doyle an irresistible $5,000 for six new stories, stipulating only that they must take place after Reichenbach, which Holmes must be shown to have survived. By accepting, Arthur committed himself to writing sporadic Holmes stories for the rest of his life. His attempts to insist that Holmes had retired only fixed the tales in the last two decades of Victoria's reign, which bathed Holmes in a soft light of nostalgia for the security of 1880s and 1890s London.

Sherlock Holmes righted wrongs in exemplary fashion. His creator's knighthood honoured his defence of the imperial administrators and soldiers who invented concentration camps. And Sir Arthur Conan Doyle continued to take up public causes.

He stood for parliament in two elections. He was a Liberal Unionist – a follower of the one-time radical Joseph Chamberlain who split with Gladstone when the Grand Old Man came out in favour of Irish Home Rule. Conan Doyle was radical Liberal in his mild distaste for the excessive pretensions of the hereditary aristocracy and in his hope that compulsory education would improve society (movingly expressed in Holmes's paean for the new public Board of Education Schools as beacons to the future). But he was an Irishman who knew full well that he and his family benefited profoundly from Union with England, Scotland and Wales. So he backed Chamberlain in supporting Gladstonian policies, except over Ireland.

By the new century, the Unionists had been forced into the corner of close alliance with the Conservatives. Conan Doyle was never malevolently partisan. He didn't mind association with Arthur Balfour, his civilised fellow-enquirer into the occult. And so he twice fought Scottish seats for the Conservatives, under the Liberal Unionist label. He lost both times.

His anti-Home Rule stance would be changed by his association with Roger Casement, the British consul in the Congo who, in 1903, exposed the atrocities perpetrated by greedy rubber- and ivory-hunters in the vast territory personally owned by Leopold II of Belgium.

Conan Doyle wrote a pamphlet attacking Leopold in 1909 (unfortunately timed, as the king had just died when it came out), and let Casement show him that sooner

OPPOSITE: Punch *satirises King Leopold's atrocious rule of the Belgian Congo, the public issue that brought Conan Doyle and Casement together.*

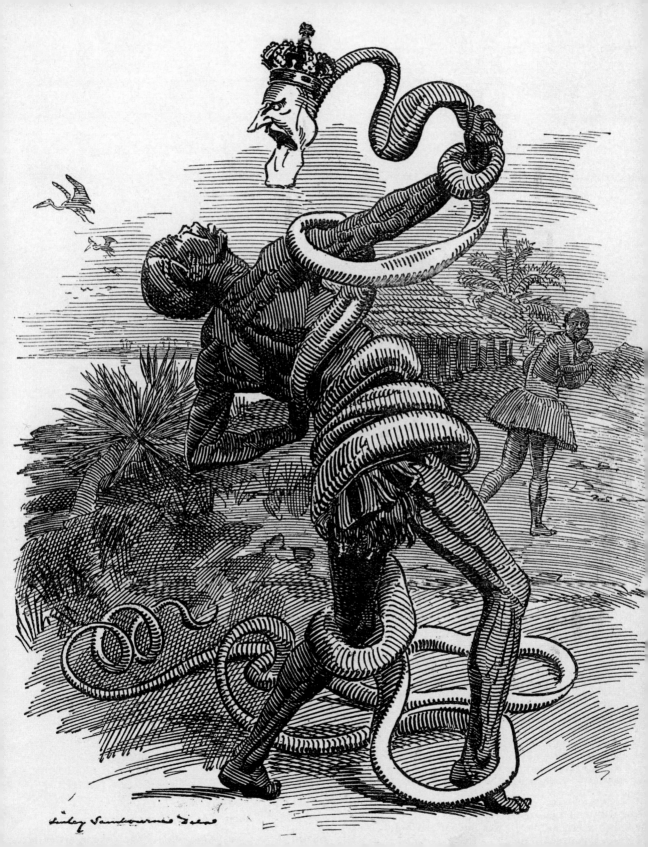

or later Ireland would have to govern itself. There seemed no great urgency in those years before the Easter Rising and the British government's foolish execution of its leaders, but Conan Doyle was happy to declare himself a Home Ruler and join Asquith in waiting and seeing. When Casement himself conspired with the German government to detach Ireland from the war effort, and was arrested and convicted of treason in 1916, Conan Doyle organised the unsuccessful petition for his reprieve. He argued that the man was honest if misguided. And the "Black Diaries", with which the government sought to prejudice sympathies against Sir Roger by exposing his homosexuality, merely showed that he was (in the mind of robustly heterosexual Arthur Conan Doyle) mentally unbalanced. And thus obviously innocent by virtue of his demonstrable insanity.

The robust heterosexual was happily remarried by this time. Louise died in 1906, and her death caused him undoubted shock and grief, though out of consideration for Jean he never expressed it loudly. He married Jean a year later, in Parliament's own church, St Margaret's, Westminster, and the two lived happy ever after, giving birth to two sons, Denis and Adrian, and a daughter "Billy".

The great detective writer turned detective in the year of Louise's death. Reading about the dubious conviction of a young half-Parsee solicitor for cattle mutilation, he went to investigate events at Great Wyrley. George Edalji, the vicar's son, had been accused at various times of harassing his own family with racist anonymous letters and finally slitting the bellies of horses, sheep and cows. Conan Doyle decided that George was too short-sighted to have made the very difficult journey to the scene of crime in the dark, too sweet-natured to have committed the barbarous crimes, and, in fact, was the victim of a former schoolmate called Royden Sharp, whose returns to Great Wyrley always coincided with the cattle-maiming.

Conan Doyle's angry articles in the *Daily Telegraph* restored Edalji's good name and his membership of the Law Society. But the police and Home Office refused to expunge the conviction, and Richard Whittington-Egan's subsequent researches have led him to conclude that Conan Doyle indeed made some extraordinary errors, including making a Holmes-like survey of the night-time journey from the vicarage to ... the wrong field!

The wrongful conviction of Oscar Slater for the murder of Miss Marion Gilchrist was another injustice to be righted. Miss Gilchrist's maid had falsely identified Slater as the man she saw leaving the dead Miss Gilchrist's apartment, and suppressed the fact that she had recognised the killer. As Slater was a foreign pimp, the authorities

ABOVE: Sir Roger Casement, idealist and friend, who persuaded Conan Doyle to favour Irish home rule.

OPPOSITE: Cover of the first edition of Conan Doyle's The Lost World.

didn't care. It took 20 years for his conviction to be overturned, and there is dispute among experts to this day as to who the real killer was.

In the years before the war, Sir Arthur took up other causes, bad and good. He firmly opposed the suffragettes. He backed the campaign against using rare birds' feathers in millinery. He defended the captain and officers of the *Titanic* against charges of bad seamanship and letting the steerage passengers drown. He became the leading light of the Divorce Reform Association. And he warned that submarines, used offensively rather than defensively, might overcome Britain's naval power.

WORLDS LOST AND FOUND

To live nearer to Jean's family and possibly to exorcise the memories of Louise at Hindhead, Conan Doyle bought a house in Windlesham soon after their marriage. In 1910, iguanadon footprints were discovered in the neighbourhood, and Conan Doyle had some casts made for his untidy, overcrowded study. They provided an inspiration. Adventure and the Mad Scientist could be combined in the search

for prehistoric creatures surviving in South America. *The Lost World* was born. Professor Challenger, the hero, was named for an exploration ship in which several Edinburgh botanists had made a well-publicised scientific cruise just before Conan Doyle's time. Challenger's appearance combined Professor Rutherford's black beard and barrel chest with George Budd's lunatic propensity for manic energy, furious overstatement and wild rage when crossed. And Conan Doyle added the true genius he naïvely believed he had seen in Budd.

As foils to this wonderful creation he devised acidulous Professor Summerlee, donnishly delighting in barking and biting, and owing much to the memory of Joseph Bell. It was a master touch to give this chairbound academic unsuspected physical stamina in the jungle. Lord John Roxton, the fearless aristocratic humanitarian, was modelled on Casement: a close friend at the time. And the narrator, Irish journalist Edward Dunn Malone, was a compliment to Edmund Dene Morel who worked tirelessly for Casement and Conan Doyle's Congolese campaign. Sir Ray Lankester, evolutionary biologist and one-time curator of the Natural History Museum, advised Conan Doyle on paleontology. It is significant of Conan

Doyle's genial good-fellowship that Lankester was once described as the only high-ranking paleontologist with a sufficient sense of mischief to have perpetrated the Piltdown Man hoax.

Good humour was a feature of this book. Challenger and his friends are intentionally funny, and it is as surprising to us today as it was to Conan Doyle at the time that many readers missed the comedy. But they loved the adventure, and Conan Doyle wrote another Challenger novel in which the professor and his friends use oxygen masks to become almost the last surviving living creatures when *The Poison Belt* drifts across the world. The happy ending, when everyone turns out to have been cataleptic rather than dead, proved a letdown to me when I read it as a small boy. And such simple critical readership was Conan Doyle's preference, so I have no hesitation in declaring the book good, but not as good as *The Lost World*.

Why didn't the unpretentious writer of adventure stories spiced with comedy become friendly with that other master of the same craft, Sir Henry Rider Haggard? It is unlikely that Conan Doyle's generous nature would have noticed how totally his own work eclipsed *King Solomon's Mines* and *She*, revealing the comparative puerility of Haggard's comedy, the adolescence of his mildly erotic moments, and the general inertia of his descriptive passages. It is probable that Conan Doyle's bluff equability over most public affairs didn't appeal to Haggard, who was to join Kipling in some anti-Semitic-tinged hysteria about Bolshevism. 1914 certainly proved Conan Doyle more balanced than the far greater Rudyard, who screamed bellicosity before hostilities opened, and nursed a sick hatred of "the Hun" when the Great War proved unlike the sporting and victorious re-run of South Africa's lighter moments he had envisaged.

Conan Doyle made a very successful visit to America and Canada in 1914. He revealed his middle-aged Conservatism when he grumbled amusingly that Mr Lloyd George had emptied his wallet: an indirect protest about the taxation financing old age pensions. His support for his country when war broke out on his return was instant. He arranged to start at once on a *History of the British Campaign*. (He had written a very successful account of the fighting against the Boers, started before

OPPOSITE: The exploring party: Professor Challenger, with Malone on his right, Lord Ruxton on his left and Professor Summerlee standing behind.

LEFT: Conan Doyle's second family looking over a wall and pointing towards New York City.

that war was complete.) He organised a local volunteer force in Crowborough, and though a knight and his county's Deputy Lord Lieutenant, he served loyally throughout the hostilities as a humble private in the precursor of "Dad's Army".

Like Kipling, he was rather too inclined to see the war in terms of quasi-South African sportsmanship at first. Unlike Kipling, who gnashed malignant teeth at most opponents of the British empire, Conan Doyle had always recognised the civilian Boers as decent farmers, entitled to shield their fighting menfolk, though necessarily to be incarcerated "for their own protection" when they did so. He enjoyed the "War Game" of moving flags over maps in his study to record the shifting front lines. He visited German Prisoners of War and reckoned them decent, brave and steady chaps. It wasn't until Zeppelin raids started that he became belligerently militant and demanded reprisals. And even then he tended to be one of those who referred carefully to Prussian militarism, distinguishing the war-based state of Frederick the Great and Bismarck from the happy bucolic souls of the Rhineland or Bavaria.

But he was an action writer, and fretted that he was unable to see action himself. Despite the horrors of Mons, where Jean's dearly loved brother Malcolm was killed, and the dreadful toll of deaths in Flanders, he detested any form of pacifism, and completely broke with his old friend and Congo Reform Association colleague Edmund Morel, when the government railroaded that idealist into jail on the specious grounds that he sent material urging a peaceful settlement of the war to Romain Rolland in neutral Switzerland.

Before the war ended, however, Conan Doyle came to believe it offered a spiritual lesson almost outweighing the healthy lessons active service might have brought to those young enough and lucky enough to survive it. A sickly, neurotic, hard-up friend of Jean's called Lily Loder Symonds had started "automatic writing" while the Doyles put her up. Jean had no belief in spiritualism at all, and Arthur thought Lily was self-deluded. Until, in 1917, Lily "automatically wrote" answers to questions Arthur put about a private conversation he had held with Malcolm Leckie many years before. He was convinced by Lily's answers that she really was in touch with the young man who had died at Mons. He was, at last, absolutely persuaded that spiritualist mediums had proved the existence of life after death. He was already writing about his newfound certainties when he heard the tragic news that both his son Kingsley and his brother Innes had died of pneumonia after surviving active service.

CRANKING UP TO OLD AGE

From the publication of *The New Revelation* in 1918 and *The Vital Message* a year later, until his death in 1930, Sir Arthur Conan Doyle seemed determined to undeceive all those who thought he was a sharp-witted simulacrum of his own Sherlock Holmes. Throughout his agnostic years, he had never doubted the existence of some incomprehensible shaping force behind nature, and as Sherlock Holmes's

OPPOSITE: Dr Conan Doyle in the simple uniform of the private field hospital in the Boer War.

little disquisition on the beauty of flowers and the non-utilitarian character of that beauty showed, he believed the force was benign. But he didn't pretend to know what the pattern was. He had been almost, but not quite, convinced by Crookes's reports on Florrie Cook. Now Lily had given him a direct personal experience. And he was sure. There was a spirit world. It communicated with ours through mediums. And it had a high purpose in doing so.

Since the guaranteed "manifestations" had all been recorded since the Fox sisters in the 1840s, Conan Doyle argued that the spirit world was suddenly bombarding humanity with evidence for its existence and messages about the afterlife. Why? Because crass materialism threatened the human race. The Great War was a demonstration that, if carried to the lengths of "Prussian militarism", scientific materialism might conjure up unthinkable means of destruction.

Orthodox Christianity had failed by concentrating on Christ's death instead of his life. Theological inanities about atonement and sacrifice had distracted attention from the example set by the Perfectly Good Man, whose powers of healing, knowledge of other people's thoughts, and appearances to his disciples after his death showed that he and they were simply the greatest mediums the world had ever known. Unitarian Christian Spiritualism would bring mankind back to the real truth.

The testimony of scientists showed that the spirit manifestations were real. Crookes had proved the reality of "Katie King". Sir Oliver Lodge had undoubtedly been in

contact with his son Raymond, killed in the war. The fact that many mediums had been exposed cheating didn't mean they all cheated. Indeed, those who had been exposed didn't necessarily cheat all the time. The suspiciously childish manifestations – flying guitars, tambourines, accordions and the like – showed only that this generation was so spiritually infantile that the spirits had to use childish toys to attract human notice. People had doubted the existence of mesmerism until it was renamed hypnotism. Photographs showing spirit faces and "ectoplasm" emerging from mediums proved that the manifestations had real existence. Ectoplasm's disappearance if exposed to daylight explained the suspicious need for darkness or dim red lighting at seances; look at the analogy of unfixed photographic images. The suspicious "conjuror's" cabinets from which mediums preferred to work concentrated psychic forces. When Assyrian cuneiform tablets produced by a famous medium in Paris turned out to be modern forgeries, this proved that the spirits found it easier to "apport" new materials which had been handled recently by the living. The extraordinary recurrence of

wise old spirit guides to direct mediums showed that Native Americans were unusually close to the natural world and so more likely than other people to come back and help its denizens. By their nature, spirits could not appear to sceptics.

Conan Doyle never budged from this self-contained, hermetically sealed philosophy. Anyone familiar with the arguments of Baconian theorists or UFO watchers or Kennedy assassination buffs or the wilder aspirants to identifying Jack the Ripper, will recognise the closed thought-patterns: the instant answer to every objection; the reliance on argument by analogy; the belief that logic-chopping constitutes a proof; the trust placed in proven liars when their statements conform to the theorist's theory; the acceptance of intrinsically hyper-dubious physical evidence; and the insistence that it is "unscientific" or "unhistorical" to rule out any possibility on the grounds of its gross improbability.

Sir Arthur Conan Doyle had become a crank. His crankiness became a national scandal in 1922 when he published his belief in the "Cottingley fairies". These had

OPPOSITE: Elsie Wright pretends to be looking at a fairy in a faked photograph.

ABOVE: George V and Queen Mary enjoyed Conan Doyle's writing, but could not support his belief in fairies.

allegedly been seen in 1917 by fifteen-year-old Elsie Wright and her ten-year-old cousin Frances Griffiths. They captured them with a Midg camera, and Elsie's father processed their plates. In 1920 Conan Doyle heard about these pictures from the editor of *Light*, and followed the progress of a theosophist, Edward Gardner, who went to investigate. Gardner was convinced by the girls and their father, and himself took some more pictures. Conan Doyle was convinced, and wrote about the girls and their fairies.

He was out on a limb this time. Sir Oliver Lodge flatly disbelieved in the fairies. Price's, the candle-makers, pointed out that some were reproductions of fairy illustrations they had used in advertisements. Mockers put together a picture of Conan Doyle himself with the Price's fairies fluttering around him. He refused to abandon his belief. The girls were too young and innocent to be lying, he insisted. Fairy folk could make themselves visible when their vibrations were in harmony with the place and the observer. It was all quite beautiful.

Old admirers like King George V, Lloyd George and Winston Churchill despaired of him. A peerage for this undoubtedly great and good man had been considered. It had to be dropped. The House of Lords could not be laid open to such ridicule as Conan Doyle invited.

Fifty years later Elsie admitted, with wicked amusement, that it had indeed been a hoax. But after Lily's death, Jean had become convinced of spiritualism and thought she too had inherited the gift of automatic writing. With her love and support, Arthur could brave any amount of public ridicule. For the rest of his life, he made it his mission to publish the good news that there was life after death and it was very pleasant. He visited mediums. He held seances at home. He became far and away the best-known advocate of Christian spiritualism, and converted the unfortunate Professor Challenger, shoving him into a book crammed with pedantic footnotes documenting anecdotal evidence of "manifestations". Sherlock Holmes was spared, though the hardening of Conan Doyle's arteries was apparent in such poor stories as "The Mazarin Stone" and "The Lion's Mane".

END OF LIFE

To spiritualists Sir Arthur Conan Doyle was neither crank nor gull, but the foremost of the celebrities who gave them confidence in their faith. He addressed annual Armistice Day mass meetings, first in the Queen's Hall, and after 1925 in the Albert Hall since audiences of 5,000 usually wanted to hear him. Sir Edward Marshall Hall, the famous barrister, was one of their number. He had visited psychics in his grief when his faithless wife died following an illegal abortion. And had become convinced when a medium told him an envelope he held had been written by a man who had died in South Africa. Marshall Hall was at that moment unaware that his brother, who wrote the letter, had died in the Union the day before, and the discovery left him understandably impressed. Sir Oliver Lodge remained true to that faith in spirits he

OPPOSITE: Conan Doyle wearing the spectacles he needed in later life.

and Conan Doyle had discussed in Buckingham Palace gardens while awaiting their knighthoods. Hannen Swaffer, the *Daily Express's* caustic drama critic, saw no reason to be cynical about seances. Hereward Carrington was distinguished as a conjuror as well as an honest psychical researcher, which marked him off from the fellow prestidigitators who usually vaunted their ability to do anything any medium did.

But the most famous stage magician of the age became paradoxically a great friend of Conan Doyle's as well as the best known debunker of mediums. Harry Houdini longed to be reunited with his mother after her death, and was concomitantly disgusted by the fraudulent conjuring he quickly found in the mediums he visited. The Fox sisters openly admitted their hoaxes to him, hardly believing that a genuine religious sect was in the making from their parlour games of table-rapping and -tilting. But Conan Doyle's simplicity delighted Houdini when the family went to see him perform on the south coast, and Sir Arthur visited him afterwards to express his positive belief that some of Houdini's best effects were the result of psychic powers! A good professional magician, Houdini did not disillusion this credulous punter but held a long discussion on spirits with him in which the two men rapidly realised that, however much their conclusions differed,

they were both seekers. When however, Conan Doyle demanded that Houdini stop pretending and admit publicly that his escape in Bristol from a carrier's sealed pallet had been achieved by psychic "dematerialisation and rematerialisation", Houdini felt it necessary to deny the suggestion and explain that he made his way out by purely natural means. It was too late. Conan Doyle firmly believed Houdini had supernatural powers that he didn't wish to disclose!

Their friendship was shaken after Conan Doyle's 1922 lecture tour of America. When the family visited Houdini, Jean offered to give him a private reading. Houdini was excited, as he knew the Doyles to be scrupulously honest. He concealed his disappointment when Jean covered pages with supposed greetings from his mother that simply had to be self-delusion. For they were all in English, which his mother never spoke; they were not the sorts of things she would have said. They were just all wrong.

Unfortunately he jotted down the name "Powell", at the end of the sitting, to remind himself to assist a friend who had fallen on hard times. But Conan Doyle believed this to be "automatic writing" sent to Houdini by a recently deceased spiritualist colleague of his own. When he published the opinion that Houdini was convinced by Jean's automatic writing and had provided the medium for spirit communication from Dr Powell, he was hurt by Houdini's public denial. But the friendship never quite died out, and Conan Doyle was saddened when the great illusionist died in 1926.

By that time Conan Doyle had been the President of the International Spiritualist Association and lectured in Paris where an incompetent magic lantern operator got the slides in the wrong order, leading to jeering and scrapping between believers and disbelievers. Sir Arthur didn't enjoy that as much as he had relished the fictional chaos when Professor Challenger released a pterodactyl on an audience of doubters. His exposure to actual seances, with physical objects "apporting" violently round the room, and once a ghostly clockwork bat clicking its way up and down a curtain rod, had made him unusually physical in some of his early ghost stories, though. "The Bully of Brocas Cowt" featured the phantom of an actual bare-knuckle champion of Regency days, Tom "the Gasman" Hickman. And it seemed a ghost boxer could deal painful physical blows. In "Playing With Fire", a seance conjured up a terrifying ghost unicorn capable of splintering a dining table. But with respect to Rosicrucianism, Conan Doyle, though inducted into Freemasonry, never took the "craft" seriously. He was a genuinely religious seeker, however unfortunate some of his findings.

He spent a good deal of money on a small museum of spiritualism in London, containing such objects as the forged Assyrian clay tablet "apported" in Paris, and a piece of muslin that once almost concealed curvy "Katie King". The last campaign of his life was a spirited attempt to get the Witchcraft Laws abolished, since they were occasionally used against innocent mediums.

A boyish sense of adventure when it came to finance left Conan Doyle less rich than he might have been. Gold mines and sunken treasure ships might be more fun than industrial chemicals or home rails. But they weren't quite such sensible savings investments. Still, he didn't have many shares to lose in the Stock Market crash of 1929.

He had put money, instead, into a second home in the New Forest; a place where he had always loved to walk. When he died peacefully at Windlesham, he was brought to the beautiful graveyard at Minstead. And he lies at peace in consecrated Anglican ground, like the conventional British gentleman he so nearly was.

OPPOSITE: Conan Doyle with the famous magician Harry Houdini in London, ca.1924.

ABOVE: Sir Arthur Conan Doyle's gravestone in Minstead churchyard, Hampshire.

THE HOUND
OF THE
BASKERVILLES

A.G.J.

CONAN DOYLE

3
THE HOLMES RECORDS

Fifty-six short stories and four short novels, all illustrated. These are the annals of Sherlock Holmes from which the Sherlockian recreates the Master's life. The general reader is not a dedicated Sherlockian. He may pick up Conan Doyle's books because he is curious about the cult figure.

But why should he go on reading, once he has identified this hero? Shouldn't a John Grisham reader throw the books down in disgust at their snail's pace and Pooterish moral naïvety? Might not an Agatha Christie fan protest that the detective puzzles are inadequately clued and poorly worked-out? Won't a Stephen King enthusiast marvel that anybody ever thought *The Hound of the Baskervilles* spooky? How did the Sherlock Holmes stories grab readers' attention in 1891? Why do they still hold it?

The generally favourable critical reception given *A Study in Scarlet* and *The Sign of Four* did not win them instant high sales. They were excellent shilling shockers. They combined Wild West or exotic Indian romance with the drabber urban crime detection starting to attract readers.

One Holmesian element drew on mere gutterpress fiction: the "penny blood" adventures for boys starring semi-criminal figures like "Charlie Wag the Boy Thief" or "Spring-Heeled Jack", a sort of precursor of Superman who jumped over high walls and low buildings to foil villains. "The Wild Boys of London" rested on the idea that the ragged street Arabs who begged in the gutters and stole from the markets by day led exciting adventure-filled lives by night. Conan Doyle, like his contemporary Baden-Powell, the founder of the Boy Scouts, saw a waste of human potential in these abandoned kids and envisaged harnessing their energy in some disciplined body. But Conan Doyle only used Wiggins and the Baker Street Irregulars in the first two books, with one additional use of a street orphan named Simpson in the story of "The Crooked Man" (1893). This may be because Dr Barnardo's steady work finally cleared the streets of outcast children after 1892. But it is equally probable that a man of Conan Doyle's humanity realised that there was nothing romantic in the life of a homeless orphan, and so he tactfully abandoned Holmes's private spy force.

Still, their presence at the outset of Holmes's career, coupled with plots and sub-plots exploiting the lawless areas of the English-speaking world, point to the fact that Conan Doyle was really writing pulp adventure stories. The detective had one kind of sensational adventure, as the empire's soldiers or the desert's explorers had another. Almost by chance, Sherlock Holmes raised the detective and his simulated puzzles to the centre of a wholly new genre.

A STUDY IN SCARLET

In fairness to Conan Doyle we must remember that this book was not intended to start a series. This was to be a one-off with a detective whose character justified his role, just for the occasion. And that role wasn't unchallenged centre-stage. Holmes's adventure was combined with a wild western romance, which itself combined the derring-do of the stories about Buffalo Bill by pulp writer Ned Buntline with the soft-centred sentiment of Bret Harte describing the harsh lives of Californian miners.

Structurally, the American characters Jefferson Hope, Drebber and Stangerson are more impressive inventions than Sherlock Holmes. Fancy a pioneering western scout turning up as a square-toed murderer, following his victims through London in the guise of a cabman! Imagine a pair of travelling American businessmen turning out to be renegade Mormons! Yet wild westerners really did journey east and dress formally and mingle with metropolitan citizens, just as the acme of urbane aestheticism, Oscar Wilde, visited the west and downed whisky with miners. English-speaking men lived in both worlds, and their paths could cross.

So it is silly to carp about "Watson's" inability to know Jefferson Hope's past. Watson wasn't yet a permanent narrator. Hope's tragic love story stood on its own merits, a piece of popular fiction much to the taste and talents of gallant, romantic Arthur Conan Doyle. Conan Doyle liked heroes and Hope is the convincing and satisfactory hero of a western weepy. And thereby the more surprising as a murderer in a familiar townscape.

Conan Doyle's suspense is as powerful in America as in England. The Mormon Avengers provide the book's most thrilling tension when they enter a locked and guarded house, undetected, night after night, to paint up the number of days remaining before John Ferrier and his daughter will be killed. And Conan Doyle's gallantry calls up our own in his anger at men who call their plurality of wives "heifers" and force unwilling young girls into their harems. The western adventure is exciting romance with a two-handkerchief love element. Sherlock Holmes had

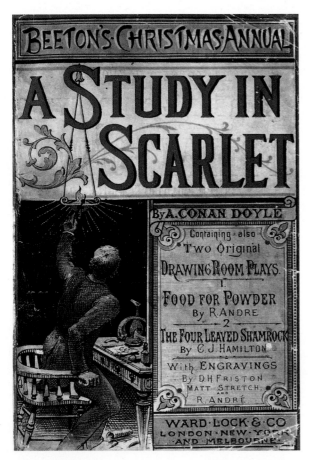

CHAPTER OPENER: The first English edition of The Hound of The Baskervilles, *published in 1902.*

to be introduced first, or he and London would have seemed anti-climactic. All credit to Conan Doyle for making him impressive enough to outlive Hope's tale.

The work is done skilfully. Watson opens in the voice of the modest British hero whose deeds speak for him. A doctor, humane by profession. A wounded officer whose loyal orderly rescued him after defeat. A traveller. But a man with his way to make in the world who welcomes the chance to share the rent with another up-and-coming professional ...

And so we meet Sherlock Holmes. He has characteristics which Conan Doyle sensibly dropped later. The hero could not go through life having his hands blotched with inkstains, pitted with acid-burns, and patched with plasters. Nor could his self-confidence find habitual outlet in the callow gesture of bowing to an imaginary audience. The superior observer shouldn't scramble over

floors with his magnifying glass, muttering, groaning and whistling to himself like a whining dog. In short, first-draft Sherlock Holmes isn't quite grown-up enough for the superior manner he is given.

But his mysterious profession lends suspense to the first two chapters. His areas of ignorance seem crippling. Yet Holmes's justification for neither knowing nor caring whether the earth goes round the sun or moon has a commonsense logic that strikes home immediately: it makes not a shred of difference to his work, a fact probably true of your job and mine.

When the secret of that work is revealed, Conan Doyle craftily adapts his own profession to make it persuasively unique. Sherlock Holmes is the world's first *consulting* detective, like the *consultant* physician to whom the ordinary general practitioner of medicine refers difficult cases. The clever wheeze proved unnecessary when it became clear that Conan Doyle's brilliant popular characterisation had made Holmes the model detective *par excellence*. He didn't need occupational elevation above his peers: he obviously was the greatest.

OPPOSITE: The 1887 edition of Beeton's Christmas Annual, *which carried the title* A Study in Scarlet.

ABOVE: A Mormon family, ca. 1870, with two wives, two servants and seven children.

The cunning presentation is twofold. First Holmes is shown to be intellectually superior to everyone else, and then he solves the mystery which is baffling us and the police. His superiority is shown, as it would be in several successive fictions, by a quick round of Professor Bell's parlour trick before the story proper begins. This "science of deduction", Holmes assures us, is his secret. But Conan Doyle does not show us the clues from which Holmes deduces his conclusion, so we cannot compete with him. We aren't told that the cab-horse has meandered while waiting outside Lauriston Gardens, proving that the man in the house with the victim was the driver. We aren't told the footprint evidence Holmes finds until he chooses to enlighten us as to how he knew who the killer was. Indeed, since he complains that the police have trampled it like a herd of buffaloes it is quite implausible that Holmes should read as much as he does from the ground! We had no idea that he telegraphed the Cleveland police and learned from them that the dead Drebber's deadly rival was Jefferson Hope. So we are amazed when Holmes says he knows the murderer's name. And we may feel aggrieved if we apply latter-day whodunnit standards and demand that we be allowed to pit our brains against the detective.

ABOVE: A scene from the 1933 film A Study in Scarlet *starring Reginald Owen.*

But how can we ordinary folk compete with this brainbox who shows his superiority to us by making scientific discoveries and playing Mendelssohn on his violin and humming that Chopin piece that Norman-Neruda plays? When he interrupts his detective work to buy an antique book, he speculates about its owner Gulielmus Whyte in ways even we humble chaps can follow. His assertive know-all personality suggests the confidence of a man using cocaine, which Conan Doyle may have tried. Sherlock Holmes didn't set the style for imaginary detectives because his detection was masterly. He triumphed as a brilliantly sketched character – the plain man's ideal of genius in a bachelor flat.

THE SIGN OF FOUR

Sherlock Holmes took his bottle from the corner of the mantel-piece, and his hypodermic syringe from its neat morocco case. With his long, white, nervous fingers he adjusted the delicate needle, and rolled back his left shirt-cuff. For some little time his eyes rested thoughtfully upon the sinewy foreman and wrist, all dotted and scarred with innumerable puncture marks.

It seems unbelievable today. The hero is mainlining cocaine. Not for the first time. Not as a scientific or detective experiment. As a habit which has marked his forearm. As a recreation. So Sherlock Holmes, with intellectual arrogance borrowed from Dr Waller, sets at defiance the conventional bourgeoisie and its timidity about experiences that relax self-control.

Holmes has to be more than the oddball intellect with tunnel vision in this book. Silently, his dedicated philistinism is shed. The man who had never heard of Carlyle now loftily places him with reference to his Swiss predecessor, Richter. The man who couldn't care less whether the earth circled the sun or the moon now recommends the rationalist Winwood Reade's attack on institutionalised religion. The consultant detective's range of knowledge has been quietly extended. For he must still seem superior to everyone he comes across. But he has moved away from the everyday criminal world where a murdered body is only exotic in that the man was once a Mormon. London itself is now a romantic world of one-legged sailors who climb on rooftops and their child-sized barefoot companions who use blowpipes. Watson will supply the love-interest.

And Watson will keep our feet on the ground. But other characters are far more theatrical than the London life around them. Thaddeus Sholto, foreshadowing Dr

Fu Manchu, has exotic rooms masked by the shabby surroundings of Brixton. His exquisite taste is shown by his possession of a doubtful Salvator Rosa, and two masters of his preferred modern French school: a Corot and a Bouguereau. Conan Doyle's doubtful taste is shown by his casually linking the perfect landscapes of the former with the saccharine sexiness of the latter.

Down-to-earth Watson is smitten by hearts-and-flowers romance as soon as he sets eyes on Miss Mary Morstan. And she reciprocates. But the case she brings to Holmes is romantically removed from the sort of criminal case that a real life Scotland Yard might associate with German socialist societies. She deals in anonymously posted pearls of great price; the mystery of a father who disappeared ten years ago; an inexplicable assignation that makes Henry Irving's familiar Lyceum Theatre into the resonant setting of a "third pillar". The wonderful combination of reality and haze that a foggy evening can cast over London epitomises Conan Doyle's achievement in casting a thoroughly theatrical light on convincingly real places.

It was a September evening and not yet seven o'clock, but the day had been a dreary one, and a dense drizzly fog lay low upon the great city. Mud-coloured clouds drooped sadly over the muddy streets. Down the Strand the lamps were but misty splotches of diffused light, which threw a feeble circular glimmer upon the shiny pavement. The yellow glare from the shop-windows streamed out into steamy, vaporous air, and threw a murky, shifting radiance across the crowded thoroughfare. There was, to my mind, something eerie and ghost-like in the endless procession of faces which flitted across these narrow bars of light.

"… a September evening …" That notorious phrase gives the first instance of Conan Doyle's incredible carelessness. Just two chapters earlier he told us the postmark on the letter Miss Morstan received in the morning was 7 July.

Nothing could make clearer the extent to which the "detective" element in the book is so much romantic window-dressing. Holmes plays Professor Bell's parlour trick in the first chapter. But the Message of Watson's Watch is no more part of the plot than are the paintings on Thaddeus Sholto's wall. And as it would be pedantry to grumble about the juxtaposition of a Bouguereau and a Corot – an obvious shorthand statement from the Plain Man writer to us Plain Men readers, "This chap is rich and has highbrow tastes" – so it would be pedantry to complain that the "detection" is unimportant to the course of the novel.

But it is. Dog Toby does most of the tracking. Our pleasure in the book is the thrill of a boat chase after an Andaman Islander down the homely London reaches of the Thames, offset by Small's narrative of exotic murder and hidden treasure. Like *A Study in Scarlet*, this is not what we now think of as a detective story, with clues laid out indicating Who Killed Roger Ackroyd or which of six suspects are the Five Red Herrings. It's an adventure romance in a loose detective aura – the format followed in all the long Holmes tales, whether they stay essentially in England like *The Sign of Four* and *The Hound of the Baskervilles*, or digress to a third-person narrative abroad like *A Study in Scarlet* and *The Valley of Fear*.

Still, the detective aura should have warned Conan Doyle. It may not matter that Wiggins hasn't aged in the years between the end of the Afghan War and 1888 when this story is set. We can forgive Holmes's character change between the two books. But our hero lectures us severely on the need to observe. So we might ask the author to observe Jonathan Small's presence in England witnessing Major Sebastian Sholto's death a couple or years before he has escaped from the Andaman convict settlement. Conan Doyle got away with it because of the rattling adventure yarn pace. Until, that is, the huge popularity of Holmes and his supposed "science of deduction" led readers to scrutinise his stories, and spot the constant hiccups.

THE ADVENTURES OF SHERLOCK HOLMES

Between July 1891 and June 1892 *The Strand Magazine* published its first twelve *Adventures of Sherlock Holmes*. Short stories suited Conan Doyle's talents for concentration on a single subject, clear unobtrusive prose, and well-sketched landscapes, cityscapes or characters. Short stories needed no love-interest, and Conan Doyle opened with the guarantee that Holmes's cold intellect would never be distracted by the tender passion. Even if his asexual admiration for Irene Adler is hard to account for. She has, after all, fallen into his trap even after suspecting his disguise, and then run away pointlessly.

But with this series Conan Doyle did something his cocksure creation had always taken for granted. Holmes knocked Dupin and Lecoq into a cocked hat. Conan Doyle took over the throne of detective fiction and established himself so securely that he could not abdicate when he wanted to.

The first three adventures start with Bell's parlour trick, practised either on Watson or the client. It is repeated in the fifth and seventh. And then apart from

ABOVE: L'Innocence, *a typically saccharine painting by Bouguereau, as collected by Thaddeus Sholto in* The Sign of Four.

a couple of observations about the way people's coats have been spattered from riding in carriages, the habit is set aside for the time being. It has served its purpose of establishing Holmes's powers of observation and deduction to new readers. It is shelved before it becomes an irritating tic.

Nor is "the science of deduction" always needed. Not all the adventures are mysteries needing Holmes to find out whodunnit – or wot they dun or how they dunnit. The first only requires him to locate and retrieve the photograph with which Irene Adler threatens the king of Bohemia. Miss Mary Ferguson, Lord Robert St. Simon and Mrs Neville St. Clair present simple missing persons cases – though foul play is suspected in the last. Mr Jabez Wilson wants to know why his cushy job has stopped, as Miss Violet Hunter wants to know whether she is safe to take the one she has been offered. Murder is threatened or attempted, and has certainly occurred in the past, in the cases of "The Speckled Band" and "The Engineer's Thumb". The threat of murder succeeds in "The Five Orange Pips". But only "The Boscombe Valley Mystery" is a straightforward murder mystery.

Holmes's detective methods seldom rest on observation and deduction. His knowledge of crime history is as important, showing him a familiar pattern in a "A Case of Identity" and a well-known master-criminal in "The Red-Headed League." The engineer loses his thumb in a virtual replay of a Wilkie Collins horror story. Holmes "detects" nothing but the probable location of the crime scene. The encyclopaedia solves "The Five Orange Pips" by describing the Ku Klux Klan. Holmes lucks out in Boscombe Valley with his wild guess that a dying Australian's mysterious last words, "a rat", are really the end of "Ballarat".

The twelve adventures bring Holmes in touch with royalty twice: definitely in the king of Bohemia; by implication in "The Adventure of the Beryl Coronet". Holmes, Watson and Conan Doyle display admirable decency and freedom from prudery or prurience when no one is shocked by the king's liaison with Irene Adler or Lord Robert St. Simon's "very friendly footing" with the dancer Flora Millar. In each case Holmes likes the lady much better than the gentleman who breaks with her to contract a respectable marriage to someone else. It's hard to believe that Oscar Wilde's scandal-threatened Lady Windermere and "Woman of No Importance" are of the same generation and culture.

Holmes catches one two-man gang of professional thieves and misses another of counterfeiters. He exposes two men who scheme to prevent their moneyed stepdaughters from marrying, and a third who follows the same motive to murder. He traces two independent amateur jewel thieves and visits an East End opium den. The wonderful variety of adventures and settings plays a great part in the series' appeal.

Three adventures direct Holmes's mind to less lawful lands. John Turner is a murderer in England because he was once the bushwhacker "Black Jack of Ballarat". The Openshaw family are pursued and murdered because Colonel Elias Openshaw's American past has led him, first to join, and then somehow to desert

NEWNES SIXPENNY COPYRIGHT NOVELS

ADVENTURES OF SHERLOCK HOLMES

BY A.CONAN DOYLE

and blackmail the Ku Klux Klan. And Dr Grimesby Roylott, after beating his native butler to death, brought back from India a baboon and a cheetah to roam around his garden, as well as the deadly swamp adder which is so useful for getting rid of unwanted stepdaughters.

Conan Doyle's wonderful howlers escaped his early fans, but delight us today. There are no baboons in India. It doesn't matter that Conan Doyle invented the

ABOVE: The Adventures of Sherlock Holmes *appears in book form for the first time in 1892.*

swamp adder as a species. But the total deafness of all snakes and their distaste for milk makes glorious nonsense of Dr Roylott's training his pet to come to his whistle for the reward of a saucerful. A carbuncle is a stone – usually a garnet – cut in a particular way; not, as Conan Doyle imagined, a crystallised carbon like a diamond. The eight-week passage of time in "The Red-Headed League" begins "in the autumn of last year" … on 27 *April*, … and runs until 9 *October*!

Nor is that writer a "lord of language" who confuses us with Holmes's "Bohemian soul" – meaning gipsyish, like the artists and intellectuals of an "alternative society" – in a story about the king of Bohemia (meaning the old Czech principality).

But, my goodness, he tells rattling good yarns

THE MEMOIRS OF SHERLOCK HOLMES

By the time the thirteen numbers of *The Strand* between December 1892 and December 1893 had completed what, omitting "The Cardboard Box", would be *The Memoirs of Sherlock Holmes*, Conan Doyle was heartily sick of his creation, and quite content to send him to a watery death in a perfunctorily imagined "Final Problem". Yet in the eleven stories of *The Memoirs* Conan Doyle confirmed his lasting reputation. He consolidated a character who would become part of the mental furniture of every Englishman and American for a hundred years – and still running! He almost perfected the detective story, a genre that would dominate middlebrow light reading for the next 60 years. Like a brilliant conjuror, he actually told his audience how the trick was done, and yet continued to deceive and amaze them from one month to the next. As Holmes pointed out to Watson,

… the reasoner can produce an effect which seems remarkable to his neighbour, because the latter has missed the one little point which is the basis of the deduction. The same may be said, my dear fellow, for the effect of some of those little sketches of yours, which is entirely meretricious, depending as it does upon your retaining in your own hands some factors in the problem – which are never imparted to the reader.

Conan Doyle wraps one more layer around this in his stories, usually allowing Holmes to withhold some piece of information from Watson so that Watson not only inevitably withholds it from us, but expresses astonishment and admiration on our behalf. The trick is at its most meretricious when, as is too often the case, Sherlock's basic "detection" is the careful examination of tracks and footprints, and he declines to share what he has seen until he flourishes his denouement.

But in the two *Memoirs* which did most to establish the detective story as a form, Conan Doyle plays reasonably fair. In "Silver Blaze" he shows the movement of the horse's prints in two directions as Silas Brown changes his mind about returning it to its own stable. And he gives us the clues of the stable boy's curried supper, the dead trainer's possession of an unsuitable surgical knife for defence, and the brilliant lateral-thinking clue that has become the hallmark of Holmesian deduction: the dog that did nothing in the night, and so revealed by not barking that no intruder came in.

And in "The Reigate Squires", too, Conan Doyle lets clues fall neatly before us, from the land dispute giving the Cunninghams their motive, through the burglary which took nothing of value and so was clearly directed at something else, to the layout of the Cunninghams's house with lighted rooms visible to any burglar, and the vital clue of the note written in two hands. This led Conan Doyle to introduce facsimile handwriting into his text: an intriguing device which would prove as popular with his successors as did the device of the sketch-map introduced in "The Naval Treaty". But in "The Reigate Squires" Conan Doyle yields to the temptation of having Sherlock read important evidence without telling us until the end: the absence of powder-blackening on the murdered man proving that he could not have been shot from close-up, and the absence of boot-marks in the ditch showing that no intruder escaped as the Cunninghams pretended.

Strangely, these are the only two stories in which detective skills solve the crime. More usually a little "Sherlocking" deduces some paltry related detail: the solution of a coded message and its author, both of which were already apparent in "The 'Gloria Scott'"; the fact that Sophy Kratides was in London when her brother came over from Athens in "The Greek Interpreter". Conan Doyle

BELOW: The Memoirs of Sherlock Holmes is a collection of Sherlock Holmes stories, originally published in 1894.

was discovering that it is very hard to invent plots which entail a perplexing mystery and a reasoned solution, even if the author starts from the end and then works out clues to lead to it. Agatha Christie made the same complaint, that detective fiction is hard work compared with writing a novel in which characters develop and events follow naturally.

But Conan Doyle's difficulties led him to slipshod writing. Though traditionalist readers have often protested that the Holmes of the later books fails to live up to the detective who went to the Reichenbach Falls, *The Memoirs* is one of the weakest of the Holmes volumes. "The Yellow Face" and "The Greek Interpreter" solve themselves once we know the characters. "The 'Gloria Scott'" might as well be a manuscript in a bottle telling us about a mutiny. "The Musgrave Ritual" is inferior to Poe's "The Gold Bug" from which it derives. Three plots use the infantile trick of giving a character temporary brain fever to create a hiatus in the action or suppress testimony and so leave a case for Holmes to investigate. Well might Conan Doyle decide it was time to stop writing increasingly tired adventures of Sherlock Holmes.

And to dispose of him he created a truly disappointing "Napoleon of crime". Holmes speaks with bated breath of Professor Moriarty's genius and wickedness. We never see either. Moriarty, supposedly Sherlock's equal, follows Watson to Victoria, arrives too late, and thereafter lures him away from the Falls with a false summons for medical help. He doesn't seem a master-criminal in the same class as John Crew of the Red-Headed League, for all the awestruck prose surrounding him.

Yet readers understandably resented Holmes's death. His personal background emerging little by little from the stories, was fascinating. Mycroft's brother visiting the Diogenes Club; Sherlock the university man; the eccentric of the Persian-slippered tobacco; the jackknifed correspondence and the patriotic VRs in the sitting-room wall: this was the character whose resurrection after his "Final Problem" was devoutly desired.

THE HOUND OF THE BASKERVILLES

Dartmoor legend presented Conan Doyle with the possibility of a new ghost story: a form he had always enjoyed writing. It was a stroke of genius to see that Sherlock Holmes might be revived to prove that the demon hound roaming Dartmoor and terrorising any passing Baskerville was owned and trained by man and not the Devil. It was a great blessing that Conan Doyle was not yet so embroiled with spiritualism or theosophy as to send Sherlock crashing down to intellectual absurdity declaiming some philosophical belief in ghosties and ghoulies and long-leggedy beasties as later happened to Professor Challenger.

The new and unexpected "early adventure" of Sherlock Holmes showed that Conan Doyle had fully recovered the skill of the first three books. Gone was the laboured pursuit of an unnecessary red herring, punctuated with false claims that some detail was "important", which had marred the two-part "Naval Treaty". The beast to be identified in The Hound is not a twaddling irrelevance like the mongoose in "The Crooked Man". The Baskervilles's curse doesn't make the family seem densely incurious and fatuously stupid like the Musgraves, solemnly repeating their "ritual" for generation after generation on without even wondering what it is all about. Instead we have an adventure crisply introduced with a round of Bell's parlour game played on the client's stick. The client himself – an evidently innocent onlooking GP – introduces the murder mystery in its historico-spooky setting, letting readers utilise what they've learned about footprints from Holmes's earlier adventures and deduce that Sir Charles Baskerville was running, not tip-toeing. And Dr Mortimer closes the first number in *The Strand* with one of the best cliffhangers in all serial fiction:

"Mr Holmes, they were the footprints of a gigantic hound!"

The next number introduces an unidentifiable villain clever enough to disguise himself in a beard and use a cab to make good his escape when he sees he has been spotted; a villain who may or may not be responsible for trying to scare off Sir Henry Baskerville with the anonymous threat or warning message clipped from newsprint.

And yet another number set in London gives us a truly puzzling mystery: why should anyone steal one boot of Sir Henry's? Why steal another single boot from another pair? Why does the first boot turn up again undamaged? The excellence of this puzzle lies in its complete relevance once it is explained. It is not a pointless coincidence or an extraneous piece of cleverness with which Sherlock can impress Watson, and us. It is an odd occurrence which, when properly understood, proves that the hound is a dog and not a demon. It is on all fours with the dog that didn't bark in the night in "Silver

ABOVE: An illustration from The Hound of the Baskervilles, *showing Holmes and Watson discovering a prostrate man.*

Blaze": a genuine clue, inviting the reader to reach a conclusion before the detective explains it. There is nothing in Dickens or Wilkie Collins, or even Poe or Gaboriau, quite like these clues: at first mystifying, then obvious and seemingly self-explanatory. There had been nothing quite like them in *A Study in Scarlet* or *The Sign of Four*. Proper clueing started in the short stories: rather limply in "The Speckled Band" where Conan Doyle's innocence of ophidian lore made his killer snake quite unguessable despite the adroitly laid fake bellpull and ventilator, the bolted-down bed, and the whistles and the saucer of milk; much better in "Silver Blaze", though racing men may find the clues lost in the welter of Conan Doyle's ignorance about racing matters; and finally perfected in this excellent clue of the stolen boots which precisely serves the threefold purpose of mystifying us at the outset, revealing something germane to the plot when explained, and impressing us with Sherlock's genius in having taken the point while we were still scratching our heads.

But if the refined detection of the short stories strengthened the London opening, Conan Doyle had not forgotten the effectiveness of contrasting metropolitan sleuthing with romance in an exotic setting. Dartmoor may lie in England, but Conan Doyle successfully makes it into a place of sinister mystery. He introduces motifs that later thriller writers would exploit when using a moorland background. The

ABOVE: Hay Tor seen from Hound's Tor, Dartmoor.

escaped convict would become almost a *sine qua non* of Dartmoor stories. The hogs fictionalised into something like quicksands were bequeathed to Daphne DuMaurier for use on Bodmin Moor, while Conan Doyle borrowed a tin mine from the Cornish moors, which would be surprising in Devon. And rightly observing the presence of neolithic monuments and iron age hut circles in the wilderness, Conan Doyle took the liberty of roofing a couple to house Selden the convict and Sherlock Holmes. In fact the only ancient man-made cover surviving on the west country moors is the occasional neolithic cromlech and a few shepherds or quarrymen's shelters which usually date from the eighteenth century.

Holmes's personal arrangements in his moorland exile are more than economical. He uses Cartwright the messenger boy to fetch his food – a rather unappetising mixture of bread, tinned meats and peaches. And he receives from Cartwright his daily clean collar. If this was his only change of linen, it is surprising that his catlike fastidiousness still attracted Watson's attention, especially as he had been lighting fires at his hideout and should, after a week without a bath, have smelled like a charcoal-burner! Yet, if Paget is to be believed, he brought his dinner jacket to Devon and wore it at Baskerville Hall. Though even above a starched and studded shirt-front he still declined to change the Bohemian habit of wearing his tie under a soft turned-down collar.

These little slips are now part of the smug pleasure of reading the period pieces, as is the quite impossible geography Conan Doyle proposes for Baskerville Hall in relation to Tavistock and Princetown, or the gallant late Victorian gentleman's uncertain romantic touch with lispy Latin Mrs Stapleton. It is kinder to note his brilliant touches like "the man on the tor"; the effective pursuit of the Barrymores as an early red herring; the entertainment supplied by the eccentric Frankland. The hound, drawn by Paget in perspectives making it look the size of a heifer, is a surprisingly effective instrument of darkness and death. And butterfly-hunting Stapleton is a jolly good smiler with the knife under his cloak.

BELOW: Holmes shoots the sinister hound in The Hound of the Baskervilles: *"Holmes emptied five barrels of his revolver into the creature's flank".*

THE RETURN OF SHERLOCK HOLMES

Accepting McClure's cheque committed Conan Doyle to a sequence of Holmes stories. And with *The Return of Sherlock Holmes* running in *The Strand* from the end of 1903 to the end of 1904, Conan Doyle risked once again tiring his imagination and producing narratives without real mystery or detection. Before the series was very far advanced, Greenhough Smith objected that there was too little Sherlock Holmes in "The Solitary Cyclist", and substantial revisions were made. "Charles Augustus Milverton" entailed no mystery at all. And "The Missing Three-Quarter" sent Holmes and Watson on a chase which, like "The Yellow Face", uncovered no crime and whose "mystery" was solved when the hunters forced their way into the house where the missing character explained everything.

As before, Conan Doyle was soon bored with inventing Holmes adventures and annoyed that his readers persisted in seeing them as his finest achievement. He didn't kill Holmes off again. It would have been difficult to win suspension of disbelief had he tried it. But he announced Holmes's retirement, and never wrote another year-long collection of stories about him.

The actual "return" from Reichenbach was rather obvious writing to order. Conan Doyle would probably have been content to go on placing Holmes's adventures in the 1880s as he had in *The Hound*. It was the decade when he himself had been in his twenties, and "all the world was young, lad, And all the trees were green". But McClure cannily saw that readers like up-to-date stories, and insisted that Holmes must come back alive from the struggle with Moriarty and the new adventures must all take place after 1891.

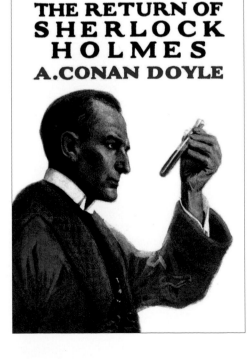

THE RETURN OF
SHERLOCK
HOLMES
A. CONAN DOYLE

Conan Doyle's solution was almost as perfunctory as had been his elimination of Holmes. The great detective's unsuspected mastery of "baritsu ... the Japanese system of wrestling" which allowed him to slither out of Moriarty's grasp leaving the "Napoleon of crime" to overbalance into the precipice, seems as simplistic as the "with one bound mighty Superman freed himself ..." form of escape. Holmes's need to hide from the Moriarty gang's revenge by pretending to be dead is absurd, since Colonel Moran has watched the entire struggle, and starts pushing rocks down at him the minute it is safe to do so. Holmes's incognito travels are full of Doylean howlers, with visits to such unlikely notables as the "head Llama" in Tibet, a Peruvian camel if spelled thus, or the Khalifa in Khartoum, a city the Khalifa and his predecessor the Mahdi had abandoned for Omdurman in 1885.

But with that duty behind him, Conan Doyle created a series of varied adventures as satisfying as the first collection. "The Priory School" and "The Golden Pince-Nez" reintroduce sketch-maps for the readers delight. "The Dancing Men" gives a

real puzzle in its sketches of pin-men, even though their letter-for-letter code would delay a cryptographer only because of the messages' brevity. "The Six Napoleons" is one of the finest examples of laterally thought misdirection: by concentrating on the apparent maniac hostility to Napoleon evinced in the busts' destruction, Conan Doyle skilfully directs us away from the real purpose, to find the jewel hidden in one of them. In "Black Peter" we see one of the first examples of the narrative clue deriving from the detective's unexplained action rather than his detection. At the

OPPOSITE: The Return of Sherlock Holmes *is a collection of thirteen short stories first published in 1905 following pressure on Conan Doyle to revive his famous detective.*

ABOVE: *Holmes trying to prevent the Russian woman Anna from poisoning herself in* The Return of Sherlock Holmes.

end we have to remember his inexplicable experiment at the beginning, proving that an untrained hand cannot drive a harpoon through a carcass.

As Conan Doyle himself advanced in success and social experience, Holmes, too, starts seeing Great Clients from a less Ruritanian background than the king of Bohemia. We meet a Prime Minister, who owes something to Gladstone, and two Cabinet Ministers, who may owe something to Lord Salisbury and Joseph Chamberlain. Holmes may not be impressed, but we are when we meet the Cambridge University rugby captain and an athletics blue from, probably, Oxford. We meet ladies from court circles and we see Holmes track down a compromising diplomatic letter which, like the Ems telegram of 1870, would precipitate a devastating war if it became public.

Chivalric gallantry becomes a little more marked in this collection. Two ladies assassinate blackmailers, one under the eyes of Holmes and Watson. After Wilde himself had fallen in the greatest scandal of the century, Conan Doyle was evidently left troubled that public airing of private peccadilloes might mean ruin. Though he was still blessedly uncensorious and incurious about Ladies who Did. The writer who was to be a great advocate of easier divorce was also willing to allow murder to pass as "justifiable homicide" if it were an honourable man's way of freeing the woman he loved from a brutal drunken husband. Yet the chivalry is far from proto-feminist. Watson, ever the impressionable male, is quick to make comparisons, even if they only put the lady's beauty higher than its reputation:

I had often heard of the beauty of the youngest daughter of the Duke of Belminster, but no description of it, and no contemplation of colourless photographs, had prepared me for the subtle, delicate charm and the beautiful colouring of that exquisite head.

Holmes, always preferring mind over matter, despairs of understanding women:

How can you build on such a quicksand? Their most trivial action may mean volumes, or their most extraordinary conduct may depend upon a hairpin or a curling-tong.

In this altogether satisfying collection, some irritating tricks of language disappear. No longer do people's eyes "sparkle" whenever they heard good news or find a wanted clue. All characters are less inclined to "spring up" to prove they have been surprised. And we lose those dialogues which opened with successions of, "Well …" answered by "Well …" or "Oh …", answered by "Oh …"

In fact *The Return of Sherlock Holmes* is as welcome today as it was when it brought a rush of increased sales to *The Strand*.

THE VALLEY OF FEAR

The last full-length Holmes novella exhibits Conan Doyle's powers at their height. The opening banter between Holmes and Watson is excellent. We enjoy the point Watson accidentally scores when Holmes leaps in too soon with a modest disclaimer of the compliment he anticipates. Conversely, Holmes's sardonic put-down is masterly when Watson naïvely suggests that the familiar columnar volume from which Porlock's cipher draws its words might be *Bradshaw's Railway Directory*:

> *There are difficulties, Watson. The vocabulary of **Bradshaw** is nervous and terse, but limited. The selection of words would hardly lend itself to the sending of general messages. The dictionary is, I fear, inadmissible for the same reason.*

The cipher presents an impressively difficult problem which Holmes solves persuasively. The unseen Porlock is fittingly named, suggesting Coleridge's mysterious visitor "from Porlock" who prevented the completion of *Kubla Khan*. And the equally unseen Professor Moriarty whom Porlock serves and betrays is an immeasurable improvement on the sinuous incompetent of "The Final Problem". The "Napoleon of crime" is sensibly compared with "thief-taker" Jonathan Wild who controlled early eighteenth-century London's underworld and enriched himself

ABOVE: Holmes leans forward and listens intently in The Valley of Fear.

by masterminding other men's crimes. Moriarty is revealed as paying Colonel Moran a higher salary than the Prime Minister's to be his chief of staff, while keeping a low financial profile himself. His arm is long and his revenge certain. And when, at the end of the novel, he engineers the death of the man Holmes set out to save, his feline and old-maidish unsigned note, "Dear me, Mr Holmes! Dear me!", suggests really sinister, controlled, icy gloating which is well matched to Holmes's razor-sharp brain and disciplined emotions.

The opening murder mystery truly is, as Conan Doyle exulted, "a real staggerer". Not until Agatha Christie's *Murder of Roger Ackroyd* and *And Then There Were None* would the reader be presented with a detective fiction leading him up so central a garden path for so long. Several commentators have wondered why Holmes abuses himself as "*a lunatic, a man with softening of the brain, an idiot whose mind has lost its grip*", at the end of Chapter 6, "A Dawning Light". The answer and the "Light" are obvious when the mystery is solved. Holmes's expedition with Watson's umbrella has fished up the dumb-bell weighted package he rightly conjectured to be in the moat. But far from proving the identity of John Douglas's murderer, it has discovered that murderer's own discarded clothes. Proving that Douglas was the killer all the time, and that the corpse confidently identified as his by Holmes and everyone else actually belonged to the supposed assassin with the yellow overcoat.

The clues to this "staggerer" are well placed: Mrs Douglas's lack of grief at her husband's death and shared secret with Cecil Harker, which make them the first suspects; Douglas's missing wedding ring, which should have been underneath the ring still on his finger, so that we ought to have surmised that the rings we see have been added to the hand on the body we see, and not have allowed ourselves to jump to the conclusion that the ring we don't see was stolen by the murderer.

"The Tragedy of Birlstone", then, is one of the great murder mysteries. But with unusual skill on Conan Doyle's part it foreshadows the related flashback adventure structurally, as well as through simple clues like the aside that Douglas's first wife was of Swedish extraction, or that Douglas's would-be killer matched his height and build, as does "McMurdo's" Pennsylvanian enemy Ted Baldwin. For "The Scowrers", too, reverses the role of the main protagonist in a startling denouement. Jack McMurdo is apparently a criminal and would-be terrorist murderer until the final moment when he reveals that he is the real Birdy Edwards, the infiltrating Pinkerton detective whom the terrorist Scowrers believed he was about to deliver into their hands. And this "villain-turned-hero" is actually the same man as the "victim-turned-killer" of Birlstone! It is, perhaps, untidy and confusing that we have to follow the fate of a man who works through three fictional names and four contrasting protagonist roles. But Conan Doyle could rightly claim that the disguise in the flashback recorded the real-life story of his generation's greatest thriller-detective's greatest adventure. James McParland's infiltration and destruction of the Pennsylvania Molly Maguires in 1875 was one of the Pinkerton agency's proudest memories. To make no mistake about the

history lying behind "Birdy Edwards", Conan Doyle had Frank Wiles draw him in the wire-rimmed glasses that famously adorned the two-fisted American he-man who quite genuinely risked his life in Pottsville, Pennsylvania.

Conan Doyle, like Pinkerton's, had wandered into a morally confused case here. McParland was exposed tampering with evidence in a later anti-union case in 1905. In 1979 the state of Pennsylvania granted a posthumous full pardon to John Kehoe, the counsellor and Ancient Order of Hibernians' bodymaster – or local lodge president – on whom Conan Doyle based Black Jack McGinty, and who had been hanged in 1877 on McParland's evidence. If "Black Jack" – the nickname was actually lifted from a western train-robber who was also brought down by Pinkerton's – was really a labour martyr to America's frightful history of industrial warfare, then Holmes and Moriarty appear to have taken the wrong sides in the struggle!

None of which weakens Conan Doyle's excellent romance. As he had done with Dartmoor and Utah, he makes a strange and sinister place of the beautiful Pennsylvania Valley. He holds our sympathy for the "criminal" McMurdo by

ABOVE: Holmes studies the cipher in The Valley of Fear. *Drawn for* The Strand Magazine.

"hormonal morality": he and Ettie fall in love at first sight, and she is obviously a heroine. So McMurdo must be okay at heart, even before we know he is a detective hero. And Bodymaster McGinty is a convincing leader of men and a frighteningly memorable villain, even if the character may libel a rather rough diamond.

HIS LAST BOW

All but the title story in this collection were written earlier than *The Valley of Fear* and appeared sporadically in *The Strand Magazine* as "Reminiscences of Sherlock Holmes", or "A New Adventure", or "A New Sherlock Holmes Story". "The Cardboard Box" is a survivor of the original twenty-four "Adventures", excluded from *The Memoirs* when they were compiled in 1894, and it is instructive to compare it with its later siblings.

First, the reasons for its belated inclusion and original exclusion. It was needed to add weight to the very short collection "His Last Bow". There are only seven stories in all, and even allowing for "Wisteria Lodge" and "The Red Circle" originally appearing in two parts each, nine stories would be only three-quarters of a full-strength Holmes book.

It seems, too, that the war's relaxation of morals played its part. In the early 1890s Conan Doyle was not expected to disapprove of Irene Adler's liaison with the king of Bohemia. Lillie Langtry, after all, suffered little social ostracism for being the Prince of Wales' mistress, and that gross gormandiser enjoyed muted public admiration for his lewd pursuit of Parisian courtesans and his friends' wives. Aristos and Royals could lead naughty lives, provided the details didn't appear in the witness box or the scandal sheets. But lower middle class persons like the Misses Cushing had to be respectable. If a woman's marriage could be broken up by her sister's lusting after her husband and deliberately driving a wedge between the couple; if marital unhappiness led through drink and adultery to murder, then Conan Doyle was questioning the validity of traditional family ties. "The Cardboard Box" leads Holmes to ponder the problem of pain in moving terms:

"What is the meaning of it, Watson? … What object is served by this circle of misery and violence and fear? It must tend to some end, or else our universe is ruled by chance, which is unthinkable. But what end? There is the great standing perennial problem to which human reason is as far from an answer as ever."

In the early 1890s it was "not nice" to ask such serious questions about a drunken seaman's wife's sordid infidelity. Common people's love-lives were merely squalid. Thomas Hardy abandoned novel-writing in disgust after the critical storm *Jude the Obscure* provoked. Conan Doyle bided his time, and allowed "The Cardboard Box" to be reprinted when the moral climate had changed and D. H. Lawrence had written things Hardy would never have imagined, and Sir Arthur Conan Doyle was starting to challenge the divorce laws openly.

The new collection also challenged legal "justice" with revitalised daring. In two of the original six "Reminiscences" a chivalrous man gets away with killing the rotter who has threatened or murdered his beloved. Scotland Yard is as casual as Holmes about such a personal vendetta when the victim is an Italian-American gangster! Given that "His Last Bow" endorses a little patriotic larceny and contempt for diplomatic privilege, two-thirds of the new stories openly prefer private violence to rule of law. "The Cardboard Box" dares not go that far. Conan Doyle might regret that a man so bitterly wronged as Jim Browner must be hanged. But he does not say so. He simply says nothing about Browner's fate after his arrest. By 1917 some of that "Bohemian" relaxation of rigid convention on which Holmes and Watson plumed themselves had spread across society.

Conan Doyle Uniform Edition

HIS LAST BOW

"The Cardboard Box"'s extended "detection" of Watson's thoughts – appearing in volume form for the second time after its transfer to "The Resident Patient" – is the only instance of Bell's parlour trick played at length in the collection. The stories now carry their own internal detection, even if some criminals seem to do irrational things especially for Holmes's benefit: Dr Sterndale pointlessly carrying gravel from his own garden to throw at the rectory window in "The Devil's Foot", for example, or Gennaro revealing his code in the message "Beware, danger" signalled to the wife he has been hiding for two weeks because of the danger of which both are fully aware ("Red Circle"). The new stories are also less inclined to give clients or captives long re-tellings of the past with a confusing proliferation of names. But more striking even than the excellent detection elements in (say) "Wisteria Lodge" or "The Bruce-Partington Plans" are the development of Holmes's and Watson's characters. Holmes's sardonic vanity reaches a momentary Wildean peak in "The Disappearance of Lady Frances Carfax":

ABOVE: In "His Last Bow" *Holmes is employed by the government to foil the German spy Von Bork.*

ABOVE: The mandrake plant, credited with magical properties in the middle ages, which probably inspired Conan Doyle's poison, Radix diaboli, in "The Devil's Foot".

Besides, on general principles it is best that I should not leave the country. Scotland Yard feels lonely without me, and it causes an unhealthy excitement among the criminal classes.

"The Dying Detective", which annoys some commentators for its lack of detection, should really be enjoyed as comedy. It is apparent enough that Holmes is not really ill. And so his delirium can be enjoyed to the full. It is merrily bizarre when the great brain babbles about oysters proliferating on the ocean floor and urges Watson to balance himself with half-crowns in his watch-pocket against the rest of his change in his trousers.

The singlestick skill with which Watson credited Holmes at the beginning of *A Study in Scarlet* is shown for the very first time in "The Illustrious Client".

Watson's and Holmes's genuine affection for each other is also discreetly developed throughout the book, with a high point in "The Devil's Foot" after Watson has saved their lives. And Holmes, with a superbly stiff upper lip, reverts quickly to mocking himself as mad to have experimented with the lethal root. The same story contains Conan Doyle's most extravagant distortion of a picturesque setting to sinister ends, when lovely Mount's Bay is turned into an "evil place" of shipwrecks.

The title story, alas, is a sadly hack job dragging Holmes into war propaganda. It was naïve of Conan Doyle to imagine the Kaiser's government as latter-day Bismarcks engineering war to further their sinister ends. It was still more naïve to retain something of the jolly, sporty attitude to war that he had brought to his Boer War propaganda, with a madly Rupert Brookean belief that the mud and blood of Flanders would prove a cleansing and rejuvenating experience for Britain. Much happier was the patriot who received an emerald tiepin from Queen Victoria for recovering the Bruce-Partington plans.

THE CASEBOOK OF SHERLOCK HOLMES

The last twelve adventures are a very mixed bunch. The war-weary public might have accepted third-person narrative in "His Last Bow" when Sherlock patriotically foiled the malign malarkey of Prussian-plotters and their Irish-American co-

conspirators. But it lacked the chiaruscuro of a dim and reverential Watson narrative. It did not merit repetition in "The Mazarin Stone", and that story's inert repetition of the "dummy Sherlock in the window" trick was not rendered more palatable by having Billy the page acknowledge that the previous use of a bust was before his time. Other details invite instant incredulity. We don't need to know, as advanced Sherlockians have established, that there was no recording of Offenbach's "Bacarolle" from *Hoffmann* arranged for unaccompanied violin solo before 1903: it seemed quite improbable enough that any disc or cylinder from that period should play continuously for the five minutes or more occupied by Merton and Sylvius's eavesdropped conversation. Nor is it really surprising to learn from scholars that historical Baker Street never contained any bow windows. Conan Doyle has evoked architectural disbelief with a bedroom door leading behind a curtain into a sitting-room window bay!

The two stories Holmes narrates himself are almost equally handicapped. "The Blanched Soldier" turns on the implausible coincidence that a man who has slept a night in a leper's bed should fortuitously contract an unrelated, non-infectious skin disease with all the appearance of leprosy. How little Conan Doyle cared about details is shown by his casually placing the story in the period of Watson's marriage, while dating it in 1903. Thus Sherlockians have their delighted excuse to speculate on the good doctor's multiple matrimonies.

"The Lion's Mane" is little better. Never mind that *Cyanea capalata* is not nearly as dangerous as the story suggests: we may forgive Conan Doyle and Holmes for being misled by J. G. Wood's somewhat hysterical account in *Out of Doors*. But Holmes says he never thought of any sea-beast causing the injuries which led to the failure of McPherson's dickey heart. Why not? Because McPherson dressed partially and snatched up his towel without drying himself on it, so that Holmes never imagined he had been in the water. Which, in turn, indicates that McPherson fought with the lethal jellyfish in the pool without getting his hair wet …

But the very worst weaknesses of the collection are linguistic. Not only does the dreaded "Well …", "Well …", return to make dialogue limp along on crutches, but there are quite horrible intrusions of a line of 1920s-sounding slang and racy talk. While "yeggman", American slang for a safe-breaker, was just current in 1903, it is a strange word to have found its way into Holmes's index prior to that date.

Misplaced modernity is at its worst when Conan Doyle seems determined to turn Holmes into a wit, but loses the terse touch which made his sardonic remarks acceptable. Now the habitual teasing of Watson can be downright rude: when he remarks that "plow" is misspelt in "The Three Garridebs" advertisement, for example: *"Oh, you did notice that, did you? Come, Watson, you improve all the time."*

And in "The Three Gables", Holmes seem about to turn into an obnoxious, xenophobic, sarcastic smartypants like Bulldog Drummond or Berry Pleydell or "The Saint". His twitting Susan Stockdale on her unsuccessful spying is heavy-handed and unpleasant: *"Now, Susan, wheezy people may not live long, you know. It's a wicked thing to tell fibs."*

But his racist banter with Steve Dixie is loathsome, and compounded by a narrative voice, as much Conan Doyle's as Watson's, calling the black boxer a "savage" and referring to his "hideous mouth" for no apparent reason but his full lips. The most devoted admirers of Conan Doyle and Holmes have drawn the line at attempting to defend this nastiness.

"The Creeping Man" is a bizarre variant on *Dr. Jekyll and Mr Hyde* prompted by Serge Voronoff's experiments in France with glandular implants from animals to men. The crude quack John Brinkley was already selling this as a rejuvenating "treatment" in Kansas. Conan Doyle had spotted the unsubstantiated claims made for Koch's tuberculin in 1891, and again he saw and exposed bad science. Though his own notion of an elderly professor developing the tastes and attributes of a large monkey is equally unscientific!

"The Illustrious Client" combines an effective offstage suggestion of Edward VII when Prince of Wales with a startlingly sadistic climax as Conan Doyle approves vitriol-throwing to ruin the looks of a calculating continental cad. The gallant writer goes a little over the top here, particularly in a story which describes the porcine Tum-Tum as loyal and chivalrous!

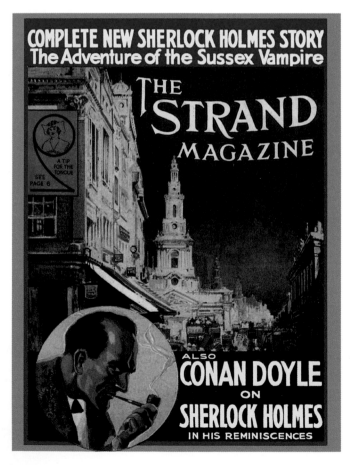

After all which complaint one has to add that "Thor Bridge" is a masterpiece: perhaps the first "whodunnit" in which learning "howshedunnit" completely changes the "who" and the victim's role as victim. And that "The Veiled Lodger", annoying to some lovers of the pure detective story, is nonetheless a very successful little soft-centred weepy. And that "The Three Garridebs" satisfactorily climaxes the spurious employment hoax Conan Doyle had pioneered in "The Red-Headed League" and "The Stockbroker's Clerk". "Shoscombe Old Place", the last story to appear in *The Strand Magazine*, and "The Retired Colourman", usurping its terminal position in the book, are worthy final pieces of detection. And Robert Ferguson's mawkish paternal blandishments in "The Sussex Vampire" contrast effectively with his manly rugger-playing past, as well as explaining and supporting his crippled son's misconduct. Such skill goes some way to compensate for the linguistic weaknesses of Doylean American and modern slang in other stories.

ILLUSTRATIONS AND ILLUSTRATORS

The first portraits of Sherlock Holmes were completely disastrous: unquestionably portraits of somebody else! Charles Altamont Doyle, invited to supply illustrations for the first volume form edition of *A Study in Scarlet*, proceeded to draw *himself* as Sherlock Holmes! A soft-bearded, glossy-haired figure lolling around in a frock coat and smart waistcoat with a broad modern type of necktie. Well might Charles Doyle's intemperate habits have landed him in the asylum by this time! His self-indulgence gives no impression of Holmes and contributes nothing to the text. The worst future illustrators did better than that.

In fact, George Hutchinson, the next illustrator was the next worst. His drawings for the third edition of *Study* are the most likely to be reproduced today, and so his dreadful picture of the great introduction in St Bartholomew's chemistry laboratory may form many readers' first impression of Sherlock Holmes. And what an impression! He smirks while crossing the room to greet the two figures who have lounged into his lab. His hair has been brushed up into a fetching little Mephistophelean quiff. He points slightly affectedly at the test tube in his left hand. This is not the Sherlock Holmes we would recognise today.

Later, when Hutchinson decides to show us the man of action, we see the "staghounds" Holmes and Lestrade leaping upon Jefferson Hope. Holmes's quiff is still upstanding, and would doubtless have become his most distinctive feature had Hutchinson remained his portrayer. The "hawklike nose" Conan Doyle liked to emphasise is big, but it is as thick and coarse a conk as Lestrade's dominating hooter. The extreme slenderness that makes Conan Doyle's Holmes seem even taller than his 6ft-plus is nowhere evident. Indeed, he seems shorter than Conan Doyle claimed given that Lestrade is a "little man". Or else, noting the severely bent knees Jefferson Hope adopts in his wild war dance attitude as he tries to throw himself backward through a window without looking at it, we must assume Hope to be nearly 7ft tall.

The pictures that do not invoke Holmes are as bad. Eugene Drebber looks like one of those children's horrid golliwog-head tin money boxes that used to swallow coins in a grinning mouth, Ferrier and Hope are a ludicrous bulbous-nosed pair goggling at each other with grotesquely caricatured whiskers and moustaches when encountering by moonlight. George Hutchinson must always be remembered as the man who created Sherlock Holmes's only unchanging feature, his bow tie tucked under its collar. But Hutchinson's departure from the canon enabled a better artist to give the final image of the great detective.

Before Sidney Paget made his own name and Holmes's face, A. Twidle had shown how effectively photogravure could evoke the dark romantic elements of *The Sign Of Four*. And happily this was the process *The Strand Magazine* preferred for its manifold illustrations. Sidney Paget and his successors would always have the advantage that their half-tone drawings of Holmes and his adventures suggested photographs more than caricatures.

The Solitary Cyclist

The Dancing Men

The Hound of the Baskervilles

The Second Stain

The Speckled Band

The Reigate Squire

The Boscombe Valley Mystery

The Red-Headed League

The Norwood Builder

The Abbey Grange

The Final Problem

The Bruce-Partington Plans

Sidney was lucky to get the commission. It was intended for his brother Walter and came to him by mistake. Walter had a double reason to regret the error. He was very good-looking, and Sidney used his features for the young Sherlock Holmes, which sometimes brought him embarrassing recognition on the street. His hair had just enough wave to suggest a muted continuation of Hutchinson's quiff if anyone remembered it. And the receding line at the temples which would give Holmes his "intellectual" brow was already starting. Charles Doyle's chosen costume of loose frock coat and well-tailored waistcoat was retained, but Hutchinson's bow appears on every single image of Holmes where a necktie can be seen. The two drawings of Mycroft Holmes, one by Paget and the other by Frank Wiles, show that this sartorial habit ran in the family. The famous deerstalker and ulster made their appearance in "Boscombe Valley", appearing for the first time in one of those first-class railway compartments Holmes and Watson liked to enjoy to themselves, and in which they looked almost exactly as they would again when travelling down to Baskerville Hall by train.

Though the attempt to make Holmes's eyes "'piercing" sometimes defeated Paget, and Sherlock could end up looking like a raccoon (in "The Resident Patient", for example), his appearance was generally lifelike and memorable. Paget gave the adventures their adventurous quality without going over the top. Melodramatic attitudes inevitably occur. But they are rarely overdone to the point of being ludicrous. The events which lift the stories out of the fireside coziness of middle-class life are shown. But there are never too many pistols. Holmes and Watson are not seen running too hectically too often. Even sinister lairs like the East End opium den are less lurid than the high-art engravings of a Doré would have rendered them.

Paget's successors followed his lead faithfully. The fine-featured, square-jawed sleuth with straight receding hair was an instantly recognisable figure. The dressing-gown, obligatory after Gillette's dramatisation, could at times make him look like a querulous valetudinarian in the hands of A. Gilbert. And Gilbert's and Howard Elcock's practice of dressing stories in the costume of the 1920s, heedless of a text which declared them to have taken place before 1903, may have lent timelessness to Homes for their generation. Certainly some of their drawings of women fainting or being man-handled by villains bring out the extent to which Sherlock Holmes prefigured James Bond as the hero of thrillers with the sexy spice of mildly sadistic threats to women.

For "Shoscombe Old Place" Frank Wiles, the best of Paget's successors, revived the deerstalker for the first time since Paget's death. And so the very last illustration of Holmes in *The Strand Magazine* is finally satisfying. His headgear and neckwear are right.

OPPOSITE: An illustration by Sidney Paget showing twelve scenes from Sherlock's career.

4
DETECTIVES AND CRIMINALS

The noun "detective" was born just three years before Arthur Conan Doyle. *The Oxford English Dictionary*'s earliest example of the word meaning "One whose occupation is to discover matters artfully concealed" is drawn from the *Annual Register* of 1856.

The adjective "detective" (almost invariably used in the form "detective police") came into being just fifteen years earlier, when Scotland Yard dedicated a small group of officers to the specific duty of discovering artfully concealed perpetrators of crime. At approximately the same time, young Allan Pinkerton was employed as Chicago's first official detective, and went on to found the first and greatest private detective agency.

So the whole idea of the detective was still something of a novelty when Sherlock Holmes was created. Charles Dickens praised Scotland Yard's detective branch in a series of articles in *Household Words* in 1850. The shrewdness of his fictional Inspector Bucket in *Bleak House* (1850) and Wilkie Collins's Sergeant Cuff in *The Moonstone* (1868) impressed readers who were unaware that the characters were based on genuine Metropolitan policemen, and such readers need not have known that most detective work was a dull business of tracing very obvious suspects. Rather different from the masterly tricks and disguises affected by Inspector Bucket or the careful deductions of Sergeant Cuff.

The private detective of 1887 was almost an unknown quantity, and if known, was probably despised as a man necessarily engaged in raking up sleazy scandals for the benefit of civil lawyers, or acting as a security guard for some business that was on the fringes of disreputability. The time had only recently passed when the employment of private detectives was quite unnecessary, for the public simply hired the services of experienced policemen if they chose, as fictional Sir Leicester Dedlock employs Bucket in *Bleak House* to hunt down his fugitive wife, and the historical Anne Buton, a poor Whitechapel Woman, hired PC Lea for a few pence expenses to find evidence against the family of bodysnatchers who murdered her grandmother in 1831.

In the year when Sherlock Holmes first appeared between the covers of a book, a private detective firm in The Strand was hired by the *Evening News* to try and catch Jack the Ripper. Mr LeGrand and his colleague Mr Batchelor found a fruiterer who had sold grapes to a man accompanying one of the

Ripper's victims. They also found some grape stalks in a drain near the murder site. They did not catch the Ripper, though the *News* used their involvement to damn Scotland Yard as incompetent. Six years later the Yard's own man on the ground in the Ripper enquiry had become a private Pinkerton's agent, guarding the casino at Monte Carlo. And the man who headed the Special Branch at the time of the Ripper murders had become the private detective with the sordid task of rounding up rent boys to testify against Oscar Wilde on behalf of the Marquess of Queensberry. It was rather a long remove from Sherlock Holmes's high-minded pursuit of justice.

SCOTLAND YARD

The English-speaking world's most famous police headquarters and the target of Sherlock Holmes's especial contempt takes its name from Great Scotland Yard, a dingy corner at the top of Whitehall where Sir Robert Peel's new Police Force established its Commissioners' Office in 1829. By 1887 it was too small for the expanding force, and a new purpose-built establishment on the Embankment at the other end of Whitehall was in the planning stages. This "New Scotland Yard", Norman Shaw's handsome edifice of striped brickwork, suffered the indignity of having a murdered woman's torso dumped cheekily in its foundations in 1888 while the Jack the Ripper scare was at its height.

Fenian bombings and the unsolved Ripper and torso murders of 1888 all contributed to growing public discontent with the Metropolitan police detectives. There was a dreadful scandal in 1877 when three senior detectives were sentenced to hard labour for having been in the pay of a notorious confidence trickster. The police made fools of themselves by arresting the wrong man for the Great Coram Street murder of 1872, in the teeth of the evidence. Sergeant Whicher, the shrewd professional on whom Wilkie Collins based Sergeant Cuff, was discredited by his failure to solve the murder of little Francis Savile Kent in 1860, although his first suspect, the boy's sister Constance, was convicted and given a life sentence on her own rather unsatisfactory confession five years later. Adolphus Williamson, the senior CID inspector when Holmes was created, was rudely described as a superannuated has-been in the press, and he was certainly tired and disillusioned by 1889. Hawklike Holmes certainly offered the public a better image than his historical professional contemporaries.

Holmes's first criticism of the police, for trampling over the path at Lauriston Gardens like a herd of buffaloes, anticipated justified concern that scenes of serious crimes were not sensibly protected by the first policemen to arrive. This led to new guidelines being issued during the Jack the Ripper case, when the amount and position of blood on the pavement in the first murder seemed to be a matter of importance which the police had cavalierly disregarded by sluicing it away with a bucket of water. The newly imposed duty to stay with a body and see that it was undisturbed until

CHAPTER OPENER: A group of perfectly turned-out police officers line up outside a barber's shop in London in the late nineteenth century.

assistance arrived led the policeman who found Frances Coles dying under a sinister railway arch in 1891 to regret for the rest of his life that he had not followed the running footsteps which he believed were those of the man who cut her throat.

But perhaps the oddest point about Holmes and Scotland Yard is his persistent use of their traditional techniques, even while he disparages official detectives. The detective department was set up in 1842 in response to public indignation about the fortnight it took to catch the murderer Daniel Good. When tracking his flight from Putney to Spitalfields, some policemen were taken out of uniform and sent to make inquiries in the guise of local tradesmen. A small permanently plain-clothed section was then established, and Inspector Field, the original of Dickens's Bucket, was almost as willing to assume a light disguise or a spurious identity as his fictional counterpart. Holmes repeatedly uses disguise and dissimulation to gain information secretly. His clumsier Scotland Yard associates never step out of character as Mr Heavy Police Investigator, even though it was well known that detectives assumed all sorts of disguises, including womens' clothes, in the fruitless hunt for the Whitechapel murderer.

An even older police technique Sherlock borrows is amassing inside information about criminals. This even pre-dated the formation of the Metropolitan police. The Bow Street Runners, who were likely to be called in after a burglary – and continued to be used as detectives for a few years after the establishment of the uniformed

ABOVE: The world-famous police headquarters, Scotland Yard, in 1808.

Metropolitan force – relied heavily on their knowledge of professional villains. Like all successful policemen, they came to know the characteristic methods of habitual thieves on their patch. They cultivated the acquaintance of petty offenders and learned from them the rumours going round the underworld. The combination of perfect familiarity with slightly chilly detachment that Inspector Bucket brings to potential informants may still be found in today's CID. And it is effectively the manner of the more highly educated Holmes with a Shinwell Johnson or, we may guess, with "Porlock".

Holmes's obsession with footprints was also something no policeman would despise. Two famous cases in the early years of the century had turned on the peculiar nails in murderer's boots: Willie Watson was hanged by a shepherd boy's keen observation – a case Baden-Powell described for generations of boy scouts – and Abraham Thornton was cleared, to everyone's fury, despite his boots matching the foot marks of Mary Ashford's killer. Sherlock Holmes was on the bookstalls, but not yet in *The Strand Magazine* when a letter to *The Times* suggested that fingermarks might make almost as good a clue as footprints!

Filing fingerprints after 1905 led to a marked improvement in detective performance, and Scotland Yard was soon as famous and respected as Holmes himself. Conan Doyle evidently spotted the trend. Inspector MacDonald in *The Valley of Fear* is the most sympathetic and least presumptuous of his CID men. *The Casebook* never mentions the Yard except to have Sergeant Coventry express his satisfaction that Sherlock Holmes has been summoned to Thor Bridge in their stead. Not because Holmes is the better detective, but because the Yard will get all the credit and the local police none if they solve the case. The unnamed inspector in "The Three Gables" is the only overconfident policeman decisively worsted by Holmes in the stories after World War I. Memoirs by Assistant Commissioner Melville Macnaghten and admiring books about the force by Major Arthur Griffith and H. L. Adam brought police detectives fresh esteem. With the Flying Squad, Sir Bernard Spilsbury and a string of classic solved cases from Crippen to Brown and Kennedy, the Yard was not like "Dolly" Williamson's CID of 1887!

HOLMES AND TRUE CRIME

Conan Doyle was high-spirited in *A Study in Scarlet* when he parodied editorials in the *Daily Telegraph*, the *Standard* and the *Evening News*, the first making use of Drebber's murder for a little xenophobia about foreign socialists; the second casting the blame on the Liberal government for slackening authority; and the third blaming the illiberalism of Continental governments, which drove potentially good citizens into violent conspiracies.

This politicising of mysterious crimes involving foreigners was not without genuine precedent. In 1854 a French mechanic called Emmanuel Barthelemy went with an unknown young woman to Warren Street, off Tottenham Court Road, to visit a soda-water manufacturer whose machinery he maintained. Within half an hour Mr Moore, the manufacturer, was savagely beaten with a lead-weighted life-preserver and shot dead; the young woman had vanished; and after killing another man who tried to prevent his escape, Barthelemy was arrested and found to be carrying a pistol, a dagger, and two steamer tickets to Hamburg.

The case is a mystery needing a Sherlock to this day. The young woman's identity was never established, nor Barthelemy's intention in going to Hamburg. No explanation of the quarrel was ever offered: Barthelemy's impassioned solicitor argued that the life-preserver was Mr Moore's, and *he* might have started a lethal assault on the young Frenchman who acted in self-defence. Despite a recommendation to mercy from the jury, Barthelemy was hanged.

But the case leaves an aftertaste of continental politics. Barthelemy was a political refugee who killed a police officer in Brest in 1839 after the man had been involved in shooting several young republicans. In 1853 he killed a Frenchman in a duel in Egham. Superficially this was a matter of honour concerning a young woman. But circumstantial evidence suggests that it was really an attempt to assassinate Barthelemy, who was initially supplied with a deliberately blocked pistol. Now, within a year, another young woman had led Barthelemy into trouble, anticipating flight to Germany: a great centre of republican and socialist dissidence.

For much of Conan Doyle's life, Englishmen feared foreign dissidents and their violent habits. While the first generation of readers were savouring the invention of Holmes, the Metropolitan Police Commissioner suspected that the Jack the Ripper murders were intended to cast suspicion on immigrant social democrats! The anarchist development of political terror as a weapon heightened such anxieties, and the classic case with a politicised background was the Houndsditch murders

of 1910, in which Russian socialists "liberating" a jeweller's property killed three policemen. But by this time Conan Doyle had turned his interest in violent foreign organisations firmly to America.

Conan Doyle's *Daily Telegraph* leader also makes play with the Camorra – an Italian secret society equivalent to the Sicilian Mafia – the German Vehmgericht (dissident socialists) and, of all people, Mme de Brinvilliers, a seventeenth-century libertine and gambler who poisoned large numbers of her family and friends. The young Conan Doyle seems to have been impressed by her sexiness: one of his ghost stories involves a vision of her questioning under torture, which is made mysteriously sado-masochistic by his declining to specify which of the lady's orifices had intolerable quantities of water funnelled into it. (It was, of course, her mouth.)

The one notorious English crime mentioned in the spoof journalism is the Ratcliff Highway murders of 1811, lastingly memorable as the first occasion when London was seized by hysterical panic and householders all over the capital tried to secure themselves against the brutal robbers who cut the throats of two entire families lying asleep in their beds. But for all the pleasure he took in the Chamber of Horrors when he visited it on that Christmas holiday spent with Uncle Dicky, Conan Doyle was not remarkably well-informed about the great crimes of his century. It was natural that a Scottish-born and -trained doctor should be familiar with Pritchard, hanged in Glasgow in 1865 for poisoning his wife and mother-in-law. But we have seen that Holmes wrongly describes him as a man at the top of his professional tree, whereas Pritchard's repellent vanity, boasting and lying perpetually damaged his practice, and his one attempt to secure a university appointment was a fiasco. He proved to have forged references from distinguished medics who had never heard of him.

The other doctor to whom Holmes wrongly ascribed professional distinction was William Palmer, one of Dickens's favourite out-and-out villains. This incompetent abortionist, gambler and rake, with fourteen illegitimate children and tens of thousands of pounds of debts, poisoned numbers of his creditors and relations. His methods were so crude and obvious that companies ceased to accept his

The Residence of the late
MR MARR,
RATCLIFFE HIGHWAY,
where he was dreadfully murdered with his Wife, Infant Child, & Apprentice, on the 7th Day of December 1811.

The Pen Maul that was used in the atrocious deed.

OPPOSITE: Marie Madeleine, Marquise de Brinvilliers being arrested after poisoning her family in the seventeenth century.

ABOVE: No. 29 Ratcliffe Highway, London, 1811. The building was the residence and shop of a Mr Marr who was murdered there, together with his wife, infant child and an apprentice, on 7 December 1811. Below the view is the weapon used in the murders.

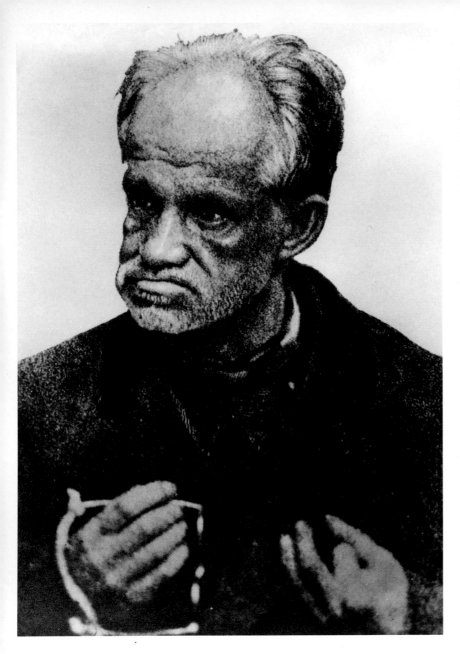

attempts to insure the lives of his nearest and dearest. To live in the same house with Palmer was an obvious actuarial risk! It is probable, but not certain, that he got rid of four of his legitimate and several of his illegitimate children; certain that he killed his wife, an uncle and three creditors; likely that he killed his mother-in-law, another uncle, and a friend who succumbed to his first experiment with strychnine in brandy. No great Sherlock was needed to bring him to justice when he laboriously dosed and redosed a fellow-gambler whose winnings he intended to steal in 1855, and Robert Graves's attempt to prove that he was an innocent man hanged in error beggars belief in its speciousness and stupidity.

The two other noted criminals mentioned by Holmes were familiar to all. "Wainewright the Poisoner" killed his grandfather for an inheritance; his mother-in-law because he couldn't afford to house her; his sister-in-law whose life he had insured. He was lucky to escape with transportation for forgery in 1831; luckier still that his minor talents as an art critic attracted intellectual interest and made him the object of an essay by Wilde. Wainewright's Wildean insouciance in pretending he poisoned his sister-in-law "because her ankles were so thick" was probably the most memorable product of his supposed creativity.

Charley Peace, cat-burglar and murderer, still holds his place in Madame Tussaud's, and his burgling tools are exhibited at the Black Museum in Scotland Yard. For some reason, this squalid killer of his unwilling mistress's husband struck Victorians as a "lovable rogue", and so Holmes calls him "my old friend".

NAPOLEONS OF CRIME

As we have seen, Conan Doyle's second thoughts about Professor Moriarty in *The Valley of Fear* were a huge improvement upon his original creation. "The Napoleon of crime", "the organiser of half that is evil and or nearly all that is undetected" is never shown winning a Marengo or Austerlitz. Nor, in "The Final Problem", is he compared with anyone whose skill and methods show just how such a genius could control all crime, "like a spider in its web".

In *The Valley of Fear*, Conan Doyle named the perfect prototype. Jonathan Wild, "the Thieftaker General", really did run London crime in the early 1720s as no man ever again ruled a civic underworld until Al Capone perfected Johnny Torrio's plan for organising crime on business lines. Wild began as a pimp practising "buttock and twang" – beating and robbing a punter when he was suitably unbreeched and incapacitated. He graduated to brothel-keeping, and then worked for London's corrupt Under-City Marshal, Charles Hitchen. In 1711 Wild started on his own in competition with Hitchen. Both men used the acquaintance with thieves their overt business of crime prevention brought them, and became receivers of stolen goods. Wild perfected the trade. He never handled stolen property himself, which left him immune to the law. He opened a "Lost Property Office", cheekily placed opposite the Old Bailey. Theft victims came to him, and for a fee he would purport to enquire among thieves and find out where they might go to have their goods restored. In fact, of course, the goods rested in his own warehouse – not that he himself either put them there or took them from it.

Wild used informing and impeachment to defeat competition. He gleaned damaging information about one thief from another, and then threatened to impeach the second if he refused to

OPPOSITE: *Charles Peace was a notorious English burglar and murderer from Sheffield.*

BELOW: *Professor Moriarty, the "Napoleon of crime", takes his leave of Sherlock Holmes.*

work for him. And he carried out his threats. He became a familiar face at the sessions, delivering up malefactors to justice and pretending to be on the side of the law. And thus he broke up the four largest gangs operating in the city, who thought they had no need of him. He acquired a crown-ended tipstaff and called himself the Thieftaker-General, deluding innocent souls into believing he and his office had legal standing. At fairs and holidays where crowds assembled, he might be seen with his tipstaff, busily indicating the fattest takings to his own pickpockets and arresting any ill-advised freelances.

In 1724, however, he impeached the popular burglar and highway robber Jack Sheppard, whose repeated escapes from gaol had made him one of the first glamorised criminal heroes. Sheppard's confederate Blueskin Blake tried to cut Wild's throat in court, and the public sympathised. Very swiftly, Parliament made it an offence to accept money for giving information about stolen goods, and the thieftaker stupidly fell into the snare of "the Jonathan Wild Act". He followed his victims to the gallows, but was immortalised as Mr Peachum in *The Beggar's Opera*, and under his own name as a satire on Walpole in Fielding's *Jonathan Wild the Great*.

Pray bring this Ticket with you

He was the perfect model for Professor Moriarty: overtly above-board, and actually controlling most of the theft in London. To cross him meant death on the gallows.

On the grounds that CID chief Sir Robert Anderson dubbed Adam Harry Worth "the Napoleon of the criminal world", and Worth's luxurious flat at 198 Piccadilly was an international meeting-place for leading thieves, he has confidently been proposed as the original of Moriarty. The Anderson citation is a red herring: Sir Robert's public comments on named criminals followed his retirement in 1903, twelve years after Moriarty's creation. It is true that, in his heyday, Worth fenced the goods in most big robberies of the 1870s. True, too, that he was widely known to be the actual (but unindictable) thief of Gainsborough's "Duchess of Devonshire" from Agnew's gallery in Bond Street, and that the theft was intended as part of a complicated blackmailing plot to secure the release of a confederate from prison. But Worth, a professional American criminal who started as a bank robber, was completely unlike Moriarty. He was extravagantly opulent, running a steam yacht with a crew of twenty. He was no intellectual. He was a hands-on thief as well as a receiver. He never ruled the underworld like a Boss of All Bosses and was never held to be involved in any murder. Attempts to make a clumsy anagram of MORIARTY out of his famous alias H[ARRY RAYMO]ND are even feebler than most anagrammatic arguments. The suggestion that Moriarty's possession of Greuze's "Jeune fille à l'agneau" points to Worth's famous theft from *Agnew's* is absurd. Conan Doyle invented Moriarty's picture 40 years after Worth's crime and sixteen years after the Gainsborough's return had been negotiated, Worth getting no more out of the deal than a "no charges" agreement. Still, a report that Conan Doyle told his friend Dr Gray Chandler Briggs he had been partially inspired by Worth must be borne in mind.

By far the most Moriarty-like London criminal of the nineteenth century was James Townsend Saward, barrister-at-law and master-forger. His totally respectable public career and circle of professional friends completely covered his nocturnal

association with hard-bitten criminals in low gin-palaces. He controlled a ramifying gang which ensured that apart from writing forged signatures on cheques, he was not directly involved with the actual practice of crime. He used corrupt solicitors to procure him genuine cheques settling genuine (but deliberately prearranged) debts. He copied the genuine signatures onto blank cheques, and had them made out for large amounts in settlement of imaginary debts to be paid into bogus bank accounts. Corrupt bank messengers and a chain of intermediaries ensured that "Jim the Penman" received only money that had been discreetly laundered. No one knew how the frauds were managed, or suspected for an instant that "m'learned friend Mr Saward" was a criminal mastermind, until the gang made the mistake of opening a bogus account in the wrong name at Yarmouth and the little empire came tumbling down. Saward was exposed and transported in 1857. Professional London was flabbergasted. And if there were a shred of evidence that Conan Doyle had heard of him we might confidently assert that "Jim the Penman" partially inspired Moriarty.

OPPOSITE: Jonathan Wild, an eighteenth-century Al Capone.

ABOVE: "The Stolen Gainsborough" (The Duchess of Devonshire) – most famous coup of "Napoleon of crime" Adam Worth.

AMERICAN ORGANISATIONS

From the outset, American crime interested Conan Doyle and engaged Holmes. Parts of the West were still Wild when Jefferson Hope came to London (whether we date from Conan Doyle's composition in 1887, or Watson's chronology placing the event in 1881). Like the Australian goldfields, it was a region where highway men still roamed, crying "Stick 'em up!" in Wyoming or "Bail 'em up!" in Ballarat. Butch Cassidy would rob trains and rustle horses for another twenty years, although the lawless postwar conditions of the 1860s and '70s had passed. Chaps and lariats and ten-gallon hats were exotic, but exotically contemporary, not bathed in the nostalgic light of Western films and dude ranches.

Likewise the nineteenth-century Church of the Latter-Day Saints did not comprise well-spoken young missionaries, politely peddling their religion from door to door. It was an exotic frontier feature. It belonged in Utah, whither it had fled from murders and massacres at the hands of hysterical anti-Mormons in the east and mid-west.

And a Mormon band led by Bishop John Lee had colluded with Native Americans to massacre 133 peaceful men, women and children whose wagon-train was passing Mormon territory. Brigham Young prevented the federal government from bringing the murderers to justice for seventeen years, and it was not until 1877, the year of Young's death, that Lee was finally executed. So Conan Doyle was not sensationalist or bigoted in believing newspapers which claimed that Young had established a terror squad called the Danites or Angels of Death to punish anyone who challenged the Mormon elders' discipline. Of course, Young had authoritatively denied the existence of such assassins to the highly respected journalist-politician Horace Greeley. But Young was not a scrupulous man. He denied Mormon involvement in the Mountain Meadows massacre.

Conan Doyle *was* scrupulous. Like Watson, he was practically incapable of dissimulation. He abhorred terrorist groups trying to force lip-service to their creeds on others. He compared the Danites to the Vehmgericht and the Italian secret societies, as well as the Spanish Inquisition. All bigotry was anathema to him, and he linked underground political organisations and atavistic peasant defenders of their rights with groups using the threat of torture and death to enforce their religious beliefs. Later works would find Conan Doyle decisively hostile to Fenians and violent working men's organisations. Odd and unyielding as his own opinions might be, Arthur Conan Doyle consistently loved freedom of thought and hated those who would stamp it out, even when they were themselves driven to desperation by oppression.

He knew, too, that successful oppression breeds corrupt tyranny, even if it starts from the immaculate scrupulosity of a Robespierre. He might have gone one stage further than Acton and said, "Absolute power corrupts absolutely. When based on and enforcing a sincerely held ideal, it is Hell's gift to Himmler."

So it should be no surprise that he was one of the first writers east of the Atlantic to spot the importance of secret Italian organisations in America. The Mafia, Camorra and Carbonari, starting as protectors of the poor against invaders and aristocrats, had deteriorated to unwelcome extortionist bandits in their own land. The Ku Klux Klan had exposed America's vulnerability to a secret society of murderous enforcers (successfully) determined to replace the black politicians of post-war reconstruction with their ideal vision of a racially segregated and stratified society. Conan Doyle, while hazy about how the KKK worked and its larger aims and intentions, had shown in "The Five Orange Pips" that he found it abhorrent for its terrorism and probably distasteful for its racism.

"The Red Circle" is the *locus classicus* for Conan Doyle's treatment of Italian-American secret societies. As he showed before in "The Five Orange Pips" and would show again in *The Valley of Fear*, he took for granted the use of a secret symbol by which such societies' dealings were identified to those in the know. The red disc and five pips are also used like the Black Spot in Stevenson's *Treasure Island* to convey a threat or confer a dreadful duty. Since the Red Circle is said to maintain itself in New York by blackmailing and threatening wealthy Italian Americans, Conan Doyle was unquestionably drawing on the wave of "Black Hand" blackmail notes which plagued immigrants, including even the Metropolitan Opera's great tenor Caruso, in the years before World War I. Like most people, he assumed the Black Hand to be an organised gang – a sub-section, he suggests, of the Carbonari – and not as the police established, the activity of freelances imitating a few Mafiosi. The general public took the terms Black Hand, Mafia, Camorra and Carbonari to be synonyms for one secret Italian society of kidnappers and protection racketeers. Conan Doyle unfortunately selected the one version which did not establish itself in America. The Carbonari had been a secret organisation of French, Calabrian, Spanish and Portuguese resistance to the Bourbon restoration. It was the Sicilian Mafia and Neapolitan Camorra which battled for supremacy in the underworlds of New Orleans and New York.

OPPOSITE: Brigham Young, the alleged controller of a band of Mormon assassins.

Conan Doyle did not underrate their murderous danger. "Lupo the Wolf" Saietta's murder stable was uncovered in New York in 1901. Sixty-one corpses showed the lengths to which the gangsters would go in eliminating opposition and terrorising recalcitrant victims. New York police lieutenant Joe Petrosino, who exposed it, was gunned down when he visited Sicily to prevent the emigration of yet more killers. This menace was a far cry from the simple gang of seven thieves or counterfeiters which boasted Abe Slaney as "the most dangerous crook in Chicago" ("The Dancing Men"). That was similar to the English gangs (other than Moriarty's) which Holmes encountered. Four Mafiosi had blasted their way to domination of such little mobs as far back as 1869 in New Orleans, using their newly invented weapon, the sawn-off shotgun.

This, too, Conan Doyle recognised as American. But *The Valley of Fear*, in which its national identity appears as a clue, was to recount very closely the exploits of one of the most remarkable detectives in the world's first and greatest private detective agency: Pinkerton's.

ABOVE: A Ku Klux Klan meeting where a new recruit swears the oath of loyalty, while a man is tarred and feathered.

ALLAN PINKERTON

Allan Pinkerton, virtually the world's first private detective, might have stepped out of a Conan Doyle adventure story. The son of a Gorbals blacksmith who was at one time imprisoned for some forgotten offence, young Allan became a notable figure in Glasgow working class political circles. An ardent advocate of the People's Charter demanding democracy, he supported the "Physical Force" Chartists led by demagogue Feargus O'Connor and the firebrand revolutionary agitator Julian Harney. In 1839 Allan joined the workers' army assembled by Newport (Monmouth) mayor John Frost to release a Chartist prisoner. Unhappily, the plan was betrayed and the workers faced a detachment of soldiers who put them to flight. Allan Pinkerton became a marked man in Glasgow, and three years later he fled to America just ahead of the police who came to arrest him as a known subversive.

He was a cooper, and paid his transatlantic passage by signing on as a ship's barrelmaker. His wife of the previous month took a passage in steerage until the captain heard they were newlyweds and gave them a little stateroom. Off Nova Scotia their vessel was forced on to the rocks and the passengers landed in Canada from lifeboats. The Pinkertons spent a couple of weeks in Montreal before Allan booked a passage to Chicago. Joan Pinkerton pleaded with him to postpone their departure: she had put down a deposit on a "wee bonnet" and wanted to collect it. Allan stormed at her, but with Scotch thrift, agreed to change their tickets. A week later they learned that the boilers of the riverboat they had intended taking had blown up, and she was lost with all aboard.

Pinkerton set up as a barrelmaker beside the Fox River, north of Chicago, and gathered wood for his work from a small island in the river. On one occasion he was surprised to find the remains of a fire. The island was not picnicking territory, nor, so far as he knew, visited by anyone but himself. He kept watch, and saw some men row furtively ashore by moonlight and start a fire. Pinkerton told the local sheriff and they arrested a gang of counterfeiters who were using the place to make bogus dimes. Counterfeiting, as Conan Doyle was well aware, was a very important branch of professional crime in the nineteenth century. Thereafter the island was known as Bogus Island, and Pinkerton was in demand as a detective.

He caught another counterfeiting gang by pretending to be in the market for forged $10 bills. He was appointed sheriff's deputy, and then "detective" to Chicago (the only one). He was no respecter of persons, and traced thefts from the Chicago Post Office to the postmaster's nephews. He set up his famous firm with its Open Eye logo and motto "We Never Sleep". And he hired and trained agents.

Like the Scotland Yard men and Holmes, he saw disguise as central to detection. His office held as many costumes as a repertory theatre. The training he gave new agents taught them to shadow suspects without being observed, and imposed the duty of sending reports frequently – daily if possible – from the field. But they also had to learn to simulate drunkenness; to loaf convincingly; to pretend to be what they were not. He believed in infiltration to crack gangs, and carried out the actual work of any firm or premises under observation. A strict teetotaller who would allow neither alcohol or tobacco in his house, he made himself drink whisky on a case if his assumed character demanded it.

And he laid down ground rules which saved Pinkerton's from the sleaziness of many of its successors. The firm would do no divorce work, and would never investigate or comment on a woman's morals unless they were absolutely germane to some crime of which she was suspected. They would never work for a political purpose or an anti-vice campaigner. They would never work for a defendant in a criminal case without notifying the prosecution that they were doing so. And the old Chartist and Coopers' Union member forbade his men to break strikes, infiltrate unions, or attend any organised labour meetings that were not open to the public.

In a good cause, however, he broke the law zealously. His house was a station on the Underground Railway smuggling runaway slaves to Canada. He hero-worshipped John Brown as he had once hero-worshipped Julian Harney. When

Lincoln was elected president he arranged for his transportation covertly through Baltimore, where would-be secessionists had threatened his life. He probably deserved the ridicule he earned for calling the threats "an assassination plot", and the derision attracted by his coded telegram "Plums and Nuts have arrived", meaning "Pinkerton and Lincoln are safe". Nevertheless, he organised an effective spy service for the Union in the Civil War.

During the war he transferred his hero-worship to Lincoln's political rival General McClellan, former chief engineer to a railroad for which Pinkerton's had supplied security. After the war Allan Pinkerton's business took on increasing amounts of railroad security, breaking the Reno gang which invented train robbery, but suffering its first real setbacks

with the Jesse James gang. "Pinkerton's men" became seriously unpopular when they incautiously firebombed a house where they wrongly believed Frank and Jesse James to be hiding. This injured the James boys' stepfather and cost their mother her right arm.

Allan Pinkerton knew the importance of public opinion. He urgently needed a popular cause to win the press back to his side. So as a successful businessman and friend of McClellan, he moved away from his former pro-labour stance. Pinkerton's started supplying guards to protect blackleg workers during strikes. The Long Strike of the Pennsylvania anthracite miners in 1874–76 brought Pinkerton's most adventurous agent into the field to infiltrate a union. And Allan Pinkerton, who had a gift for flamboyant prose, wrote up James McParland's adventures in Pottsville and Reading as exaggerated heroics. Which suited Conan Doyle's tastes perfectly.

OPPOSITE: Allan Pinkerton during the American Civil War.

ABOVE: The heads of the James Gang – (left to right) standing, Cole and Rob Younger; seated, Jesse and Frank James.

JAMES MCPARLAND AND THE MOLLY MAGUIRES

Sherlock Holmes's first encounter with a Pinkerton's man comes in "The Red Circle". "Mr Leverton of Pinkerton's American Agency" is disguised as a cabman in the pursuit of "Georgiano of the Red Circle". Holmes has already heard of both Leverton ("the hero of the Long Island Cave mystery") and Georgiano. (Pinkerton's agent Frank Dimaio successfully infiltrated the Mafia between 1891 and 1908, and was one of the few people who realised that "Black Hand" notes were the work of individuals and not Mafia family business.)

Historically, Pinkerton's American agents rarely travelled to Europe. The Agency employed Europeans as agents, ex-Inspector Abberline, famous for his detective work on Jack the Ripper, being the best-known. Nor did Mafiosi (or Neapolitan Camorristi) come to England until the 1960s. They went to Sicily and Italy, where Lt Petrosino followed them to his death. Mr Leverton was obviously not Frank Dimaio or Joseph Petrosino.

But "Birdie Edwards", alias "John Douglas" the Pinkerton man who infiltrated "the Scowrers" as "John McMurdo", was clearly based on the Pinkerton operative James McParland, who infiltrated the Mollie Maguires as "James McKenna". And in making this man a hero in *The Valley of Fear*, Conan Doyle unwittingly stepped into a hornets' nest.

We have said that Conan Doyle's story usefully simplifies the events of 1874–76. Allan Pinkerton's *The Mollie Maguires and the Detectives* told a long and complicated story that still needs cautious interpretation. The Pennsylvania hard-coal district runs from Reading in the south to Scranton and Wilkes-Barre in the north, between the Blue Mountains and the Tuscaroras in the Upper Appalachians. A few years after the Civil War, the miners formed a union, the Workingmen's Benevolent Association, and the union organised sporadic strikes against atrocious working conditions and debt-controlled wage-slavery of a kind England had legislated away in the 1840s. In 1870, Franklin Benjamin Gowen, a former Schuylkill County District Attorney, became President of the Reading Railroad, and as mediator in the mining disputes set a sliding wage-rate tied to the price of coal. This led to trouble as coal prices fell immediately and the miners' pay dropped by 8%. Gowen then made things worse by doubling rail freight rates, which put many small mine owners out of business. And the Reading Railroad took over their mines.

Gowen claimed that the labour problems arose from too many men chasing too few jobs, and only large companies could resolve this. The WBA believed that Gowen was determined to establish his own monopoly. A "Long Strike" was called in 1875, and under pressure of hardship, some miners assaulted and even murdered foremen, managers, and blacklegs. Killing with impunity on the open street was effected by bringing in outsiders who could not be recognised. The technique continued in American Organised Crime, earning the nickname "Murder Inc."

und giving semi-mythical status to Albert Anastasia and the Brooklyn Mafia family when the press caught up with Conan Doyle's knowledge in the 1930s.

To the mine-owners it seemed that the Irish-American friendly society "the Ancient Order of Hibernians", with its secret passwords and signals, was the body most likely to be responsible, and Gowen asked Allan Pinkerton to investigate. Pinkerton sent the Irish Catholic McParland to pass himself off as an unemployed labourer and infiltrate the organisation. McParland did so, much as Conan Doyle describes Birdy Edwards. Despite his spectacles, he was ready with his fists, and he merged easily into the hard-drinking life of the "Wild Irish" miners. Conan Doyle added the colour of branding with a red hot iron for the initiation ceremony, and giving Edwards the spurious secret occupation of counterfeiting to provide visible means of support. The Ancient Order of Hibernians themselves supplied the colourful feature of genuinely naming their lodge presidents "Bodymasters". And Conan Doyle created the memorable villain "Black Jack McGinty" by combining the Bodymaster who owned a saloon which the Hibernians used as headquarters with the influential Councilman whom the owners believed was using political influence to protect the assassins he directed.

Pinkerton also supplied a body of special policemen to guard the mines and their managers and to carry out arrests based on McParland's evidence. Their leader and Gowen were the only locals who knew that the terrorist "McKenna" was really the Pinkerton's spy McParland. And McParland and Gowen were the only locals who knew that Captain Linden and his men were employed by Allan Pinkerton.

It was Pinkerton, however, who supplied Conan Doyle with the misleading idea that, at least in the Shenandoah district, the Hibernians were identical with the "Molly Maguires": Irishmen who adopted the name and terrorist methods of an underground band of landless peasants in Ireland in the 1850s. The Molly Maguires undoubtedly existed and were likely to be members of the Ancient Order. Like the IRA later, they were condemned by the church, and having made himself prominent in their councils, McParland, a devout Catholic, really did

ABOVE: *The detective James McParland, who was responsible for infiltrating and dismantling the Molly Maguires.*

suffer the humiliation of hearing a sermon directed against him by a priest who disapproved of the terror. But reading between the lines it seems that everybody missed the real point of the Mollies. They don't seem to have made their prime purpose the assassination of managers or even blacklegs until the Long Strike. They look far more like a strong-arm extension of the Hibernians: a group of Irishmen determined to protect their fellow-nationals against miners from Wales and Germany. The ethnic problems of the great American melting pot led to racially based gangs and politics among immigrants in the cities; and these in turn developed into the Italian and Irish and Jewish and German gangs of syndicated crime. Pinkerton, unfortunately, simply turned his organisation against organised labour: a police the agency finally dropped forever in the late 1930s.

Shortly after Conan Doyle completed his manuscript, he travelled across the Atlantic with one of Allan Pinkerton's sons, and heard from him more Agency scuttlebutt about the Long Strike and James McParland. Unfortunately when *The Valley of Fear* came out, young Pinkerton concluded wrongly that Conan Doyle had exploited a private conversation for gain, and Conan Doyle's friendship with the sons who now ran the agency never recovered.

OPPOSITE: The Molly Maguires were a secret organisation of Irish immigrants who worked in the anthracite coal region of Pennsylvania. In the 1870s, they used sabotage and assassination against coal companies to gain better wages and working conditions.

BELOW: James McParland, being initiated into the Irish secret society, the Molly Maguires.

SHERLOCKING AND MODERN DETECTION

For many years informed opinion held that Sherlock Holmes and true crime detection were poles apart. Sherlock's lofty superiority to the ordinary police seemed ever more misplaced as this or that "Knacker of the Yard" produced memoirs detailing memorable cases solved and real villains sent to the gallows. Fingerprinting was central to detection. Sherlock Holmes seemed locked in admiration for Bertillon's system of identifying individuals from exhaustive lists of head and body measurements. Worse still, the great scientific mind dropped hints of admiration for Cesare Lombroso, the Italian founding father of scientific criminology. Lombroso's science was vitiated by the nineteenth-century predisposition to think of taxonomy, ordering things in related groups and species, as the heart of scientific method. And so he persuaded himself that he identified "criminal types", recognisable by their rather primitive simian features! A thick-necked, low-browed, generally shtoopid face for Burglar Bill was a gift to cartoonists. It bore little relation to America's most famous and glamorous thief, the handsome and daring robber and jail-breaker Gerald Chapman whose image was the first ever to be cheered by audiences when it appeared on film screens in newsreels, and whose cell was filled with flowers sent daily by admirers when a clumsy confederate brought about his conviction for murder. Nor was Britain's good-looking and fastidious housebreaker Steinie Morrison a Lombrosian type whose unsafe conviction for murder might be ascribed to a villainous appearance.

The weakness of Lombrosian criminal typing was made clear to Conan Doyle in Egypt in 1895. He was unimpressed by the discovery that his Sherlock Holmes stories were being put before police recruits as part of their training. He was even more unimpressed when a young officer studied his face and told him it showed criminal tendencies!

Holmes's search for a reagent to prove that stains were really blood reflected a far more genuine approach to forensic science. A complicated test to crystallise haemoglobin had been in existence since 1850, and a really skilled practitioner might be able to distinguish microscopically between human and some animal blood. But it was too expensive and unreliable to be used by the police. Nor did they employ spectroscopic analysis, though this might have definitely identified blood (without distinguishing between human and animal) after 1859. A proper test, based on the properties of blood serum, was discovered in France and used by the French police in 1902. But as late as 1911 the British still depended on crude tests like pouring hydrogen peroxide onto a stain, which would foam if it were blood; or mixing turpentine and either benzedrine or a guiaiac extract with the stain to see whether it turned blue, indicating that it was mammalian. The continental police were already determining whether the mammal was human, and by 1928 were testing to see whether the blood group matched their suspect's. Britain caught up in 1934.

Holmes's famous magnifying glass also reflected trends in detection, though the further refinement to microscopic examination was yet more important. The Duc de Praslin's scandalous murder of his wife in 1847 had been solved in ways that were truly Holmesian. The Duc's bloodstained pistol, with which he claimed to have defended his wife from intruders who killed her, was examined under a magnifying glass, and a chestnut hair, the colour of the Duchess's, was found on the butt. Under the microscope this proved to be definitely human and to have been beaten out of the scalp with the pistol. With the case against him hopeless, the Duc de Praslin committed suicide before he could be brought to trial.

Two years after Holmes "died" at Reichenbach, Hans Gross published a *Handbook for Magistrates*, which was translated into English ten years later as *Criminal Investigations*. This shared Holmes's interest in footprints. And it highlighted the value of microscopic examination of fibres, hairs, dust and pieces of wood. All these would play a lasting part in forensic science, though the impossibility of positively identifying one hair as coming from the same head as another reduced the evidential value of the stray hair until DNA comparisons made all previous forms of body cell identification secondary.

By that time, most informed students of crime took it for granted that Sherlock Holmes was played out, and a joke. Policemen rightly deplored Holmes's tendency to reach conclusions from one set of clues and restrict his lines of enquiry accordingly. They had given up disguise for casual inquiries. The forensic science laboratory was a better instrument of detection than Holmes's magnifying glass, and his table of scientific instruments.

Yet one influential detective approach of the 1980s and '90s proved a genuine throwback to Holmesian method. "Psychological profiling", developed by the FBI in America, was credited with astonishing results. In fact the psychological element was far less important than the intelligent Holmesian analysis of clues.

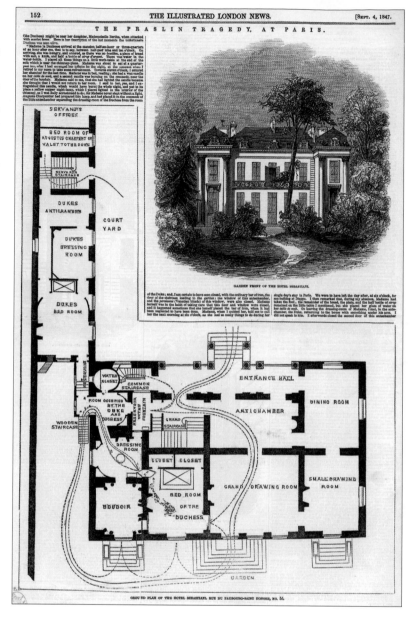

OPPOSITE: A magnifying glass – one of the objects with which Sherlock Holmes is most closely associated.

ABOVE: A floor plan and view of the front garden of the Hotel Sebastiani, Paris, where the Duchess of Praslin was found dead in her bedchamber in suspicious circumstances. Her husband, the Duc, was accused of her murder but poisoned himself before the full truth was revealed.

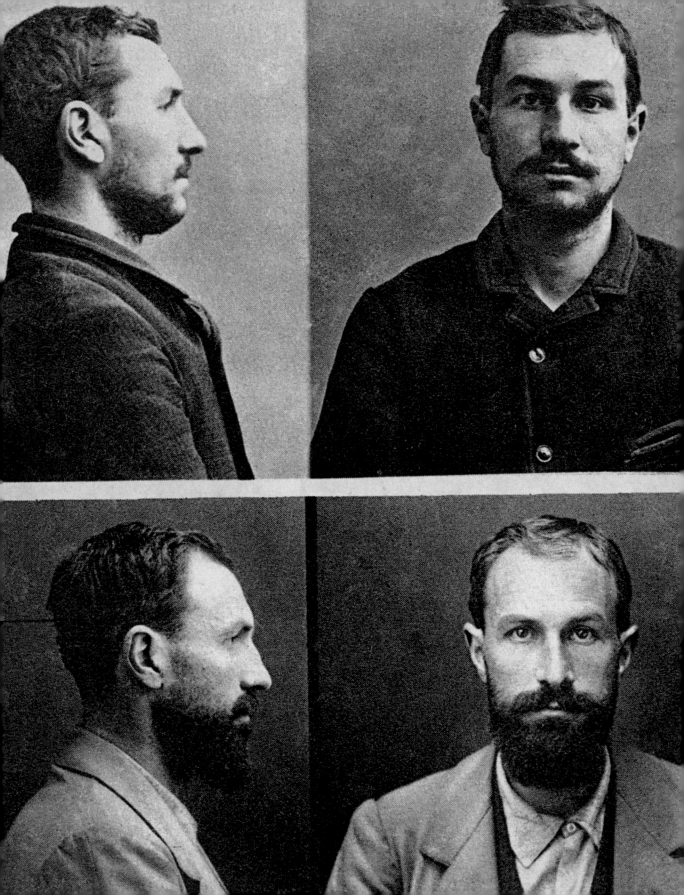

Professor David Canter who was associated with the British development of Criminal Identification Analysis (as it came to be called) proved this when he and his police associates correctly identified the "railway rapist" and murderer as a man whose work brought him into contact with the London overground railway system and the Post Office; whose hobbies included oriental martial arts; and who lived in a very precise area of North London. Psychological data played little part in the ultimate arrest of John Duffy. Professor Canter noted that the crimes frequently took place in little known approaches to railway stations; that he bound his victims' hands in a manner taught by martial arts classes; and used a paper string preferred by the Post Office. And the almost miraculous pin-pointing of Duffy's residence was a matter of consulting maps and noting the positions of his earliest known assaults. Sherlock would have been proud of the methodology, as might those few crime historians who devote similar study of maps and actual clues to historical mysteries like the Whitechapel Murders or the death of Sir Edmund Berry Godfrey.

DETECTIVE DOYLE

Arthur Conan Doyle's son Adrian insisted that Conan Doyle, and Conan Doyle alone was the model for Sherlock Holmes. He recorded that his father turned his detective mind to problems sent by distressed victims, and that on these occasions he shut himself up in his study, and ate his meals from trays left outside his locked door. Certainly Adrian was describing behaviour very different from that Conan Doyle evinced when writing. He was famous for working in company, and even contributing to conversation without breaking off composition.

The rehabilitation of George Edalji's reputation was his best public triumph. The Oscar Slater case was less satisfactory. Elderly Miss Marion Gilchrist was killed in her Glasgow flat by a man who ransacked the place, smashed open a wooden box of papers, and passed Miss Gilchrist's maid, Helen Lambie, outside the apartment door. Helen said the only thing missing was a crescent-shaped brooch, and the police arrested Oscar Slater who had pawned such a jewel before crossing the Atlantic. Slater came home voluntarily, for he could prove that his brooch was not Miss Gilchrist's, and there was no other evidence against him. Except that Helen Lambie and two other witnesses identified him as the man leaving the murder scene.

But Helen Lambie told a relative of Miss Gilchrist's that she recognised the murderer. Since the broken box suggested that the killer was looking for Miss Gilchrist's will, the old lady's family were suspected by those who saw that Slater the pimp had been railroaded for a crime he never committed. Conan Doyle believed that Miss Gilchrist's step-nephew, the distinguished Dr Francis Charteris, was the killer. Others thought that another relative, Austin Birrell, had murdered her. Or

OPPOSITE: Photographs taken at a ten-year intervals, and analysed using the Bertillon system, reveal it is the same man by the spiral lobe of the ear and the angles of the face.

yet another relative who was a sailor. Or two of them acting together. Perhaps if Richard Whirtington-Egan's 500,000 word study of the case is ever published, we shall finally be satisfied that we know who killed Marion Gilchrist.

Conan Doyle was dissatisfied after Slater's release. He spent a good deal of money publicising the injustice done to a man he disliked, and hoped for some reimbursement when the government granted Slater £6,000 compensation. Slater, who had written grovelling letters of gratitude from prison, demurred. He felt that he had done the time and he deserved the money.

Conan Doyle had no success in saving his neighbour Norman Thorne from the gallows. The young Methodist chicken farmer lived in a shack near Crowborough and wanted to shake off his clinging London fiancée, Elsie Cameron, in favour of a local girl. But Elsie wouldn't be shaken. She pretended to be pregnant, packed her suitcase, and came down to Crowborough. Never to be seen again. Thorne said she had not arrived, but had to change his story when Elsie's suitcase and her body, sawn in three, were dug up under his chicken run. Now he claimed he went out after a quarrel, returning to find her hanging from a beam …

Pathologist Sir Bernard Spilsbury made a duff job of examining Elsie's remains, though the police confirmed that there was positively no trace of a rope ever having passed around the beam. Conan Doyle thought Thorne was probably guilty, but his story was *possible*.

"Brides-in-the-Bath" George Joseph Smith fell victim to Conan Doyle's Holmesian habit of keeping newspaper cuttings about oddities. When he read that a Mrs Lloyd had been found drowned in her bath in London by her grieving husband, he was forcibly reminded of the strikingly similar case of a Mrs Smith in Blackpool. He sent his cuttings to Scotland Yard, as did Mrs Smith's father-in-law, who had also noticed Mrs Lloyd's death. And when the bigamist Smith was shown to have had an earlier wife still, who died in identical fashion after he had insured her life, the evil murderer's fate was sealed.

It is often said that Conan Doyle declared that Jack the Ripper might have escaped detection by disguising himself as a bloodstained midwife. Conan Doyle may have said this, but neither I nor Ripperologists I have consulted can find the source. Conan Doyle certainly did observe, sensibly, that the "Jack the Ripper" letters were on good paper in a literate, clerkly hand. And he thought the police ought to have published facsimiles of them – quite unaware that they had done so!

Conan Doyle was unhappily unable to help his mother's second cousin, Sir Arthur Vicars, the Chief Herald of Ireland, when the Irish crown jewels were stolen from a safe in his office. Vicars had appointed some rummy assistants, and was rumoured to be involved with some of them in a flagrant homosexual circle. He and Conan Doyle came to believe that Francis Shackleton, Dublin Herald and brother of the Antarctic explorer, was principally responsible for the theft, aided and abetted by the sexually suspect Captain Richard Gorges, and possibly even the Viceroy's son, Lord Haddo. But the plot had been well managed. Shackleton and Haddo were out of the country when the theft was discovered. And Vicars was made scapegoat for his carelessness in letting his keys out of his permanent possession.

The Langham Hotel looms large in Conan Doyle's and Holmes's lives, and Conan Doyle solved a mystery for them. A guest disappeared one night, leaving his evening clothes behind. He had been wearing them early in the evening, whereafter neither he nor his luggage were seen again. Conan Doyle deduced that he would be in Edinburgh or Glasgow, leading a limited social life. The reason? He must have left unseen while the lobby was full of returning theatregoers. If he travelled a short distance to a minor station, he would have been seen getting off the train. He must have gone to a major terminus. Only Edinburgh and Glasgow were possible destinations at that time of night. And his social life would be reduced, as he didn't need white tie and tails.

It proved just as he had said. Elementary, my dear Sir Arthur ...

Conan Doyle could be obtuse. He was astonished to learn that his French chauffeur became a noted anarchist terrorist. He could be absurdly romantic, postulating that the unfortunate Mrs Luard (shot, almost certainly by some passing vagrant who stole her rings) was the victim of revenge perpetrated by some exotic oriental enemy her husband had made when serving in India (where Major General Luard had never been)! And for the last ten years of his life he confidently passed over criminal problems to mediums to bring the truth from the other world. It must have disappointed the famous Crime Club "Our Society" when this celebrated founder-member gave a paper about spiritualists predicting correct solutions to obscure crimes!

OPPOSITE: Marion Gilchrist, who was murdered in 1908 during a robbery at her home in Glasgow.

ABOVE: Oscar Slater was wrongfully convicted of Miss Gilchrist's murder.

5
CRIME FICTION

There was no such term when Sherlock Holmes was created. There were a few detective stories and novels. Edgar Allen Poe's *Tales of Mystery and Imagination* were accorded the prestige status of "art", especially as the French, deaf to Poe's dreadful jingling rhythms and tiresome repetitions, thought of him as a great romantic poet.

Nobody else had created detective fiction that won international respect, and Poe himself mixed his handful of crime and detection stories indiscriminately with tales of horror, psychological disturbance, spookiness and hair-raising peril.

Yet today "Crime" enjoys its own labelled sections in public libraries, booksellers' shelves and publishers' lists. And "Crime" means "Crime Fiction". It was awarded its own instantly identifiable green covers in the heyday of Penguin Books. It was read by virtually everybody who read any fiction at all, from the most highly educated to the barely literate, throughout the mid-twentieth century. It still holds pride of place with situation comedy in British television series. It has been accorded its own special cable television channel in America. Actual serious crime impinges on most people's lives far less than road traffic or housing conditions or garbage collection. Yet crime holds a quite disproportionate place in our diet of fiction. Romantic love, its most serious rival, is something most people can reasonably expect to experience, probably more than once. But very few people will meet a murderer in their lifetime; it would be most unusual to be on familiar terms with more than one. And private detectives are almost an unknown quantity, except as adjuncts of solicitors who may take statements for divorce proceedings.

And this triumph of crime is entirely owing to the success of Sherlock Holmes. When his *Adventures* started in *The Strand Magazine* he had no serious competitors. Before long, other writers were imitating Conan Doyle, and *The Strand* used their work when there were no Holmes stories flowing from his pen. By the last decade of his life, when spiritualist Conan Doyle produced *The Casebook of Sherlock Holmes*, his hero was an international byword and his adventures appeared alongside those of Hercule Poirot and Inspector French and Lord Peter Wimsey. Ellery Queen was invented before Conan Doyle died. Agatha Miller was born before *The Adventures* started in *The Strand*, and became Mrs Christie twenty-four years later. Her early work mentions Holmes as a model and Conan Doyle as a living celebrity.

As we shall see, in one way or another, the Sherlock Holmes canon anticipated many devices that his successors were to use, and stimulated others to create deliberate contrasts. Later writers might be cleverer and more accurate than Conan Doyle in arranging their mysteries; their characterisation might be more interesting to some readers; their psychology more profound; their realism more convincing: their comedy funnier. But Conan Doyle's successors owed him more than the creation of a readership for crime fiction. In every way, he created a hugely successful genre of prose fiction as few other writers have ever done.

BEFORE HOLMES

Paul Clifford, Bulwer-Lytton's romantic life of a highwayman appeared in 1830, and should probably be seen as the first English crime novel. Two years later, his *Eugene Aram* fictionalised the life of the eighteenth-century murderer with most appeal to intellectuals: a scholarly schoolmaster who wrote articles on philology but was arrested in 1758 for the murder he had committed years previously while secretly one of a gang of thieves. In 1834 Harrison Ainsworth had an instant success with his first novel, *Rookwood*, glamorising the life of the brutal and bloody robber and murderer Dick Turpin. Dickens was next in the field, starting the serial novel *Oliver Twist* in 1837, but taking fright when hostile critics dubbed the crime fiction school, "Newgate novelists". Dickens was at pains to point out that he did not glamorise Fagin and Bill Sikes. And his treatment of the prostitute Nancy changed adroitly from a man-of-the-world's amusement at her occupation and pretensions to a sentimental moralist's presentation of a "tart-with-a-heart-of-gold". Finally in 1839 Ainsworth gave Jonathan Wild's most famous victim heroic treatment in *Jack Sheppard*. And then, for the time being, serious crime novels dried up in England.

The genre went effectively underground. In France, Eugène Sue, sensationalist author of *The Wandering Jew*, took on his fellow-countryman Paul De Kock's mantle

Oliver Asks for More.

Dickens.

of soft-core suggestiveness, and in *The Mysteries of Paris* and *London* travelled through sexy, exciting and improbable urban underworlds. In England, the sub-literary fictions of G. W. M. Reynolds and Thomas Peckett Prest (criminous creations like "Varney the Vampire" and "Sweeney Todd, the Demon Barber of Fleet Street") paved the way for "penny dreadfuls".

But, truth to tell, Dickens was genuinely fascinated by crime and went on putting it in his novels. Murder in *Barnaby Rudge, Martin Chuzzlewit, Bleak House, Little Dorrit, Our Mutual Friend* and *Edwin Drood*. Theft, fraud and forgery all over the place. And in *Bleak House*, though it is at best a sub-plot, he has Detective Inspector Bucket investigate and solve the undoubted murder mystery of Who Killed Mr Tulkinghorn?

Balzac, the greatest French contemporary of the early Dickens, also included crime in his *Comédie Humaine*, with the recurring character of Vautrin the master-criminal. Vautrin was based in part on Balzac's personal friend Eugène Vidocq, a

OPPOSITE: Wilkie Collins, who centred The Moonstone *on a crime solved by a police detective.*

ABOVE: A scene from Oliver Twist *by Charles Dickens, depicting Oliver Twist demanding more food.*

poacher-turned-gamekeeper who started his career as a criminal but became the first head of the Sûreté in 1811, and after he had been forced out of office in 1832 under suspicion of setting up the crimes he solved, started his own detective agency. Vidocq's *Mémoires* (1829) were unreliable and self-serving. But they contributed much to later writers of detective fiction. In particular, he was intimate with the underworld and its denizens, and was (by his own account) a master of disguise which he used to penetrate criminal haunts. He favoured the dramatic moment when his disguise could be cast off, and with the announcement "I am Vidocq!" he could arrest all those who had believed him to be a fellow-criminal. Holmes matched him in the use of wigs and walnut juice and fake wrinkles, though he tended to be more discreet in his moments of self-revelation.

The Notting Hill Mystery by Charles Felix appeared in 1862, and is an astonishing sport. The first real detective novel, it is narrated through the letters of an insurance investigator looking into the suspicious case of a lady who has died after her sinister husband took out five large policies on her life. The "howdunnit" proves to be one of those Victorian quasi-scientific impossibilities like human spontaneous combustion: "mesmerism", being thought of as a physical current of "animal magnetism", allows the villain to give poison to one sister and transfer its effects mesmerically to another! But the narrative includes a map and facsimiles of a marriage certificate and part of a letter: devices that Conan Doyle and his successors would use. And the proof of a murder and whodunnit and how is the central subject of the book. If Conan Doyle knew it, we may be sure it influenced him.

Before the decade was out, Wilkie Collins had written *The Moonstone*, using various colourful narrators to solve a death and a robbery. Sergeant Cuff, his canny investigator, owed his appearance and manner to Scotland Yard's Sergeant Whicher. And like Felix (and as Dickens probably intended in *The Mystery of Edwin Drood*) Collins used notions about hypnosis, drugs or sleep-walking to create the "impossible" situation at the heart of the mystery. Conan Doyle, as a doctor, wisely resisted the temptation to plot in this way, although we have seen that he could make unhappy use of "brain fever" to give himself elbow-room.

In 1872 "dime novels" started to appear in America: the equivalent of the "shilling shockers" whose ranks *A Study in Scarlet* was expected to join. These gave a recognisable form to the "crime novel", akin to the *roman policier* which was well established in France. The prolific Anna Katherine Greene produced a series of detective novels with city detective Ebenezer Gryce as her hero. The first, *The Leavenworth Case* (1878), has the triple distinction of anticipating Holmes by ten years, being the first detective novel by a woman, and being Stanley Baldwin's favourite detective novel. Unfortunately, it is described by Julian Symons as "drearily sentimental" and "extremely feeble".

Nor have most commentators thought highly of the detective novel which immediately preceded the emergence of Holmes. *The Mystery of a Hansom Cab* (1886) is mentioned, without much enthusiasm, in every survey of the detective novel, because, according to its author, it achieved the highest sales of any such novel ever written, and yet he made a mere £50 from selling the copyright. Frankly, this seems to me suspiciously like Conan Doyle's £25 payment for *A Study in Scarlet*, and my suspicions are increased by the surprise expressed by every writer who comments on the *Hansom Cab's* sales. The writer was a New Zealand barrister; the tale is set in Australia; and the discovery of a body in a hansom cab is generally acknowledged to be a good way of kicking off the mystery.

DUPIN AND LECOQ

It is not moving backwards to take up the Chevalier Auguste Dupin as Holmes's most important predecessor. Conan Doyle acknowledged as much himself and claimed more when, in 1894, an American lady journalist asked him, "Are you influenced by Edgar Allan Poe?"

"Oh, immensely", Conan Doyle replied. "His detective is the best in literature."

"You mean except for Sherlock Holmes?" the lady returned archly·

Caught in the intolerable situation of being asked to boast, Conan Doyle stood up furiously, and shouted, "I make no exception!"

Holmes, fantastical and conceited, was allowed a more self-indulgent outburst when Watson innocently remarked that he thought deductive gifts only existed in stories like Poe's.

"No doubt you think that you are complimenting me in comparing me to Dupin", he said. "Now, in my opinion, Dupin was a very inferior fellow. That trick of his of breaking in on his friend's thoughts with an apropos remark after a quarter of an hour's silence is really very showy and superficial. He had some analytical genius, no doubt; but he was by no means such a phenomenon as Poe appeared to imagine."

The primitive example of "the science of deduction" to which Holmes refers runs thus: Dupin tells his astonished companion that he agrees with his silent thought that a cobbler, recently turned actor, was deservedly panned in the press as too short for the heroic role he essayed. He explains that he has followed his friend's train of thought from the moment when he slipped and turned his ankle slightly. This led him to look at the road for a little, until a stretch paved with dressed blocks reminded him of the pretentious word "stereotomy' for this kind of masonry. "-otomy" suggested "atomies" and Epicurus's scientific theories. Dupin and his friend had recently discussed their recent confirmation by astronomy which, as Dupin expected, led his friend to glance up at the stars and see Orion which, in turn, reminded him that the previous day Dupin had told him that a Latin quotation in the press attack on the cobbler's acting referred to Orion. Thinking of the cobbler's inadequacy made the friend smile, and as he then drew himself up to his full height, it was clear that the cobbler's diminutive stature was in question. Elementary, my dear chevalier!

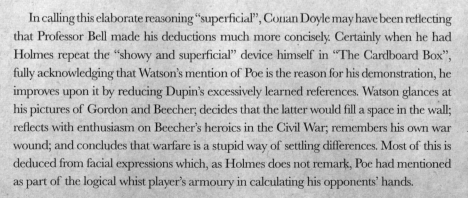

In calling this elaborate reasoning "superficial", Conan Doyle may have been reflecting that Professor Bell made his deductions much more concisely. Certainly when he had Holmes repeat the "showy and superficial" device himself in "The Cardboard Box", fully acknowledging that Watson's mention of Poe is the reason for his demonstration, he improves upon it by reducing Dupin's excessively learned references. Watson glances at his pictures of Gordon and Beecher; decides that the latter would fill a space in the wall; reflects with enthusiasm on Beecher's heroics in the Civil War; remembers his own war wound; and concludes that warfare is a stupid way of settling differences. Most of this is deduced from facial expressions which, as Holmes does not remark, Poe had mentioned as part of the logical whist player's armoury in calculating his opponents' hands.

ABOVE: The French writer Émile Gaboriau, a pioneer of the detective story. His Mystery of the Yellow Room *remains one of the finest tales in the genre.*

Poe was prone to show off too much knowledge as he was prone to florid writing and prone to allow Dupin deductions that were rather too laboured. Yet to his undoubted credit, the three Dupin stories clearly invented the detective genre in which a super-intelligent sleuth works out and explains, stage by stage, how a crime must have been accomplished. The first, "The Murders in the Rue Morgue" also invented the "locked room mystery".

Conan Doyle copied Dupin's intellectual superman status, wisely turning it into a more accessible matter of casual (if sometimes inaccurate) references to names and things the man-in-the-street might have heard of. He copied and fleshed out the simple-minded narrator to be astounded by the great detective's genius. He made the two room together, with the detective rather eccentrically cut off from the world, though he improved on Poe's explanation – that Dupin was so financially incompetent that he had lost most of his money, and so aristocratic that he would not stoop to work!

The other fictional detective admired by Watson, and, indeed, by Conan Doyle, though despised by Holmes, is the French sensational novelist Emile Gaboriau's Inspector Lecoq.

> *Lecoq was a miserable bungler … he had only one thing to recommend him and that was his energy. That book made me positively ill. The question was how to identify an unknown prisoner. I could have done it in twenty-four hours. Lecoq took six months or so.*

Gaboriau's use of a policeman hero was original in France, where the police were so despised that even in the 1940s the great moral philosopher Simone Weil noted that they suffered instant and excessive stigmatisation to the same degree as prostitutes! Gaboriau's first detective novel had an amateur detective putting Lecoq's stupid superior on the right lines, and Lecoq himself was said to have a Vidocq-like criminal past. This was quickly dropped, but Lecoq retained the contempt for his superior which Holmes would transfer to most police detectives. And Lecoq is simply characterised by confident conceit and the habit of sucking lozenges. From his success the *roman policier* became the essential French detective form.

Lecoq moves more slowly than Dupin because his initial (Bell-like) deductions about the criminal, instantly explained from the clues left at the crime site, are structured to lead him on a convoluted chase. Conan Doyle actually copied this in his novels: we have seen that *The Sign of Four* is more chase than detection. He copied, too, Gaboriau's tendency to have crimes committed in response to some past event which is then explained in long flashbacks. It is hardly (if ever) remarked that Monsieur Lecoq uses the format which Conan Doyle was to follow in *A Study in Scarlet* and *The Valley of Fear*: a two-volume structure in which the first volume shows the detective tracking down the criminal, and the second entirely excludes the detective, making the background to the crime a sensational novella in its own right.

RIVAL AND COUNTER-TRADITIONS

One of *The Strand*'s more unusual substitutes for Sherlock in the years after Reichenbach was created by Conan Doyle's brother-in-law E. W. Hornung. A. J. Raffles, *The Amateur Cracksman*, was a gentleman-jewel-thief. A stylish ex-public schoolboy, the finest slow bowler of his generation, and a welcome guest in white tie and rails at the houses he burgles, Raffles casts an interesting light on High Imperial England's possible boredom and dissatisfaction with the conventions and caste-habits by which it assured itself of its superiority over "lesser breeds without the law". Raffles's "Watson" is his old school fag, Bunny, who mingles, in almost equal measure, shock at his friend's apparent amorality, and completely submissive hero-worship for his daring. Although Bunny's admiration and Raffles's patriotic respect for the queen are intended to make us like him, his extreme moment of Flashmannish disloyalty is really distasteful. It is impossible to forgive Raffles for making good his escape and leaving Bunny to serve a long prison sentence, even though Bunny vapidly returns to his master's feet on his release. There is a faintly homoerotic tone to Bunny's love for Raffles, quite unlike the brisk bachelor sexlessness of Holmes and Watson's affection for each other. Conan Doyle disapproved of the

BELOW: Le Bouchon de cristal *(The Crystal Stopper), featuring Arsène Lupin, the gentleman-thief turned detective.*

stories, telling Hornung he should never make the criminal a hero. Hornung may have bowed to his brother-in-law's superior morality in "redeeming" A. J. Raffles with a heroic death in the Boer war. Probably neither man could conceive how dated and disappointing the stories would ultimately seem to a generation which was taught by another of Conan Doyle's *Strand* and cricketing protegés, young P. G. Wodehouse, to find Edwardian aristocratic conventions the hallmark of the upper-class twit!

A better and, indeed, *overt* anti-Holmes was the French writer Maurice Leblanc's *Arsène Lupin, Gentleman-Cambrioleur*. Unlike Raffles, he concentrated his talents for disguise and burglary on helping damsels in distress and victimising those who richly deserved some punishment. A master of make-up, he operated internationally and infiltrated the police, once posing successfully as head of the Sûreté and taking command of the hunt for himself! But, most memorably, he pretended to be a Scotland Yard detective and ran rings round "Herlock Sholmès". His British translator, blenching at the sacrilege, disguised the defeated Englishman a *little* more discreetly as "Holmlock Shears". But Germany was unblushing in titling the adventure "Arsène Lupin kontre Sherlock Holmes". It was a daring literary venture in 1907 when Holmes's popularity was at its height.

Five years before Lupin emerged, R. Austin Freeman, already aged 40, wrote his first book in collaboration with prison doctor J. J. Pitcairn. As "Clifford Ashdown" the two created Romney Pringle, a literary agent with a decidedly shaky sense of honesty.

But he is not a professional criminal like Raffles or Lupin; rather he turns things to his own advantage when some unexpected trouble lands in his lap. In addition to his inferior morality, he reverses the Holmes pattern by his drug free, clean-living habits and going early to bed and early to rise.

Five years later Freeman created his most important character, the forensic scientist Dr Thorndyke. Drawing on Freeman's knowledge of pathology and admiration for its great Victorian practitioner Dr Alfred Swayne Taylor, Thorndyke was able to grip readers by his careful demonstrations of the way scientific detection was *really* undertaken. Indeed, Freeman went so far as to devise the "inverted" detective story, where the criminal is shown committing his crime at the beginning, and leaving what will prove to be clues; and although the reader knows from the start "whodunnit", he is held by following the way Dr Thorndyke runs him down. This compensated for Freeman's very pedestrian prose and characterisation in the books he produced almost annually for more than 30 years.

Before Thorndyke, Holmes's rival detectives had, like him, no official standing. Arthur Morrison produced the first of these. Martin Hewitt stood in for Holmes in the *Strand* as early as 1894. And Sidney Paget drew him. Unlike the master, Hewitt was a deliberately commonplace chap who explicitly went no further, intellectually, than "the judicious use of ordinary faculties." Some very successful detective stories resulted. But Morrison's real forte was the depiction of London life. He was concerned about the poor and concomitantly uneasy about making

OPPOSITE: G. K. Chesterton, the creator of the clerical detective Father Brown.

light entertainment out of crime. His most lasting work lay in fictional accounts of life in the East End, and his stories of the most notorious slum in Shoreditch were so effective that, to this day, many readers believe that the area was known by the name he gave it, "the Jago", and not its true popular name, "the Nichol".

The "commonplace" detective was raised to the height where his ordinariness became extraordinary in G. K. Chesterton's Father Brown. The untidy, clumsy, podgy little priest, with his unlovely shovel hat, badly folded umbrella, and awkward habit of loading himself with brown paper parcels, was the absolute reverse of the elegant, hawklike agnostic Holmes. His pursuit of the exciting master-criminal Flambeau in the early stories ends, perhaps unfortunately, when (like Vidocq) Flambeau reforms and turns his alert mind and knowledge of crime to the side of the law. Chesterton, a serious moralist for all his love of paradox and absurdity, may well have felt Doylean misgivings about letting a criminal seem too admirable.

Father Brown's best purely detective observations are quite secular: that a uniformed functionary going about his normal business is effectively invisible, or that a diner in evening dress will be indistinguishable from a waiter if only his legs are seen. But Chesterton was not content to keep the little priest's observations at this simple and potentially Holmesian level. He was more interested in "good and evil" than law and justice. And so Father Brown's detection comes to rely more and more on his immense knowledge of the human soul, gleaned from the confessional. Understandably, it makes him a little sad when he solves a crime by uncovering a little bit more of the banality of human wickedness. For admirers, this gives the stories a strength that few in the genre can match. For others it makes them repetitious, as they spread through five volumes, and real detection diminishes while Father Brown becomes ever more inclined to a creditably Christian weariness of the ways of the world.

THE GOLDEN AGE OF DETECTION

A very different priest laid down a code of rules by which the proliferating "whodunnit" novels should be written if they were to remain a fair test of the author's wits pitted against the reader's. Fr Ronald Knox wrote light-hearted detective novels himself, reverting to Charles Felix's idea of an insurance company to provide the mystery's investigating hero, and seizing the chance to reiterate his facetious observation that insurance was just a form of gambling. After his translation into modern English of the Vulgate (St Jerome's Latin version of the Bible, which was the only approved ancient scriptural source for lay Catholics at the time) Knox was recognised as a leading Catholic intellectual, promoted to Monsignor, and made Catholic chaplain of Oxford University. There, during the "Brideshead" years, "Father Ronnie's" services were annually in demand at the Oxford Union's Eights Week debates: by tradition, occasions for frothy wit rather than serious argument.

OPPOSITE: Reverend Monsignor Ronald Knox was a priest and author of detective stories.

Knox's commandments of detective fiction, propounded in 1928, might have been drawn from the Holmes canon. The criminal must be introduced early in the book, and must not be the detective. The detective could keep his deductions and even some facts to himself, but his Watson (if he had one) should never deliberately mislead or conceal information from the reader. (Though he might be wrong in everything he deduced!) Nor, if the criminal's thoughts were given, should they ever run counter to his being the criminal. (Though his non-criminous thoughts were perfectly fair.) Supernatural events, whether ghosts, magick, or Christian miracles, should not be used. The murderer's motives should be personal and rational: not, that is, political or religious or cranky or in the service of professional crime. The detective should not come across the truth by some remarkable accident, nor should he reach his conclusions by "unaccountable intuition". (Father Brown's knowledge of the human soul came from saintliness and confessional experience, not lucky hunches.)

BELOW: A. A. Milne, creator of Winnie-the-Pooh, and a prolific general writer with one famous whodunit to his credit.

These peculiar (though intelligent) "rules" show how crime fiction, or at least a part of it, had become an intellectual puzzle, like the newly invented crossword, with particular appeal for the literate middle classes. The settings and characters of run-of-the-mill or light-hearted whodunnits often exhibited the appeal to the same readership. A country house was a favourite setting. The occupants could display a range of easily differentiated characteristics, motives, and potentially lethal skills. A body in the library was a promising start. (And the idea of a domestic residence with its own library shows how far the genre aspired upward socially.) A sinister butler or footman could be included among the suspects, though as a rule servants were restricted to petty crimes: murderers had to come from what Q. D. Leavis approvingly remembered being called "the Quality". And – an interesting sidelight on the conventional morality which the books rarely challenged – while "the vicar" was (as might be expected) a frequent character and sometimes mildly suspected, I can't offhand think of a "Golden Age" writer who made a parson the killer. It is the world of Cluedo, with Colonel Mustard and Miss Scarlet and Mrs White, except that Cluedo abbreviates the Rev Mr Green to the Rev Green (which Golden Age writers would have known as a solecism), and may let him be the murderer (which they would have considered improper). Intellectuals (apart from the brilliant detective), radicals of any kind, persons of profoundly religious or mildly criminal or provocatively sexy temperament, artists, and even foreigners, were all social oddities and might be automatically suspect for being "different". They made useful red herring suspects in books which took for granted the confidently educated but essentially Philistine attitudes of ambitious suburbia. The *Just William* books exploit the same ethos, and despite her light surface of futuristic metropolitan sophistication, Flora Post brings it to *Cold Comfort Farm*.

Thus A. A. Milne ventured in to the field with *The Red House Mystery*, making some commentators feel that he had produced the puzzle-whodunnit's most entertaining book ever; others feel that he should have stuck to *Winnie-the-Pooh*, and a devastating attack on his carelessness, improbability and general incompetence came from the hard-boiled thriller writer Raymond Chandler. Thus, too, Philip MacDonald (grandson of the Victorian moral fantasist who created *The Princess and the Goblin*), made himself a substantial reputation with books that I find, frankly, unreadable. In America, the art critic Willard Huntington Hart, who wrote detective fiction under the *nom-de-plume* S. S. Van Dine, declared that the puzzle element was, or should be, the essence of the detective story. Everything else was extraneous. (By which standard, of course, nothing whatsoever counts in the first Holmes short story composed, "A Scandal in Bohemia", or the last supposedly occurring in his lifetime, "His Last Bow"!)

Van Dine was, in fact, extremely good at the puzzle element, working out plots and clues in exemplary detail, and often surprising in ways which were absolutely legitimate by the "rules". But his huge readership in the 1920s and '30s probably responded to the snob appeal of his detective, Philo Vance, an Oxonian art-lover with a residence in Florence (though his cases all took place in America). With an exasperating line in affected facetious dialogue, a monocle, a habit of parading his knowledge of art and the art world, he is like an American version of Harold Acton, the original of *Brideshead*'s Anthony Blanche. Most people today probably agree with Ogden Nash's summary:

Philo Vance
Needs a kick in the pance.

At the opposite extreme, Freeman Wills Crofts's Inspector French laboured his way colourlessly through case after case. He evinces no mark of genuine police work, but an astonishing knowledge of travel timetables. Crofts specialised in the mystery which depended on breaking an alibi, and this was usually done by finding an unexpected train service to get the villain to point B when he shouldn't possibly have been able to leave point A. Tediously establishing how-he-dunnit *then* became one of the great bores of the Golden Age.

But we have looked at an important era without considering its noted jewels: the four Queens of Crime.

THE QUEENS OF CRIME

In 1916, a year before Sherlock Holmes took "His Last Bow", twenty-six-year-old Mrs Agatha Christie took a break from her war-work as a pharmacist's assistant, and wrote a detective novel. *The Mysterious Affair at Styles* has a sketchy war-time background. Captain Hastings, the "Watson" who narrates, is recuperating from the western front. One suspect is a landgirl. Another turns out to be a German spy. Mrs Christie's pharmaceutical experience gives the murder a cunning twist with far more scientific accuracy than Dr Doyle brought to his curare in *The Sign of Four*. The detective is a Belgian refugee.

Yet the feeling of war-time is conspicuously absent from the book. Although practically every family in England lived in dread of bad news about some relative, such tension is markedly absent from Styles. There are none of the deprivations of war: dried eggs and cocoa-butter never appear. Instead we are safe in Cluedo-land; in a big country house with a plan of the bedrooms to show where everyone slept. It is a locked room mystery, worked out in a plausible way. The immediate suspect proves to be guilty, despite having been *obviously* unable to commit the crime. His confederate is the one character no one ever thought suspicious for a moment. A definite new talent to puzzle had emerged.

The detective, Hercule Poirot, was a brain-box like Holmes, but stood on his dignity in explicitly refusing to make Holmes-like scrambles on his hands and knees studying carpets through a magnifying glass. Simple characteristics are tacked on to him: outrageous conceit; a passion for tidiness and symmetry; an urban distaste for country life; a huge black moustache and an "egg-shaped" head. Hastings is a jolly good chap, bluffly dim-witted, with an eye for (especially red-headed) ladies. Nothing suggested that this was the beginning of a career which would make Mrs Christie the most widely published author *ever*. Everything augured, rightly, that when this became the case, Poirot would never match Sherlock Holmes as a legendary figure capturing the universal imagination. *The Mysterious Affair at Styles* did not find a publisher till 1921, and then enjoyed a fair success.

In 1926 Mrs Christie broke a rule. Following a suggestion from Lord Louis Mountbatten, she wrote a brilliant book in which the "Watson" concealed some thoughts, words and deeds, to become the absolutely surprising murderer. It was slickly plotted, and it set off a furore. Some readers felt cheated. Others thought this was the greatest detective novel ever. Thereafter Agatha Christie was famous, and by such remarkable devices as having *all* the suspects participate in a murder, or *all* the characters *including* the murderer die according to his plan, she became the greatest of all puzzle-makers, fully earning the title "the Queen of Crime" from Penguin, when they published ten of her books at once.

Later they invited her to share the throne with Dorothy L. Sayers, a vicar's daughter who lacked Mrs Christie's intimate knowledge of poisons but devised strange alternative means of murder: injecting air into the victim's vein, or having a man die with no apparent injuries because he could not escape the overwhelming din of an all-night bell-ringing session in the church tower where he was imprisoned.

OPPOSITE: Two queens of crime: Agatha Christie (left) and Ngaio Marsh in 1960.

Miss Sayers was at her weakest when puzzle-solving was to the fore (in *The Five Red Herrings*, say, or *Have His Carcase*). Her strength lay in brilliantly realised settings drawn from her experience: an advertising agency; a women's college in Oxford; or her own Lincolnshire village background, a strange flat land of dykes and straight roads and churches.

Her fans also loved her detective, Lord Peter Wimsey: an aristocratic Raffles on the side of the law. A first-class cricketer and excellent scholar. The fraightfully posh brother of the Duke of Denver with mouthfuls of facetious upper-class-twitspeak which Miss Sayers offered as wit. In successive novels, Lord Peter saved Harriet Vane from a murder charge, courted her, and married her. And then, giving up hope of persuading the world to value crime fiction for its backgrounds rather than its crimes, Miss Sayers eschewed the genre for her last twenty years, writing instead a series of radio plays dramatising the life of Christ, and translating the *Chanson de Roland* and the first two books of Dante's *Divine Comedy*.

The other two Queens of Crime anointed by Penguin also created aristocratic detectives whose courtship and marriage trailed through several volumes. "Albert Campion" was the incognito name of highborn "Lord Rudolph" Something in Margery Allingham's novels. Like Lord Peter Wimsey he was willowy but fit and strong. Unlike Lord Peter he wore spectacles, was not cursed with toffspeak, and aged at the same pace as his creator. The London arts world, familiar to Miss Allingham and her husband, often made a change from the old country house in her pre-war novels. The home front of World War II, effectively erased from Mrs Christie's sanitised Cluedo-land, made a realistic appearance in the Campion books. *Tiger in the Smoke* gave a foggy London chase with more thrills than *The Sign of Four* and a profounder moral centre than publicly Anglo-Catholic Miss Sayers ever achieved. And *More Work for the Undertaker* was a wonderfully wacky development of the use of coffins to transport people, invented by Conan Doyle in "The Disappearance of Lady Frances Carfax". Generally Miss Allingham's puzzle element was subordinate to her interest in character. And that was weakened by undue class consciousness and hints of racism. Not that she ever matched Mrs Christie's vicious anti-Semitism.

New Zealander Ngaio Marsh bequeathed to Michael Innes and P. D. James the bad habit of making her police detective hero "acceptable" to upper middlebrow readers by bestowing on him a very unpolicemanly upper-class family. She also let Roderick Alleyn court and marry Agatha Troy through several novels. The irritating young journalist she described as his "Watson" in the earlier novels did not narrate them, and contributed little to the work, which ran the risk of many early policeman-detective novels, and could decline to a series of repetitive interviews with suspects, from which the reader could select his facts and take his pick. But she was exceptionally good at devising complicated booby-traps which allowed the "obvious" yet "impossible" suspect to prove, convincingly, to be the murderer after all.

OPPOSITE: Peter Ustinov was Hercule Poirot in the star-studded film version of Death on the Nile, *1978.*

DIFFERENT DIRECTIONS

The "crime" shelves in your public library hold many different types of fiction, not all of which follow the simple Holmesian pattern of "A Detective Solves a Mystery". Yet even within that easy plot line, several possibilities emerge. The detective may be a private-eye, a policeman, or an enthusiastic amateur who just "happens" to keep stumbling across crimes. This last type of detective – Agatha Christie's Miss Marple or Edmund Crispin's Gervase Fen – has rather fallen out of favour on the ground that it is quite improbable that an Oxford don or a little old lady should find murders happening wherever they go.

The "enthusiastic amateur" sleuth is, however, peculiarly fitted for one form of crime fiction that Conan Doyle could never have attempted. Dorothy L. Sayers once

said her intention was to place the comedy of manners in a detective framework. This form makes the people with the best glamorous style in the work the heroes and heroines. It carries the concomitant danger that the reader may not actually *like* their particular "manners". Miss Sayers apparently thought Bertie Wooster with an Oxford double-first and a cricket blue was the *beau ideal*! Sarah Caldwell's two glorious murder mysteries solved by the witty "kindergarten" of young barristers similarly delight those who share their sense of humour, but fall flat for those who don't. Conan Doyle's simple and robust comedy was safe from such dangers.

And lacking any sense of irony, Conan Doyle could never have written books like Sarah Caldwell's or Edmund Crispin's which reveal, by their extravagant plotting, sophisticated references, and detached amusement, that the whole form of detective fiction or adventure story is something to which the author is superior. Conan Doyle really believed in healthy adventure and was proud of his appeal to the athletic young. Nor, despite the odd quotation from Goethe, did he make a bid for bookish readers with a constant parade of literary reference like "Michael Innes" or "Nicholas Blake", respectively the Christ Church don J. I. M. Stewart and the subsequent poet laureate, Cecil Day-Lewis.

The "hard-boiled" school of private eye fiction which emerged in the 1930s, headed by ex-Pinkerton's employee Dashiell Hammett and Raymond Chandler, accepted Conan Doyle's premiss of a professional detective who was a decent man in a wicked world. "Down these mean streets a man must go who is not himself mean", Chandler famously wrote. It could define Sherlock Holmes. And the hard-boiled writers' distaste for puzzles which were ever more stylised and unreal led them to follow Conan Doyle in giving priority to suspense and the chase: leading their heroes into and out of tough spots. "Who cares who killed Roger Ackroyd?" asked Chandler.

The search for realism led other writers to prefer detectives who were actual policemen. Georges Simenon's Inspector Maigret led the field for years. Simenon's economical prose, drizzly urban settings, and down-to-earth professional hero set a standard which could be followed by other continental-based policemen: Nicholas

OPPOSITE: Dashiell Hammett, pioneer of "hard-boiled" detective fiction.

ABOVE: Humphrey Bogart as Raymond Chandler's classic hard-boiled private eye, Philip Marlowe, in The Big Sleep *with Lauren Bacall.*

Freeling's Van der Valk, or Per Wahlöo and Maj Sjöwall's Inspector Beck. Ed McBain widened the range of crimes investigated and gave added realism by putting within the covers of one book the work falling to one New York city precinct's detective department over a short given period. On television, in particular, this found many imitators: *Hill Street Blues*, *The Bill*, *NYPD Blue* and *Homicide*. It seemed to have moved a great drama-documentary distance from the cosy old *Dixon of Dock Green* police series or the more '"realistically" aggressive *Z-Cars*. Yet at the heart of all of them lie a sequence of murder mysteries to be solved by unravelling clues and eliminating suspects. And the outright triumphs of Rupert Davies's Maigret performances in the 1960s and John Thaw's Inspector Morse in the 1980s showed that the basic Sherlockian approach, translated to a professional police setting, still worked best.

The seemingly quite different line of "crime fiction" – spy stories and thrillers – are also kin to Holmes. Suspense, danger and some sort of chase are paramount in the four novels. Foreign agents stealing armaments plans or draft treaties feature in two of the best stories. "His Last Bow" has neither detection nor plot: just a series of cameos showing sinister Germans revealing their evil intent; a disguised Holmes revealing that he has undermined them; and Holmes and Watson summing everything up as they make off with their easily taken captive. The subject of anti-British spying (perhaps understandably in wartime) gives suspense and excitement enough. The later masters, Len Deighton and John le Carré, took this as a *donné*; added mystery and villainy to be unravelled in the manner of the better Holmes stories,

ABOVE: John Thaw as Morse: Sherlocking under the aegis of policing.

and lifted their writing to a higher plane with psychological density owing much to Joseph Conrad's perception of the subversive spy's world.

The unrealistic thriller reached huge heights of popularity in the hands of Edgar Wallace. He, too, often set a puzzle to be solved, though never with the complexity and ingenuity of Holmes or the Golden Age detective writers. But his reduction of all the elements of style, characterisation and setting to the barest minimum in the interest of sustaining pace has let his work slide out of print, while Conan Doyle and Agatha Christie are still readily available. For one horrible moment, in "The Three Gables", Sherlock Holmes seems to have come under the influence of the 1920s thriller. Tough talk and crudely racist gibes were the supposedly debonair staples of "Sapper's" Bulldog Drummond and Dornford Yates's Berry Pleydell. Although Conan Doyle was far more liberal than those xenophobic reactionaries, and even in "The Three Gables" tolerates a foreign adventuress they could never have stomached, his brief elderly slip under their spell has led most readers to judge this story a failure. Probably the younger writers' stress on patriotic "sportsmanship" misled him into thinking their style was the modern form of his healthy adventure for athletic youth. In the hands of Eric Ambler and Hammond Innes, however, the pure thriller moved "crime fiction" away from the consistent unreflecting conservatism of the Golden Age. Conan Doyle, the lover of freedom, would surely have approved of Ambler's drafting the thriller into service against Fascism; and Innes's apolitical left-of-centre decency was very close indeed to Sherlock Holmes's basic position.

DEBTS TO CONAN DOYLE

Does crime fiction ever stray really far from Conan Doyle and Sherlock Holmes? In many ways it does, as specialist interests attract readers who, by now, might be bored with the simple detective puzzle. The thriller in particular has wandered into some explicitly political fields that would have astonished Conan Doyle, who took it for granted that *almost* every little boy and girl born into this world alive was either a little Liberal or a little Conservative, but had no difficulty in maintaining friendly disagreement with Bernard Shaw and discounting his socialism as an eccentricity like his vegetarianism. Conan Doyle was the last man on earth to condemn another morally for mere eccentricity.

A writer who contributed much to the rise of the thriller by straddling detection and suspense was Peter Cheyney. On the whole he upgraded Edgar Wallace's *oeuvre*, improving the class and social *savoir-faire* of his characters, and enriching his style. He could move easily from the casual elegance of Slim Callahan to the fast-paced Americanism of G-man Lemmy Caution, and he anticipated his successors' growing fascination with the secret services in the "Dark" novels. Far racier and obliquely sexier than Conan Doyle would ever have been, he nonetheless stayed securely within the upper-middle and governing class world that Holmes occupied, though he tainted it with the reactionary snobbishness that the Golden Age had introduced.

James Bond, superficially worlds away from Sherlock, is in fact a fairly obvious descendant, via Buchan and Sapper and Cheyney. He doesn't detect, but he chases or is chased. His free-ranging sexual adventures are the 1950s and '60s parallel to Holmes's Bohemianism. His constant dropping of familiar brand-names and street-names exaggerates a trait of Holmes's. His travels to exotic locations parallel the exotically located flashback adventures in three of the Holmes novels, and the transmogrification of Dartmoor in the fourth. SPECTRE and SMERSH are for Bond what Foreign Agents are for Holmes: their and Bond's greater violence and callousness are the inevitable product of the generation which lived through or actively participated in two World Wars, only one of which was witnessed by Conan Doyle, and that from the misleading position of the homebound armchair patriot.

Perhaps most obviously, Ian Fleming genuinely believed that he was creating a traditional patriotic hero of a kind that was needed by an unheroic Welfare State England. Like Sapper and Dornford Yates, he shared to the hilt Conan Doyle's belief that a criminal should never be idolised, and thought his own hero a model of exemplary true-Brit decency. Arthur Conan Doyle's personal life was so remarkably unblemished that it should, perhaps, come as no surprise that few of his successors could match the unpretentious moral rightness he bestowed on Holmes. Only another fine moralist like Eric Ambler could get away with the deliberate creation of such a well-perceived sleazy (and actually smelly) anti-hero as Arthur Abdel Simpson.

If the Holmes stories took a few things from penny dreadfuls and shilling shockers, sub-literary pulp fiction took back from him with interest. Within a couple of decades of Conan Doyle's death, a marketing survey discovered, to its surprise, that when asked to name a famous detective who lived in Baker Street, more people named Sexton Blake than Sherlock Holmes! Written by a sequence of hacks, the "Sexton Blake Library" ran and ran, well past the mid-century. They were highly competent popular imitations, as the detective's name showed. Its rhythm was exactly that of Sherlock Holmes, and Blake, too, had an unusual forename. Which, by a masterstroke is very lightly sinister.

The stories were not an absolute rip-off. Blake's cockney assistant Tinker was no copy of Watson. The pair simply updated their habits and surroundings, smoothly and unobtrusively belonging to any date at which any adventure was published. Like his pulp rivals, Blake did not do a great deal of elaborate deduction. But he carried the undemanding reader very satisfyingly from an initial mystery posed to a final criminal caught. *The Mystery of the Missing Angler* from the Sexton Blake Library was the first detective novella I read (when I was nine or ten); a couple of years earlier I first encountered the idea of the "detective" as a man with a magnifying glass in the exploits of Colwyn Dane, narrated in the *Champion*, one of the last boys' comics to consist of prose stories with no strip cartoons.

In some ways, nothing is more surprising than Sherlock Holmes's influence on children's fiction. Penny dreadfuls and shilling shockers, in their day, were regarded with something approaching the contempt now reserved for porn on the Internet. Decently educated children were not supposed to see them. (They had Arthur Mee's instructive publications instead, and the BOP.) The best non-magical fiction for children stayed much within the plausible bounds laid down by *Little Women* or *The Secret Garden* or *The Treasure Seekers*. Ballantyne and Henty offered a variant on Captain Marryatt's adventurous novels, at once watered down and spiced up for boyish consumption. A *burglar* in the house was unheard of in middle class fiction written for middle class children.

Within ten years of Conan Doyle's death, all that had changed. Enid Blyton, whose use of a deliberately simple vocabulary and clear sentence structure won plaudits from educationists at the start of her career, was soon confronting her breezy, out-of-doorsy (and, alas, irritatingly

class-conscious) "Famous Five" with more thieves and smugglers than the average village policeman might come across in a lifetime. "Norman and Henry Bones, Boy Detectives" entertained children on "Uncle Mac's" wholesome BBC Children's Hour. The Hardy Boys, the Bobsy Twins and Nancy Drew, Girl Detective enthralled their transatlantic cousins. Nobody turned a hair. It was, surely, Conan Doyle's most staggering achievement to give crime fiction such respectability that a diluted version became an accepted staple of educated children's reading while purists who battled against giving children Angela Brazil's innocent school stories were still active.

6

THE IMMORTAL REPUTATION

Try this test. Can you think of another fictional character whose image would be instantly recognised all over the world by so many people? Mr Pickwick? Fagin? Bill Sikes? Not in, say, South America, surely? Maybe not even in England. Falstaff? Same objections.

Let's leave English fiction, then. What about Don Quixote? Possibly … but while I'm sure anybody who could identify the Don would also be able to recognise Sherlock, I doubt it's true the other way around.

Doesn't the world know the striking classical gods and goddesses? Mercury, perhaps, with wings on his heels and helmet, and snake-entwined wand in his hand? Well … he *might* have been part of everyone's mental furniture when he was the emblem of National Benzole Petrol. But since that disappeared from the filling stations and Mr Mercury dropped off the advertisement hoardings and classical education is a rarity, I suspect the kids who congregate under the Shaftesbury Memorial in Piccadilly Circus couldn't tell Mercury from Eros.

It's extraordinary, but I really believe that the only imaginative creations that could be so instantly and universally recognised from their appearance are the early Disney cartoon characters: Mickey Mouse, Donald Duck, Pluto and Goofy. And what does a cartoon mouse do if he wants to solve a mysterious problem? He frowns, dons a deerstalker and oversized ulster, and glares through a magnifying glass, peering at the carpet for clues.

The magnitude of Conan Doyle's achievement becomes more apparent when we remember that Walt Disney's real talent was as a businessman and promoter. It was animator Ub Iwerks who actually designed the brilliant combination of circles forming The Mouse. Disney, who could never reproduce Mickey's head properly, created the megabucks industry that ensures we never ever lose sight of his creation in some advertisement or promotion every day. Sherlock Holmes's fame came without the aid of corporate selling.

And that may explain why the two characters are household names with a difference: the adjective "Mickeymouse" is derogatory and dismissive, usually paralleling the old-fashioned British "Heath Robinson" ("Don't sell me that Mickeymouse equipment"). The noun Sherlock is wryly admiring – "It didn't take a Sherlock to know that …" – even though wryness passes to outright sarcasm in the New York vulgarism, "No s—t, Sherlock!" to be thrown at anyone who states the obvious as a discovery. Conan Doyle himself learned that South Americans used the term "Holmitos" to describe ingenious but irrelevant observations, like Sherlock's little uses of Professor Bell's parlour trick, which didn't contribute to his cases.

"Elementary, my dear Watson!" Everybody knows the quotation. Probably most people know Holmes never said it, just as most people who know Mae West was famous for saying, "Come up an' see me some time", know that she never said it in those words. That really is a remarkable double whammy: it is achievement enough for Conan Doyle to have created a character that virtually everybody recognises when they hear the tag-line; it is more amazing that large numbers should know the words are an adaptation rather than a quotation. These things are real fame.

WILLIAM GILLETTE

Of course, it is the image rather than the writings that commands universal recognition. And the image, as we have seen, owes much to its diffusion over stage and screen, and its refinement by the first actor to make his name as Sherlock Holmes. The American William Gillette saw the dramatic possibilities in the character at exactly the time that Conan Doyle himself was completing a dramatisation, and had discovered that the great English master of make-up and melodrama, Herbert Beerbohm Tree, could not possibly star in it. Tree wanted to play both Holmes *and* Moriarty, distinguishing the two by giving Holmes a beard! The year was 1897 and Conan Doyle hoped to scotch the belief that he was tired of, or disliked, the *character* of Holmes.

It was the chore of inventing a new short plot every month that had led him to kill off the great detective in Switzerland.

A. P. Watt, Conan Doyle's literary agent, sent the manuscript of his play to a New York impresario who liked it and, with Conan Doyle's approval, suggested Gillette for the role. Gillette was touring in his own thriller, *Secret Service*, and with his tall, lean figure and handsome, intelligent face he certainly looked the part. Once he had made it his own, the part came to resemble Gillette, for artists drawing Holmes after Sidney Paget's early death tended to base their illustrations on Gillette's appearance.

The Americans felt there should be a romantic interest. Conan Doyle disagreed, telling the impresario, "There must be no love business!" But when his and Gillette's original drafts had been lost, and the actor was rewriting from memory, he yielded temporarily. "MAY I MARRY HOLMES?" Gillette cabled him from New York, and received the generous response, "MARRY HIM OR MURDER HIM OR DO WHAT YOU LIKE WITH HIM." In the event, he rather disliked Gillette's romantic ending, even though it allowed Holmes to remain a bachelor as the curtain came down. But the play's use of Moriarty as the villain determined the permanent fixture of "the Napoleon of crime" as Holmes's chief opponent. And Gillette's

CHAPTER OPENER: British actor Basil Rathbone as fictional detective Sherlock Holmes, ca. 1939.

OPPOSITE: American actor and dramatist William Gillette, in the role of Sherlock Holmes.

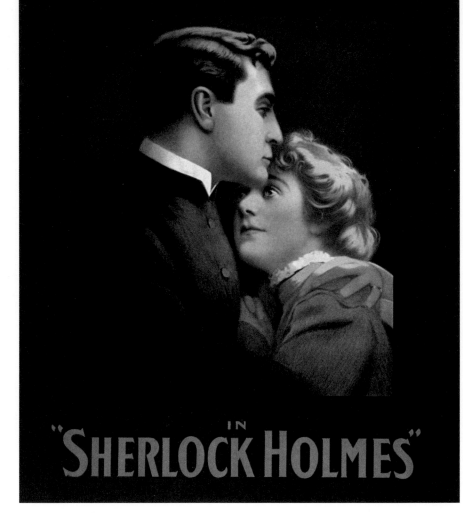

device at one point, of having Holmes put a wax model of himself in his window for Moriarty to shoot at, was subsequently used by Conan Doyle in the short story that brought Holmes back from the dead, and again in the less happy one-act play *The Crown Diamond* (1921) and its derivative story "The Mazarin Stone".

Gillette's melodrama took off from the "Scandal in Bohemia" situation. Some compromising letters from a Very Important Person had passed to the recipient's sister, and she, in turn, had fallen into the clutches of Moriarty, who was determined to use them to destroy the VIP. Innocent Alice Faulkner, the sister, was being held captive – shades of "The Copper Beeches". And the play drew on a notorious case

*ABOVE: A poster for
William Gillette's play*
Sherlock Holmes.

of 1877, which had been in Conan Doyle's mother's mind when she proposed the plot of that tale to her son as he was baulking at having to invent new stories to order. Louis Staunton, a young estate agent, had married a mentally retarded girl with a small private income and, having got control of her money, paid his brother a small sum to look after her in a farmhouse while he settled down with a mistress. The unfortunate Harriet Staunton was sequestered from her friends and relations, and treated so badly that she died of neglect. The Stauntons were convicted of her murder, but reprieved from the gallows on medical evidence that Harriet *might* have succumbed to meningitis. And (as Conan Doyle never knew) Louis became a deeply penitent and devout Catholic who, after serving a long sentence in Dartmoor, died in the odour of sanctity.

Naturally, Conan Doyle and Gillette's "Alice Faulkner" was not feeble-minded and did not evince any of the distasteful personal habits that led Harriet's husband and brother-in-law to lock her up in a room away from company! She won Sherlock's heart, if not his hand.

Gillette was a man after Conan Doyle's heart. He dabbled in spiritualism. He adored miniature railways, and (like Conan Doyle) constructed one on his own property. He had the Holmesian habit of taking long walks through the city at night, sometimes falling asleep on park benches until dawn. And, like Arthur Balfour, he cherished so consuming a passion for the deceased love of his life – in Gillette's case, his wife – that there was never any subsequent romantic entanglement for him. Like Balfour, he was led to the psychic through his longing for reassurance that his beloved still lived.

With a rather biting sense of humour, an actor's presence, and no fear of startling the public, he determined his vital contribution to the Holmesian image before he had even appeared on stage in the role. He had all Sidney Paget's illustrations to choose from when he went to meet Conan Doyle off a train for the first time. Understandably, he eschewed the unremarkable elegant frock coat, which was Holmes's usual attire. Instead he settled on his more striking travelling garb. Conan Doyle was greeted by a tall figure with an aquiline face, garbed in deerstalker hat and matching ulster, who pulled out a magnifying glass, scrutinised the new arrival, and said, "Unquestionably an author".

Conan Doyle's amusement and instant recognition of his own creation ensured that Holmes's outdoor wear for stage performances was decided, even though such country garb in the city was a dreadful breach of Victorian and Edwardian gentlemanly conventions. Indoors too, the stage Sherlock established a new convention for "the detective", unlicensed by Paget. Holmes's resplendent purple dressing gown was widely known to be exaggerated from one owned by Conan Doyle himself. The modest, tweedy public author sometimes allowed himself a little more splendour when relaxing at home. A generation later, the silk dressing gown, worn indoors in place of a jacket became a hallmark of matinee idols like Noel Coward, who had no aspirations to be viewed as detectives, but emulated Holmes's

image of frozen, superior, intellectual detachment. This was a particularly useful way of disseminating sex appeal to women for a homosexual like Coward.

Holmes's drop-stem pipe, as we have seen, was a stage convenience for Gillette. Think about it. It is impossible to deliver lines and seem superior if a straight-stemmed pipe is bobbing up and down in your mouth with every syllable!

LATER STAGINGS

After a successful tour of America, Gillette opened *Sherlock Holmes* at the Lyceum Theatre in London on 9 September 1901. The theatre was where Conan Doyle saw Irving's *Hamlet* as a boy, and where Miss Mary Morstan waited with Holmes and Watson under "the third pillar".

The play was a hit. Edward VII and Queen Alexandra loved it, as did Prime Minister Balfour. The king stirred a little incipient republicanism in the audience by unconscionably extending the interval while he chatted with Gillette about monarchical elements in the play: the character made up to look like his cousin the Kaiser, and the hints that he himself was Holmes's "Illustrious Client".

Gillette played Holmes to great acclaim almost until his death in 1932. His skill on the violin compensated for his occasional inaudibility from the gods. In the London revival of 1905, a juvenile called Charles Chaplin took the part of Billy the Page. Gillette also wrote a one-act farce called *The Painful Predicament of Sherlock Holmes*, in which Irene Vanbrugh played a talkative client who never let Holmes get a word in. (This was not the first comic Holmes on stage. Gillette's impersonation was parodied almost as soon as it opened in the burlesque *Sheerluck Jones: or Why d'Gillette Him Off?*)

In 1909 Conan Doyle indulged his love for an adventurous investment. He leased the Lyric Theatre for a year to mount a drama he had written about English tourists kidnapped by dervishes in Egypt. With full control, he insisted on perfect realism. He spent a fortune on sets and costumes, and demanded that the dervishes actually beat and whip their captives. Not only did this bruise the unfortunate actors, it prompted a young Guards officer in the audience to try and jump on the stage to shoot the cads who so abused an English woman!

But although the small audiences enjoyed it, an unusually hot summer meant that very few people were willing to sit in a stuffy theatre. Conan Doyle had to send the play quickly on a provincial run and replace it with another, which glorified the old-fashioned, bare-knuckle boxing he admired. Again, he made his actors administer real drubbings to each other, and cover their weals with make-up. This time his success was foiled by the death of the king, which cut down London's theatre going. Conan Doyle seized the chance for an excellent and constitutionally important agitation: the late king's favourite writer persuaded the new king to remove anti-Catholic passages from the coronation oath, which they had blemished since William and Mary.

OPPOSITE: Eille Norwood, the great 1920s interpreter of Sherlock Holmes.

But there was only one way for Conan Doyle to recoup his investment and save the theatrical season. He would have to bring Holmes back to the stage.

This meant a new play. So he set about dramatising "The Speckled Band", which he and many admirers saw as one of the very best Holmes mysteries. H. A. Saintsbury had understudied Gillette and taken the role on provincial tours, and he was cast as Holmes. Lyn Harding was one of the best Demon-King-like melodrama villains in the business, and he played Dr Grimesby Roylott. The character was renamed "Rylott" in the play: another example of Conan Doyle's habitual pernicious carelessness. But it was "Rylott" who saved Conan Doyle's bacon as a theatrical impresario. A competent critic advised Sir Arthur to leave Harding alone in rehearsals and stop trying to make him into a perfect facsimile of the Roylott of the story. Conan Doyle, chastened perhaps by his two flops, agreed. And the role, which overshadowed Holmes's in the script in any case, was a mighty success for Harding.

Conan Doyle's passion for realism extended to using a real snake for the first few performances. Although this evoked genuine horror from the unfortunate actress playing "Enid" (as Rylott's stepdaughter was renamed), it refused to slither down the bellrope prepared for it, and a critic denounced the live boa as an obvious inanimate fake! Conan Doyle rapidly agreed to substitute a real fake, which satisfied the audience it was a true "swamp adder".

In 1923, J. E. H. Terry and Arthur Rose concocted a script from "The Empty House", "Charles Augustus Milverton" and "The Disappearance of Lady Frances Carfax", with dashes of Gillette's play. They called it *The Return of Sherlock Holmes*, and cast Eille Norwood, better known for his silent film interpretations of the stories, as the great detective. The play worked so well that Conan Doyle and Norwood were given standing ovations. Conan Doyle modestly checked his to transfer the credit to Terry and Rose. Their play succeeded again when revived in Bromley as late as 1953. Norwood went on to become the "perfect" Sherlock Holmes for his generation, though to a jaundiced later eye, still photographs suggest that he continued playing it when his figure had lost the lathlike slenderness of the original. But he was a master of stage make-up, and so was utterly convincing when Holmes assumed his various disguises.

There was a serious flop involving two fine actors three years after Conan Doyle's death. Nigel Playfair and Felix Aylmer appeared in *The Holmeses of Baker Street*, which adventurously, but absurdly, portrayed Holmes as an elderly widower with a grown-up daughter!

And Margaret Dale, doyenne of television choreography, had little more success with her ballet *The Great Detective*, created for Sadler's Wells in 1953. Kenneth Macmillan's "Detective" was approved, but not his doubling the role with the "Professor". Moriarty's control of characters as marionettes probably owed more to *Coppelia* than to Conan Doyle. And everyone hated Stanley Holden's Watson, which seems to have been more like the dapper little Snob from Massine's *Boutique Fantasque* than Sherlock's stolid companion.

After these failures, it is happy to report success. Provincial and repertory theatres of the 1940s and '50s, which throve on comedy thrillers and whodunnits, almost invariably found that revivals of the great original stage detective worked. And the lavish musical *Baker Street* was a Broadway hit in 1965, though Fritz Weaver's Holmes carried out the constant wish of American impresarios, and dutifully fell in love with Inga Swenson's Irene Adler.

HOLMES ON FILM

Foreigners probably got there first. It is claimed that a silent British Sherlock Holmes film was made in 1906, but no details of it have survived. Thirteen Sherlock Holmes films were produced by Nordisk Film Co. of Denmark between 1908 and 1910. Other countries spotted their success and imitated them swiftly. Copyright and original plotting meant little to catchpenny German, American and Italian film-makers. *The Great Murder Mystery* was synopsised for distributors as "Holmes goes into a trance, to pin a murder on an escaped gorilla" and added, for the benefit of those who had never heard of "The Murders in the Rue Morgue", " – not based on Conan Doyle"! The Eclair Cie. of France bought the rights to make nine good versions of original stories in 1912.

At last in 1914 Britain caught up. The Samuelson Film Company produced *A Study in Scarlet*, using the Cheddar Gorge for the Rocky Mountains and Southport sands for Death Valley. Nobody knows who they used for Sherlock Holmes, except

ABOVE: John Barrymore, perhaps the most famous actor ever to play the great detective.

that he was an accountant in Samuelson's Birmingham office. He is said to have played the part very well, and surviving stills show that G. B. Samuelson was quite right to think that this complete amateur's looks fitted the role perfectly. Two years later the same company made *The Valley of Fear*. And in that year, Essanay Films recorded Gillette's performance on film.

The breakthrough came after the war. Starring in 1921, the Stoll Film Company made 47 *Adventures of Sherlock Holmes* featuring Eille Norwood, who really rather resembled Professor Bell. These were well-made, reasonably faithful renderings of the original stories, with slightly updated settings to harmonise them with *The Strand*'s completely up-to-date illustrations of the same period. Conan Doyle thoroughly approved of Norwood's performances. He was further delighted when Hollywood rather romanticised his character to fit it to the perfect profile of John Barrymore in 1922. Both had rightful places in his oeuvre, he chuckled. Jonas Oldacre, who faked his own murder to escape his creditors and avenge himself on the son of the woman who rejected him, was "The **Norwood** Builder". And **Barrymore** was the name of the sinister butler at Baskerville Hall. Barrymore's film was shown in England under the title *Moriarty*. *Sherlock Holmes* probably already seemed a little hackneyed.

Talkies were obviously of great benefit to Holmes filming. The master's words were as effective as his appearance in establishing his superiority. But for a few years producers were at a loss to find the perfect impersonator. Clive Brooks made two reasonable adventures: *The Return of Sherlock Holmes* and *Sherlock Holmes*. But he was not really sufficiently hawklike. Raymond Massey in *The Speckled Band* was disastrously unconvincing, despite having the support of Lyn Harding, the stage's

RIGHT: A poster from the 1959 horror film The Hound of the Baskervilles, *starring Peter Cushing as Sherlock Holmes and Christopher Lee.*

OPPOSITE: The 1946 film Terror by Night *uses elements from Conan Doyle's story "The Adventure of the Empty House", "The Sign of Four" and "The Disappearance of Lady Frances Carfax".*

Dr Grimesby Rylott. Robert Rendel was as bad in *The Hound of the Baskervilles*. Reginald Owen was indistinct enough to play Watson to Brooks's Holmes, and then take the role of Holmes himself in a version of *A Study in Scarlet*.

But in 1931 the perfect Holmes came to the screen. Arthur Wontner made the part his own for the rest of the decade, winning plaudits from Conan Doyle's daughter Jean (formerly "Billy"). Wontner's interpretation, like nearly all stage and screen Holmeses, sacrificed some of the original's frigidity. Unhappily, his films have not been given frequent re-airing on television like those of his successors, so it is not possible to judge his performances. But audiences thought them perfect, unless they remained completely besotted with Eille Norwood's work. It is possible to say with certainty from the stills that there has never, ever been a Holmes who looked so perfectly and exactly Paget's illustrations brought to life: figure, profile, hairline, and even, unusually, the bow tie tucked under the turned-down collar.

Yet Wontner was upstaged in 1939 when Basil Rathbone starred in *The Hound of the Baskervilles*. For the first time, a production took real care with the work as a period piece, as well as following the text fairly closely. And Rathbone's clean-cut features and chilly manner suited Homes admirably. Enjoyable today, this was the best Sherlock Holmes film that had been made to date. It was followed a year later by an almost equally careful, almost equally successful *The Adventures of Sherlock Holmes*. And then it all fell apart with the war. Rathbone's acting still impressed Holmesians. But the settings underwent a rapid updating, and Sherlock was to be seen foiling the machinations of Nazi spies and voicing patriotic sentiments, or battling against American strip cartoonish, monstrous villains.

One very important convention was established by these films. Nigel Bruce's Dr Watson reflected the jazz age's opinion that anyone with an Afghan War wound must be a silly old buffer. Bruce exaggerated the occasional obtuseness for which Holmes mocked Watson. Henceforth it was open to any actor to portray Watson as a well-meaning comic blunderer: something Conan Doyle never did.

In the 1950s Peter Cushing starred in many Hammer horror films, and created Holmes in *The Hound of the Baskervilles*. The actor who casually swapped the roles of dreadful Dracula or hero Harker with Christopher Lee was well fitted to play a hero who throve on tension by keeping his cool truly icy. And with clear blue eyes that could relax into gentle benevolence, he let the fundamental humanity

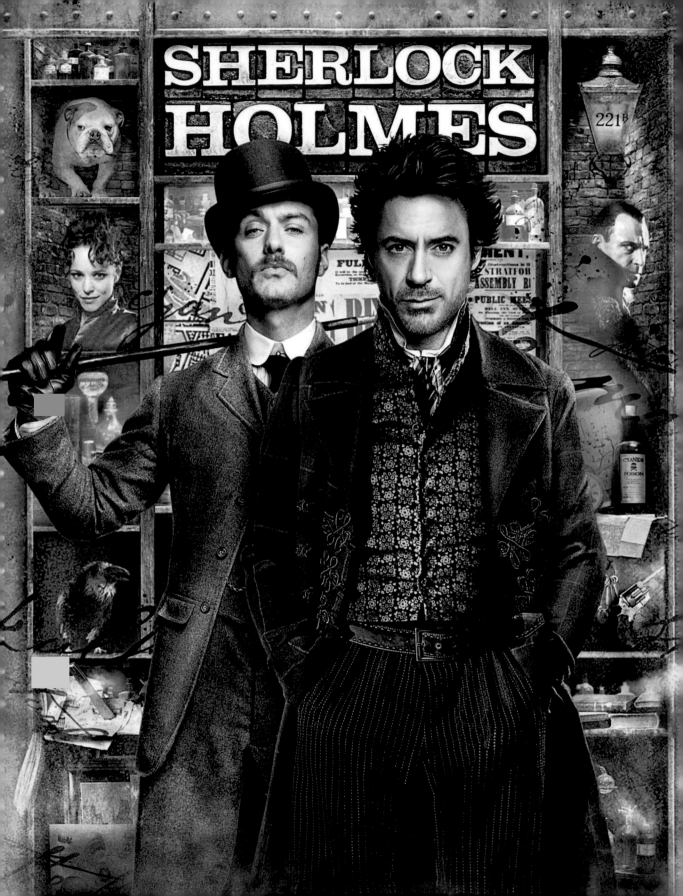

of Holmes emerge from time to time. But above all, Peter Cushing was a genuine Holmesian enthusiast who knew the books intimately and collected Sherlockiana. It was presumably his influence that ensured that his final outing in the role (*The Masks of Death*, 1984) visualised Holmes as Conan Doyle's character, and not the Mickey Mouse variant of the popular imagination. He wore a frock coat and soft hat more often than a deerstalker and ulster. His ulster was hooded not caped. He wore spats out of doors and changed his jacket for a grey dressing gown indoors. His pipes were straight. His Watson (John Mills) was no buffoon.

In 2009 Robert Downey Jr. launched his bid to become the internationally recognised Sherlock Holmes, with Jude Law as his Watson and Rachel McAdams as Irene Adler – the adventuress Holmes nominated "*the* woman" in "A Scandal in Bohemia". She, like the British government, needs Holmes's help to foil criminal Lord Blackwood's sinister attempt to combine science with necromancy, and rule first Britain, and then the world. The film is very much a would-be twenty-first century blockbuster with explosions, special effects using national icons (like Tower Bridge still under construction), and a 'Perils of Pauline' moment when Irene is dragged toward the teeth of an enormous buzz saw. Holmes the cold brain is not much in evidence.

Most interestingly, James Fox, as a pillar of the establishment, is given the name 'Sir Thomas Rotherham', which was also the name of one of the co-founders of

OPPOSITE: The 2009 Sherlock Holmes *film directed by Guy Ritchie and starring Robert Downey Jr as Sherlock and Jude Law as Dr Watson.*

ABOVE: Noomi Rapace, Robert Downey Jr and Jude Law in the 2009 film.

Holmes's putative Oxford College as suggested in this book's section, 'Education and Early Years'. And at one point Downey wears an ascot tie in Lincoln College dark and light blue. Could *The World of Sherlock Holmes* have been the designer's source?

At the end of the film it is revealed that Irene Adler, despite have enjoyed a steamy romance with Holmes after the end of her marriage, is now working for Professor Moriarty. This signalled a pretty clear intention to develop a series if the casting and scripting worked, and in 2009 *Sherlock Holmes: A Game of Shadows* was released. Irene Adler was assassinated quite rapidly, as Moriarty (Jared Harris) wove a string of assassinations around the world in his plot to start a World War and profit hugely. The attempted kidnapping and assassination of Dr and Mrs Watson, and Holmes himself, was foiled by derring-do and explosions, but Stephen Fry as Mycroft Holmes, added a little more brain power. And after the famous, fatal trip to the Reichenbach Falls, Holmes silently reappeared to add a question mark to Watson's "The End" on his typed account of the master's adventures.

A third Sherlock Holmes film is planned, but will not meet its once-projected deadline of 2014, and it remains to be seen whether Downey and Law will rank up there with Rathbone and Bruce.

But another medium has long dominated: when Peter Cushing died, his obituaries noted that he had played Holmes often, in films *and* on television.

RADIO AND TELEVISION

The figures are astonishing. Sherlock Holmes has appeared in 200–300 films, and made 1,000–2,000 appearances on radio and television! Basil Rathbone alone is said to have broadcast over 200 performances as Holmes.

The first radio Holmes was Orson Welles in 1934. His Mercury Theatre pioneered richly imaginative drama in sound until, notoriously, he went too far with *The War of the Worlds*, and spoofed a good many citizens of the east coast USA into believing that they really were being invaded by Martians. The Holmes stories obviously lent themselves to radio. Conan Doyle always used dialogue extremely effectively to sweep his narratives along and lend pace and tension to the stories. "The game's afoot!" is worth paragraphs of lurid description. "I have the threads almost in my hand!" is a recurrent image, redolent of the detective's mind mastering the case. We recall that *A Study in Scarlet* was originally to be entitled *The Tangled Skein*. Well-bred British voices, rising to crescendos of excitement on the trail, sinking back to careful thought, backed up by the sound effects of a gigantic snuffling hound, creeping footsteps, sudden pistol shots: these things were wonderfully exciting during the two or three decades when the wireless supplied the family's normal domestic entertainment. We probably owe the tag "Elementary, my dear Watson!" to radio scriptwriters, adapting and dramatising the stories for the sound medium. Welles returned to the microphone in 1957 to play Professor Moriarty.

OPPOSITE: Jeremy Brett as Holmes with Edward Hardwicke as Watson in the late 1980s television series.

The BBC first broadcast Carleton Hobbes as Holmes in 1947. With Norman Shelley as his Watson, the great radio actor went on supplying the voice of Holmes until 1969, by which time television had conquered all. Producer Raymond Raikes made the first experiment in stereophonic sound broadcasting with Sherlock Holmes extracts in 1958. Listeners who had television sets were invited to turn on their sound at the same time as the radio played, and listen to a hansom cab's wheels move from one speaker to the other; a pistol shot ring out at one side of the room while a voice cried from the other.

But television has given most people their image of Sherlock Holmes for the last 50 years. The Basil Rathbone films became staples of American afternoon TV and viewers were quickly able to see the difference between 20th Century Fox's reasonably respectful treatment of Sherlock, and Universal's crude exploitation

of the character in such un-Doylean adventures as *Sherlock Holmes and the Spider Woman,* or *The Scarlet Claw.* However, Rathbone's playing was consistent and intelligent, making him many people's preferred Holmes to this day. He himself came to regret the inescapable typecasting, especially when autograph hunters asked him to sign his name as "Sherlock Holmes"!

The BBC produced its first televised Holmes adventure in 1958. In 1964, Douglas Wilmer starred in a series of twelve. He was firm and incisive, but perhaps a little blunt for the mastermind. The adventures gripped. But for many, the most memorable feature of the 1960s televised adventures was Nigel Stock's Watson. This raised Bruce's comic treatment to new heights. Stock was sublimely dim-witted; unfailingly astonished by the simplest explanations of things; a bewildered foil who gave conviction to Holmes's vaunted intellectual superiority. And withal, Stock's Watson, doggedly following his friend on the perplexing paths of adventure, shone with the essential decency that had always made Conan Doyle's creations lovable. Though the

THE JACK THE RIPPER MURDERS.
Sherlock Holmes lifts the veil of
secrecy, corruption and terror at the
heart of the throne of England itself.
Clue by clue...murder by murder...

MURDER
BY
DECREE

Robert A. Goldston Presents A Film By Bob Clark
Starring CHRISTOPHER PLUMMER · JAMES MASON
DAVID HEMMINGS · SUSAN CLARK · ANTHONY QUAYLE
JOHN GIELGUD and FRANK FINLAY
and DONALD SUTHERLAND as "The Psychic" Robert Lees
and GENEVIÈVE BUJOLD as Annie Crook
"MURDER BY DECREE"
Screenplay By John Hopkins · Music By Carl Zittrer and Paul Zaza
Executive Producer Len Herberman
Produced by Rene Dupont and Bob Clark · Directed By Bob Clark
A Highlight Theatrical Productions Production Produced in Cooperation
With The Canadian Film Development Corp. and Famous Players Limited
AVCO EMBASSY PICTURES Release

PG PARENTAL GUIDANCE SUGGESTED
SOME MATERIAL MAY NOT BE SUITABLE FOR CHILDREN

Read the Ballantine Paperback

ABOVE: A poster for the 1979 film Murder by Decree, *starring Christopher Plummer, James Mason, Donald Sutherland, Geneviève Bujold, Susan Clark, David Hemmings, John Gielgud, Anthony Quayle and Frank Finlay.*

OPPOSITE: The recent BBC series Sherlock *has re-invented the character for the modern age. This new Sherlock Holmes, played to huge critical acclaim by Benedict Cumberbatch, and supported by Martin Freeman as Dr Watson, solves mysteries in a modern-day London using all the benefits of digital technology.*

character was in most ways a travesty of the original, it had merits of its own that led a lot of viewers who never read the books to feel let down when more perfect dramatisations came to the screen 20 years later. In 1968 the BBC started Peter Cushing on another fifteen Holmes adventures, fixing him in the popular mind as one of the great Sherlocks.

Granada's series with Jeremy Brett weaned many fans away from their attachment to Basil Rathbone. Brett's features, like Cushing's, were suitably hawklike: an obvious improvement on Douglas Wilmer's more oval face. His playing suggested real intelligence, as Rathbone's and Cushing's had. But to it he added the melancholy sensitivity that made Conan Doyle's character so memorable. Jeremy Brett was genuinely sensitive to his surroundings. When location filming for the series look him to Carn Galver on the West Penwith moors, he was so struck by that eerie, romantic landscape, its desolation relieved by the huge crags of the Great Galver, the minestacks of Ding Dong West and Greenbarrow, the broken toothed stone circle of the Nine Maidens, and the sea to north and south, that he decided on the spot that one day he would have a house in the district. Unhappily, he did not live to realise the ambition.

The excellent use of locations in the series was a mark of the distance television had come from cardboard studio scenery with the microphone boom casting its occasional shadow. Direction was by professionals who had progressed well beyond the old sneer, from film-makers, that television didn't know how to pick out a character from a crowd without using close-up. Sets and costumes were created with a serious eye to the period and the illustrations in *The Strand*. This Holmes wore top hats and soft hats and elegant frock coats, not just the familiar deerstalker and ulster. And Watson retreated back from a comic mainstay to being the simple and straightforward companion in adventure. It was possible for the role to be recast in mid-series, David Burke and Edward Hardwicke respectively taking the part. Had Basil Rathbone lost Nigel Bruce, the fans would have been appalled and half the audience could have been lost. The Granada series was truly the *Adventures of Sherlock Holmes*, and it was the adventures and the Sherlock, both admirably true to the originals, which held attention.

Another actor was to become noted as a great Sherlock Holmes: Christopher Plummer took the part in a television version of *Silver Blaze* in 1977. This succeeded so well that he was cast in the role again, two years later, in the film *Murder by Decree*. But this went as far beyond Conan Doyle as Universal had done in pitting Rathbone against the Spider Woman and the Creeper. It was one of the most successful thefts of Sherlock Holmes.

Benedict Cumberbatch's series *Sherlock*, starting in 2010, was different. It updated the adventures to the present day. Its hero was a young Sherlock, in some ways reminiscent of the young Inspector Morse featured in its contemporary series *Endeavour*. Cumberbatch, however, was immensely successful in conveying a character whose immersion in his own unsurpassable intellect detached him from easy normal association with his fellow beings. Indeed, his icy remoteness has been compared with some aspects of Asperger Syndrome. Such a chilling individual urgently needed a humanising Watson, and perfect casting came in the form of Martin Freeman, fresh from large screen success as Bilbo Baggins in *The Lord of the Rings* series. (In the subsequent trilogy *The Hobbit*, Cumberbatch gave voice to the dragon Smaug.)

Three 90-minute episodes, rather than the usual six of 60) minutes each, permitted more elaborate psychological development in stories that took inspiration from Conan Doyle originals. The producers tried to make modern London as iconic as the original Sherlock's city of fogs and cobblestones and hansom cabs. They startled most viewers with the utterly convincing leap to his death from a high building with which Cumberbatch ended the second series in "The Reichenbach Fall". Ending the third with another cliff-hanger as Sherlock appeared to have been outwitted, arrested, and fated to suffer conviction for murder was less satisfying, as it promised a year's wait for a resolution without the justification of Conan Doyle's original. But the producers had certainly succeeded in their avowed aim of breaking away from treatments of the detective that were too reverential and slow-moving in their determination to recapture Victorian times.

When SBS announced its intention of producing a modernised Sherlock Holmes based in America, they were criticised for imitating *Sherlock*. In the event, *Elementary* proved so different that it won critical approval and repeat seasons. Johnny Lee Miller's Sherlock is an Englishman with a serious drug problem living in New York and applying his old deductive skills from his days as an English police detective. His Dr Watson, played by Lucy Liu, is a surgeon. Irene Adler has formerly been Sherlock's lover, but is belatedly identified as the real Moriarty. Mrs Hudson retains her own gender, but is now the tenant of Sherlock and Watson and cleans up for them rather than being their landlady. Both modern Sherlock television programmes can probably anticipate reasonably long-running new series.

OPPOSITE: Jonny Lee Miller as Sherlock and Lucy Liu as Dr Watson in the hit American series Elementary *first broadcast in 2012.*

PARODIES, TRAVESTIES AND THEFTS

Basil, the Great Mouse Detective was the Disney studio's Christmas offering for 1987. In a relatively lean period when they seemed to have lost some of the zest of their better creations, it was a thoroughly entertaining cartoon. The evocative animation of 221B Baker Street in foggy London was particularly effective. And nobody protested that there was any impiety in translating the Great Sherlock into a squeaking caricature like the little French mice in Disney's *Cinderella*.

For the theft of Conan Doyle's character had become almost a literary genre of its own. Holmes has probably appeared on the sidelines or in the foreground of more books and stories by later writers than any other fictional creation. I cannot pretend to have surveyed them all, and doubt whether even the most dedicated Sherlockian researcher would ever guarantee having picked up all his posthumous reappearances. I recall a pulp sci-fi story which had an alien or future researcher interested in the mighty human "Sherk", it being obvious to such a scholar that "Sherlock" and "Shakespeare" were corruptions of the name of the same man, immediately identifiable by the idolisation in every reference to him. I recall another entertaining novel in which Sherlock himself was a time traveller stranded from the future, where his real occupation was to be the greatest actor of his aeon.

A pleasantly entertaining combination of sci-fi and Sherlock was put together by CBS Entertainment in 1987. Margaret Colin, as Watson's American grand-daughter, inherited the doctor's abandoned home in England, and found there Sherlock's cryonically preserved body, awaiting a time when the march of science would permit his revival and resurrection. After which, Michael Pennington in deerstalker and Norfolk jacket accompanied Miss Watson to America, overcoming his fear of flying and general bewilderment at twentieth-century inventions, to help her set her failing private detective agency back on its feet.

The Seven-Per-Cent Solution, written by Nicholas Meyer in 1974, and filmed by Universal two years later, carried Holmes back into a world of science fact. The cocaine habit, it seemed, had turned Holmes's brain. Moriarty, "the Napoleon of crime", was a complete fantasy arising from drug-induced paranoia. There was a Professor Moriarty and he *did* have a guilty secret. But he was no criminal: just a harmless maths coach who had once been Sherlock and Mycroft's private tutor. Mycroft and Watson, appalled by the deterioration of the great detective's mind, rush him off to Vienna to be treated by … Sigmund Freud! The use of Freud as a great genius in historical fantasies and parodies curiously started just as feminists perceived his sexism, biographers exposed his mistakes and moments of intellectual timidity, and scientists accepted the statistical evidence that psychoanalysis was of little more value than conversation with a sympathetic friend: all combining to topple the man from the pinnacle of esteem where he sat during the 1950s and '60s. Alan Arkin played Freud in the highly entertaining film, with Nicol Williamson as the neurotic Holmes, and Laurence Olivier as a memorable Moriarty, convincingly pleading that he was no criminal and suffered dreadful persecution on account of the great detective's obsession! Nicholas Meyer returned to successful pastiche of Holmes with *The West End Horrors* in 1976.

Peter Cushing's *The Masks of Death* was another pastiche, true to the character and period, but inventing a new story. This was sensibly and persuasively placed in 1913, deliberately overlooking the fact that Conan Doyle's Holmes was supposed to be wearing a beard and posing as Altamont the Fenian in that year. For Cushing was now too old to look convincing as Holmes in the years before his retirement.

Christopher Plummer's version in *Murder by Decree* introduced the fictional character of Holmes into sheer fiction that already masqueraded as fact and deceived a great many people. An elderly gentleman calling himself Joseph Sickert told a pack of lies on television in 1973, the gist of which was that his grandmother had secretly and illegally married Queen Victoria's grandson, and the Jack the Ripper murders were perpetrated by Freemasons led by the royal physician, Sir William Gull, to eliminate prostitutes who knew this guilty secret. More people read and believed Stephen Knight's book developing this twaddle than took in Sickert's confession in *The Sunday Times* that it was untrue. And *Murder by Decree* discreetly changed the names, but sent Christopher Plummer and James Mason on the trail in 1888 to unravel this mystery. It must be hoped

OPPOSITE: Robert Duvall, Nicol Williamson and Alan Arkin in the 1976 film The Seven-Per-Cent Solution, *in which Dr Watson is convinced that Sherlock's mind has been turned by a severe drug addiction.*

that the 1980 film may prove the last time that directors send Holmes careering through the city in the costume he rightly reserved for the country!

Witty travesty is possibly commoner than serious exploitation of the Holmes character. M. J. Trow's delightful "Inspector Lestrade" books take Sherlock's rival; make him a bungler; but have him stumble on the right solutions by a combination of luck and judgement. Regrettably, the splendidly absurd character of Sherlock Holmes himself is dropped after the first adventure, in which Lestrade, too, catches Jack the Ripper. Trow's Holmes is a glorious figure of fun, prancing around London brandishing the wrong end of the stick, but fully persuaded by his toadies, the two doctors, Watson and Doyle, that he is a great universal genius.

The 1988 film *Without a Clue* also proposed an amusing travesty. Dr Watson is offered as the real detective brain. But having discreetly ascribed his published adventures to the imaginary Sherlock Holmes, he has been forced to employ an actor to learn his lines, follow his cues, and appear before the press in the guise of the Great Detective. Unhappily, the actor Reginald Kincaid is a drunken, womanising disaster. But Watson is stuck with him, since the press refuses to believe in "the Crime doctor". Despite excellent performances from Ben Kingsley as Watson and Michael Caine as Sherlock/Kincaid, the film did not really work (for me, at least). And unlike the almost simultaneous *Basil the Mouse Detective*, *Without a Clue* did provoke some rumbles from dedicated Sherlockians.

ABOVE: Michael Caine as Sherlock Holmes and Ben Kingsley as Dr Watson in the 1988 comedy Without a Clue.

THE SHERLOCKIAN GAME

The great Sherlockian Game was invented by Fr Ronald Knox. Or, at least, he believed it was when he claimed to have grown tired of it. It consists of pretending that Holmes and Watson were real people and the Holmes canon the historical documents from which their lives may be reconstructed. (Cf Chapter 1 of this book!) Conan Doyle, in this game, becomes Watson's "literary agent" who placed the documents in *The Strand*.

The game is enormous fun because of Conan Doyle's ubiquitous inaccuracies. Where real historical documents show lacunae, hiatuses and contradictions – and many do – it is the duty of the historian to explain how they occurred, and tease out the probable truth. Errors in the text may have come from the writer's faulty memory. (Watson was looking back 30 or more years when he published stories in the 1920s.) Or his bad handwriting. (Watson's inability to write clear numerals has been blamed for many misdatings.) Or his deliberate suppression of sensitive facts. (Since Watson does this quite openly in "The Illustrious Client", and "Charles Augustus Milverton", why shouldn't he have done it elsewhere?) Truly daring Sherlockian scholars may rest their case on that obtuseness which Sherlock criticised in Watson, and assert that the good doctor simply "didn't understand".

Then the Sherlockian may enjoy a little genuine historical research. Or a lot. Those dedicated to dating the stories have worked through almanacs to decide in which year "the 15th fell on a Tuesday", and so ascribe a precise time-frame for every adventure. If Sherlock and Watson take a train to Dartmoor, old *Bradshaws* may be combed to decide exactly which train they took, and when they departed and arrived. When Conan Doyle uses the fiction writer's common device of grounding his work in reality by naming some real places, but then saves innocent householders from nuisance visits by making up a nearby location, the Sherlockian turns to old maps or walks over the terrain to decide where "Watson" really meant.

Factual historical dates can be mixed, *ad libitum*, with dates in the stories. If an "Adventure" was published in 1892, it must have taken place before that date, even if internal evidence suggests that it followed some event that is dated later in another story. The Battle of Maiwand seems to pinpoint the date of Holmes's meeting Watson. But time has to be allowed for Watson's treatment and convalescence from his wound. Time for him to return from Afghanistan. Time for him to live in London. There is room for happy disagreement.

And, as we have seen, the more egregious mistakes invite imaginative invention. In true historical scholarship, too, this may happen. If it is labelled "speculation" it can be ignored. But a "hypothesis" should be formed when sources clearly contradict one another, and there is no clear reason for preferring one over the other. "Deduction" is admissible but not conclusive. No conclusion should ever be reached by piling one deduction on another, let alone as is all too common, a chain of speculations leading to a triumphant assertion.

Sherlockians are not limited by these cruel laws of history, and may speculate to their hearts' content. Was Watson married once, twice or three times? Deduction and speculation can prove any of them. Why did Mary Watson call her husband James, when he was really called John? Any answer to that question is bound to be invention; even the simple suggestion that it was Watson's slip of the pen or a printer's error, for the true Sherlockian is not allowed to say, "Conan Doyle was careless, and wrote each story for its own immediate purpose of publication, without reference back to earlier pieces."

The Sherlockian game has been running for more than 80 years now. This seems astonishing, until one realises that people who like mystery stories and enjoy solving puzzles have the sort of curiosity which naturally lends itself to scholarship. If they enjoy teasing out "the truth" of an Agatha Christie plot, they will derive even more satisfaction from chasing down the truth of a real historical puzzle. But historical scholarship is time-consuming and expensive. And historical mysteries are often insoluble from the data at hand, which can lead to bad-tempered quarrelling among scholars who think they've found the answer. Disraeli warned people never to give an opinion as to the side of Whitehall on which Charles I was beheaded. Today, anyone who wants a peaceful life might be well advised not to postulate an identity for Jack the Ripper, or dip a toe into the acid bath of supposed mystery surrounding President Kennedy's assassination, or try to establish the exact details of Elvis Presley's or Marilyn Monroe's deaths. The emotional charge, which was the largest reason for those deaths becoming "mysteries", made it immediately predictable that an industry of silly conspiracy theorists would grow up around the self-explanatory death of Princess Diana.

Other "mysteries" seem transparently absurd to the world of common sense. While it is obvious (by definition) that some flying objects have been seen but not identified, UFOlogy is not a field attracting our down-to-earth neighbours. From Flying Saucers, through "the Roswell incident" and its ludicrous film of "scientists" dissecting an obviously manufactured "alien", to the accounts of those who genuinely believe they have met Little Green Men and gone up in their spaceships, this is a realm of transparent fantasy. The belief that Elvis is still alive belongs to the same dreamland. So, probably, does the Loch Ness monster, which must have died by now, if it really existed in the 1930s when the most persuasive sightings were reported.

Sherlockians have all the fun of "solving mysteries" with none of the penalties. Since they know it is all a game, they are incapable of "faking" or accusing each other of doing so. Since their "solutions" will never change history or make them great reputations or large sums of money, they are not tempted into the vicious ego-clashes which have marred recent Ripper research. Since they deal with fictitious characters, they will slander neither the dead nor the living, as Kennedy buffs and Presley murder freaks do.

They are sometimes criticised by humourless outsiders for treating fiction as fact. Why shouldn't they, as long as they know what they are doing? They almost invariably prove to be jolly, good-natured people having a lot of friendly fun.

OPPOSITE: An illustration from the story "The Sign of Four", showing Holmes and Watson examining footprints in the attic.

WORLD-WIDE SHERLOCKIAN CLUBS

Maybe Monsignor Knox really had lost interest in the Sherlockian game by the time he reached middle age. But soon after he had proposed the rules by which it might be played – and what a passion that man seems to have had around 1928 for inventing rules to govern the pleasures of light literature! – he and Dorothy Sayers and a few friends formed themselves into the Sherlock Holmes Society. Dorothy Sayers, as we have seen from her suggestions about Holmes's university and Watson's middle name, was a player of great distinction. But the society did not survive the outbreak of war.

Already, however, what would become the most important Sherlockian group had started in America. Bibliophile Christopher Morley founded the Baker Street Irregulars on 6 January 1934, "to perpetuate the myth that Sherlock Holmes is not a myth". 6 January is the Sherlockian choice for Holmes's birthday, on the slender grounds that he left his breakfast untasted on 7 January at the beginning of *The Valley of Fear*, so he may have been celebrating the night before; and he quotes from *Twelfth Night* more than any other Shakespeare play, and *Twelfth Night* is 6 January, and so … Ever since, the Baker Street Irregulars have held their annual dinner in New York on the Friday falling closest to 6 January. About 500 people have been elected to membership since 1934, and they include many names of distinction. Greatest of these was Franklin Delano Roosevelt, five of whose letters mentioning Sherlock Holmes became such valuable collectors' items that a limited edition of 150 facsimiles was printed in 1949, half of which were presented to the then members of the BSI, and the other half sold to the public at $15.00 each.

Other notable Irregulars included Rex Stoute, the creator of Nero Wolfe; Don Marquis, the creator of *Archy and Mehitabel*; one of the two cousins who were "Ellery Queen"; Isaac Asimov the science fiction creator of robots *par excellence*; writer and critic Anthony Boucher, who gave his name to America's most successful convention of crime fiction fans and to the "Anthony", one of the three most prestigious crime writing awards. (The other two being the "Edgar" and the "Agatha", it is perhaps time the Sherlockians established an "Arthur".)

William S. Baring-Gould was the Irregular who gave Sherlockians their "Bible". His two-volume *Annotated Sherlock Holmes* (1968), picked up and cross-referenced allusions throughout the canon, offering a usable tool for the scholar (with a sense of humour) as well as a pleasure for enthusiasts and an invaluable basis from which to write Sherlockian scholarship. The Irregulars have been publishing "Writings about the Writings" since 1940, and a quarterly *Baker Street Journal* since 1946. Baring-Gould also wrote an exceptionally jokey biography of Holmes in 1962, postulating an eldest brother Sherrinford to inherit the family estate in Yorkshire, and identifying Inspector Athelney Jones as Jack the Ripper, with *Watson* rather than Holmes catching him!

Membership of the Irregulars is by invitation. The current membership stands at about 250. But since 1935 the Irregulars have supported "scion" societies open

DOROTHY L. SAYERS

to everyone. They meet on their own terms and at their own convenience: publish their own Sherlockian journals if they so wish, and often have wonderful names drawn from The Writings. "An Irish secret society at Buffalo" is a particularly attractive example, neatly snipping a phrase from "His Last Bow". E-mail addresses among the mass of Sherlockian information on the Internet reveal still more eccentric scion societies: "The Three Pipe Problems of Nashville", "Von Herder Airguns Ltd", "The Red Circle of Washington", or "The Crew of the Barque Lone Star".

Baker Street Irregular John Bennett Shaw was interviewed on television for the Holmes centenary in 1987. He was introduced as a leading light of the most peculiar of the American scion societies: a little group who meet in the tiny New Mexico town of Moriarty every November to dump bags of manure on the marker they declare to be Moriarty's grave, and wish him "Unhappy birthday, you bastard!"

Mr Shaw's more significant claim to fame was as one of the greatest collectors of Sherlockiana. In fact, as his collection increased he had to extend his house to hold it. First and most important come the texts of the canon, in as many editions as possible. First editions, of course, are subject to the same inflationary pressure as the Roosevelt letters: dedicated Sherlockians are competing with other types of collectors for their possession. When a *Beeton's Christmas Annual* for 1887 last came on the market, its estimated value was £10,000–£15,000. It auctioned for nearer £25,000. The library becomes more extensive as other works by and about Conan Doyle are added, together with the multiplicity of books about Holmes. In death as in life, the creation has outweighed the creator, and far more has been written about Sherlock Holmes than about Sir Arthur Conan Doyle.

Artefacts, games and puzzles contribute the next collectable area of Sherlockiana. There are statuettes, pictures, toby jugs and pieces of Sherlockian pottery. There are boxed board games, card games, and more recently boxed detective puzzle games with cards of clues and bits of stories and characters for players to assume at "murder mystery" dinner parties. These have evolved from the very popular "Murder Mystery weekends" organised by tour companies in England with the American market especially in view. A Sherlock Holmes murder mystery weekend at the Sherlock Holmes Hotel in Baker Street was one of the first of these.

The Baker Street Irregulars have always taken a generous interest in Sherlock's London, subscribing to have plaques placed on important Sherlockian sites. And they correspond with national Sherlock Holmes societies in France and Australia. A more surprising development in the Sherlockian world is the huge Japanese interest. Postwar tour companies were surprised to find how many Japanese visitors put Baker Street above the Tower of London as a place of pilgrimage. Japan's Sherlock Holmes Club is now the world's largest: it must have been an error in translation that had their spokesman claim this was because members wanted to understand Holmes as "part of the history of their culture"!

SHERLOCKIANS IN LONDON

221B Baker Street. One of London's most famous addresses. It did not exist when Holmes created it. The house's situation was then in Upper Baker Street, and its number did not exist.

In 1932, the Abbey National Building Society moved into a large building numbered 219–229 Baker Street. They rapidly discovered that people from all over the world were writing to the address asking for Mr Holmes' attention: people in search of missing relatives and lost contacts; admirers who sent greeting cards; even the occasional befuddled police chief hoping for help. The Abbey National

OPPOSITE: Franklin D. Roosevelt, statesman and Baker Street Irregular.

BELOW: Anthony Howlett as Moriarty and Philip Porter as Sherlock Holmes at Reichenbach.

appointed a staff member to receive and reply to this mail, usually intimating that when last heard from, Mr Holmes had retired to Sussex where he kept bees. The postbag rose to 20 to 40 items a week, swelled by schoolchildren whose teachers encouraged them to write to Sherlock Holmes. The children ultimately received a gift pack with a badge, a bookmark, commemorative stamps and a booklet, as well as a letter.

Confusion began in 1991, when the recently opened Sherlock Holmes Museum at 227 Baker Street was given permission to change its address to 221B. They then demanded that Abbey National cede to them the right to receive the mail. Abbey National refused, and the dispute over the right to receive the correspondence of a non-existent man, who would have been nearly 140 years old if still living, found its way, astonishingly, to the law courts. The wrangle went on until 2005, when Abbey National moved to new premises, and since then the Museum has had the unchallenged right to receive mail addressed to Sherlock Holmes.

Marylebone Borough Council had the idea of making a Sherlock Holmes exhibition its contribution to the Festival of Britain in 1951. This has survived in two places. The serious and scholarly collection of books, magazines and other writings has been held in Marylebone Public Library and kept up to date. The curator gives knowledgeable assistance to the many students, ranging from keen Sherlockians researching Watson's wives, to serious scholars examining literary history. And the demands on the limited space resources available are such that it is necessary to telephone her in advance and make an appointment in the queue of researchers wanting to use the facility.

The other Festival of Britain exhibit in Marylebone was a loving recreation of the sitting-room in 221B Baker Street, with pipes, jack-knifed correspondence, chemistry bench, and Persian slipper carefully placed in the clutter of Holmes's notorious untidiness, and a few extra goodies like the skin of the "swamp adder"

stretched on the wall and the slightly kinked poker, which Dr Grimesby Roylott bent threateningly into a hoop, only to see the equally strong Holmes unbend it again. The room was housed in the Abbey National's building, and stayed there until 1957, when it was transferred to the Sherlock Holmes public house in Northumberland Street.

This was a refurbishment of the Northumberland Arms, itself part of the former Northumberland Hotel where Sir Henry Baskerville stayed on arriving in England, and Stapleton purloined his boot to let the Hound learn his scent. Whitbread's brewery, the pub landlords, would have liked a Sherlock Holmes pub in Baker Street, but no licensed premises were available. So they added to the Baskerville connection the suggestion that the hotel might have been visited by Holmes and Watson before they took the Turkish baths they both loved in the establishment opposite. (The stories never say which baths the pair visited.) A disgruntled barmaid at the time complained that the room in the corner of the dining room took up space where she could have run a sandwich bar that would have brought in £50 a week. But it must have paid for itself over and over again in the number of tourists (especially American and Japanese) who have dropped in and supped their pint for the privilege of seeing the famous room. The success of the new pub became manifest early in the 1960s, by which time it was normally so crowded that the London branch of Truro School Old Boys' Association had to abandon it as the venue for their informal monthly gatherings.

The Festival of Britain also led to the formation of England's premier Sherlock Holmes Society. Some Marylebone Councillors had opposed the Holmes memorial project in 1950, sniffily dismissing "this character, associated with murky crime". The stuffy Library Committee wanted "something on public health" instead!

They reckoned without Holmes-lovers in the Establishment. Seventeen letters of protest appeared in *The Times*. "Watson", "Mycroft" and "Lestrade" were among the signatories. When Marylebone Council yielded, they took the advice of the weighty Holmesians on setting up the exhibition. And when their efforts were crowned with success, the Holmesians formed themselves into "the Sherlock Holmes Society of London" (the last two words becomingly differentiating themselves from Fr Knox's and Miss Sayers' original group). Sir Sydney Roberts, Vice-Chancellor of Cambridge University, was the first president. He was succeeded by Sir Paul (later Lord) Gore-Booth, head of the Diplomatic Service. The lovers of the "murky crime" character rather outweighed the councillors of Marylebone!

The London Holmes Society produced its own *Sherlock Holmes Journal*. It held regular meetings to hear papers and debates. It organised tours to places of Sherlockian interest. The most famous came in 1968, when Sir Paul (dressed as Holmes) wrestled with Charles Schofield QC, Master of the Middle Temple (dressed as Moriarty) on the edge of the Reichenbach Falls. They were photographed by over 100 journalists and appeared as the first item on the BBC news that night. The Society has revisited Reichenbach four times since then, the latest occasion

OPPOSITE: A silhouette of the Sherlock Holmes statue outside Baker Street station, London.

being in 1991 when the present chairman, barrister Anthony Howlett (at that time Remembrancer to the Lord Mayor of London), re-enacted Moriarty to businessman Philip Porter's Sherlock. They and 100 Sherlockians, all in glorious Victorian garb, had come to support Dame Jean Conan Doyle (little "Billy" being honoured in her own right, now, as an Air Commandant), who opened a Holmes Museum in the town of Meiringen at the foot of the falls.

Like the Baker Street Irregulars, the 1,000-strong Sherlock Holmes Society of London welcomes and encourages provincial branches with Holmesian names: "The Northern Musgraves" or "The Poor People of the Moor".

SERIOUS SCHOLARSHIP

Lovers of light literature are often annoyed when academe refuses to take their subject seriously. Sherlock Holmes did not feature on university syllabuses until American universities began offering courses on popular culture. Thereupon Ph.D theses on the Holmesian canon and the life and works of Sir Arthur Conan Doyle started to appear.

England is more cautious than America in admitting unusual fields of study. When Jonathan Cape issued a new edition of the complete Holmes with introductory critical essays, the only one-time academic among their contributors was Kingsley Amis, who had notoriously proved unacceptable to Cambridge University. But the roster of writers contributing was impressive: Graham Greene and his brother Sir Hugh, John Fowles and C. P. Snow, Angus Wilson, Julian Symons, Len Deighton and Eric Ambler. Len Deighton produced a particularly intelligent and insightful essay on *The Valley of Fear*.

In the early 1990s the books received the accolade of publication by the OUP as the Oxford Sherlock Holmes. To edit and introduce them, the press selected one of the finest and most influential postwar critics and teachers to emerge from Oxford, Professor W. W. Robson of Edinburgh. "Robbie" had an amazing and omnivorous memory for minor prose – not that he ever mistook it for major literature – and had always admired Conan Doyle's intelligent approach to detective fiction and his ability write evocative passages economically. Unhappily, he died with only *The Hound of the Baskervilles* and *The Case-Book* completed.

The series was finished by his colleague from Edinburgh's history department, Professor Owen Dudley Edwards, whose masterly study of Conan Doyle's life before 1887, *The Quest for Sherlock Holmes*, had given due weight to the importance of Bryan Charles Waller for the first time, and rigorously investigated Stonyhurst to look for possible originals of Conan Doyle's characters and outlook. Professor Edwards, however, was affected by a peculiar bug, which attacks many of us who write on Conan Doyle. Studying this benign and large-minded gentleman, for some reason, seems to induce an indefensible asperity in to our writing. I recognised this in myself when I had to erase some extravagant expressions of contempt for Edward VII from my first draft of this book. And until I wrote them, I had

never realised I despised the king so deeply! Professor Edwards bad-mouths almost all previous biographers of Conan Doyle, suggesting that they are unworthy of comparison with Dupin or Lecoq!

The biography of Sir Arthur Conan Doyle has always been dogged by problems. Adrian Conan Doyle guarded his father's reputation jealously. And, like Oscar Wilde's son Vivian Holland, he rather came to feel that his father's work owed him a living. Conan Doyle's books, papers and personal possessions had been divided equally in his will between Adrian, his sister Jean, and their brother Denis. Adrian effectively took charge of the papers.

He let his friend Hesketh Pearson use them for a biography in 1943. And the book ended their friendship. Pearson, the first really successful popular biographer in England, has always aroused differing reactions. By his immensely readable lives of Wilde, Disraeli, Shaw, and others, he put basic facts about those worthies into the public domain. But he was jokey, opinionated and inaccurate. He drew some completely unjustified and untrue conclusions from writers' fictional creations, and to many readers, he seemed to diminish the subjects for whom he professed

ABOVE: Len Deighton, whose introduction to The Valley of Fear *is one of the most perceptive critical essays on Conan Doyle.*

admiration by a cocksure certainty of his own superiority whenever he disagreed with them. Moreover, he sometimes gave them opinions they probably never held.

Adrian wanted a hagiography of his father. He rushed into print to say that his father was not vague and unobservant even though he also recalled his once going out wearing one brown and one black shoe! He tried to stop Pearson's biography from being reprinted. And he threatened lawsuits against Pearson.

In 1947 he made the papers available to John Dickson Carr, master of the "locked room" detective story, with whom he had collaborated to produce some pleasant pastiche "new" adventures of Sherlock Holmes. Carr's life of Conan Doyle was the standard biography until very recently, though it was quite unduly reverential and followed a bad convention of its time in making up conversations to dramatise events.

Charles Higham's 1976 biography was a great improvement, though he tended to proffer very dubious "originals" of characters. And he was never accepted as "standard" because he lacked access to the papers. First Adrian and then Denis's widow, the Princess Mdivani, entangled the memorabilia of the Conan Doyle estate in questionable sales, which tied up the papers in legal proceedings until

ABOVE: Conan Doyle with his second wife, Jean, and their family.

OPPOSITE: Statue of Sherlock Holmes by Gerald Ogilvie Laing, Picardy Place, Edinburgh, Scotland.

1996. Biographers had to work from the rather inadequate use Pearson and Carr had made of them.

Ronald Pearsall's biography of 1977 outraged fanatical Sherlockians. It was a debunking job and produced Professor Edwards' loudest outcries of protest and contempt. Yet Pearsall supplied necessary correctives to the extravagant respect in which Conan Doyle was generally held. Doyle was, after all, the admirer who was quite unaware that some of Major Drayson's astronomical theories were highly controversial, and rated the man with Copernicus. He was the writer whose carelessness allowed Martin Dakin to produce a quite fascinating Sherlockian work, methodically and entertainingly exposing the oversights and internal contradictions to be found in every single piece of Holmes fiction! He was far more of a dully conventional conservative imperialist than acclaim for his courage in taking up unpopular causes allowed. And he was the naive twerp who doggedly believed in the Cottingley fairies!

Unluckiest of Conan Doyle's biographers was Martin Booth, whose painstaking reassessment of his predecessors' work should have become standard, only to be put at risk by the donation of the Conan Doyle papers to the British Library within a few months of his publication. Access to these enabled Jon Lellenberg, Daniel Stashower and Charles Foley to produce in 2007 *Arthur Conan Doyle: A Life in Letters*, which cast a warm and human light on Conan Doyle's relations with "the ma'am", gave a clearer picture of George Turnavine Budd's abilities and eccentricities than previous lives had done, and enhanced the impression that Arthur Conan Doyle was, above all, a really decent human being.

BAKER STREET TODAY

Sherlockians visiting London today will probably make a beeline for Baker Street. Outside the underground station they will see an imposing bronze statue of Sherlock Holmes, the second such effigy created by sculptor John Doubleday. Although G. K. Chesterton had suggested in 1925 that London ought to have a statue of Sherlock (and been laughed at for his pains in *The Bookman*), funds had never been available. And so on the centenary of the first Holmes publication, the little Swiss town of Meirigen unveiled Doubleday's first effort in the presence of Dame Jean Conan Doyle, and went on to re-create the famous study in a Sherlock Holmes museum.

A few months later, in October 1988, Karuizawa Town in Japan, noted for its many statues of literary figures, unveiled Satoh Yoshinori's conception of Holmes, in honour of the translator of the adventures into Japanese.

In 1991, Edinburgh was the next to honour Sherlock, putting his statue near Conan Doyle's birthplace in Picardy Place. By this time the campaign to make smoking history had succeeded to the point that the great detective's love of a "three-pipe problem" was a bad example to children. This was wittily dealt with by inscribing on the pipe Magritte's famous surrealist title, "Ceci n'est pas un pipe."

And finally in 1999, London got its own 9-ft effigy where everyone expected it, at Baker Street Underground station.

Practically all the highly competitive walking tour companies in London offer Sherlock Holmes walks. It is the third most popular subject, after Jack the Ripper and Ghost walks.

There is one problem. Walkers *expect* that the tours will start from Baker Street. But apart from 221B there is not a great deal of Holmesiana in the vicinity to be shown. Oxford Street, where Holmes and Watson followed Sir Henry Baskerville, and Stapleton followed them in a false beard. Wigmore Street Post Office where Watson sent a telegram. Bentinck Street, where Moriarty tried to have Holmes run down, and Vere Street where a brick was dropped from the roof in another attempt on his life. After these locations, even John Muffty's Historical Walks, perhaps

the most learned of the companies, are reduced to mentioning Holmes's grandfather, the French painter Vernet, as they pass the Wallace Collection.

Richard Jones, proprietor of City Walks when it was the most successful group in London, once confided that the lack of genuine sites made Sherlock Holmes walks exceedingly difficult. Basically, he felt he had to get his walkers from 221B Baker Street to the Sherlock Holmes pub. On the way he used the stops to lay out Sherlock Holmes mysteries, and subsequently present their solutions. When I myself took three Sherlock Holmes walks for him in 1983, I offered the walkers the option of a walk around local true crime sites after they had seen "221B", and to my considerable relief, all accepted.

The obvious local alternative to looking at the Abbey National office in Baker Street is to go to No.239, which now bears the number 221B and a plaque identifying it as Sherlock Holmes's address, and houses the very successful Sherlock Holmes Museum. This began quite humbly with the first-floor front room made into a facsimile of Holmes and Watson's sitting-room. And another room holding a small case of exhibits like the birth certificate of an unfortunate Mr Holmes whose parents christened him Sherlock, and a letter from a naive small-town American police chief who thought that a real Sherlock Holmes in London might be able to help him in criminal investigation.

Mr John Aidiniantz was the man who set up the museum in 1991. He played the Sherlockian game to the hilt when callers came, pretending that Mr Holmes had just gone out, but visitors might go up the – "count them!" – seventeen stairs to his room.

The business looked likely to come to a sticky end in 1994, when Mr Aidiniantz was arrested for fraud. It was shown in court that he had taken out second mortgages on 238 Baker Street and two other properties in London, falsely claiming that any first mortgages had been paid off, and producing false references. Fortunately for Sherlockians, his mother Mrs Grace Riley was able to establish her title to the building, and with John separated from the business, she led it from strength to strength. Four more exhibition rooms were opened, and a fifth is expected next year. "Mrs Hudson's Restaurant" serves good traditional Sherlockian food to visitors. Two souvenir shops sell Sherlockian knick-knacks. And a Museum booklet expounds the influence and importance of Sherlock Holmes.

Aware that the Sherlockian clientele is likely to comprise serious students, Mrs Riley keeps her exhibits tightly related to the canon, and feels no serious regrets that space limitations prevent the use of waxworks and holograms and sounds and smells, such as those that feature in so many exhibition centres for today's tourists.

Further down the road, the Carlson Rezidor Hotel Group's deluxe associate hotel, the Sherlock Holmes, features memorabilia and Sherlockiana in its public places and 126 rooms. The luxury suites are the Baskerville Suite and the Reichenbach Suite. Moriarty's Restaurant never allows the evil professor's hand to

OPPOSITE: A view of 221B Baker Street – the London address of the fictional detective Sherlock Holmes.

influence food or service. And Dr Watson's Bar is available for those who feel the need of the gazogene and the spirit-case.

The serious Sherlockians, too, are bent on making a contribution to the Baker Street environment. Almost 90 years ago, G. K. Chesterton complained that a statue of Sherlock Holmes in Baker Street ought to match the statue of Peter Pan in Kensington Gardens. With the millennium approaching, the Sherlock Holmes Society of London commissioned John Doubleday, the sculptor of Leicester Square's Charlie Chaplin. They obtained the promise of a site on the slip-road by the station from London Underground. Finally they were able to gain planning permission and raise £10,000 to elevate Doubleday's creation from a 12-in maquette to an 11ft bronze on a plinth. This shows the long sweeping caped ulster, the deerstalker, the hawklike features, and the drop-stem meerschaum pipe.

Baker Street Irregulars and Sherlock Holmes Society members alike are apt to become a little earnest in praising their hero's immaculate virtues, hoping that their games do not really persuade misguided nutters to believe Sherlock Holmes really exists, and confidently assuming that he will survive as a glory of our literature well in the next century and beyond. In embarking on this book, however, I asked a fifteen-year-old pupil what she knew about Sherlock Holmes and whether she could describe him. She knew nothing and could offer no description. When I described the deerstalker, cape and magnifying glass, she immediately recognised this as a caricature of "a detective". So maybe all those advertisements and parodies mean that Paget's drawings and Gillette's selection from them will in fact outlive the real Sherlock Holmes. The immortal memory may become the memory of an immortal appearance.

RIGHT: Located in Karuizawa Town, Japan, this sculpture was erected to commemorate the work of Ken Nobuhara, who translated 60 Sherlock stories into Japanese.

OPPOSITE: A bronze statue of Sherlock Holmes in the town of Meiringen, Switzerland.

INDEX

Page numbers in *italics* type refer to illustrations. Holmes and Watson are indexed under their own names: other characters from Sherlock Holmes stories are indexed under "characters in Sherlock Holmes stories".

ACKNOWLEDGEMENTS

Grateful thanks to John L. Lellenberg of the Bakers Street Irregulars and Commander G.S. Stavert of The Sherlock Holmes Society of London for information generously supplied. Also to Geoff Drew, Glory Ward and Gug Kyriacou (the current "Secretary to Sherlock Holmes", all of the Abbey National Building Society. And to Mrs Grace Riley of the Sherlock Holmes Museum. And to Julia Clark and Alison Atkins of the Hilton Hotel Group.

To Paul Begg for trawling through recent publications and ensuring that I did not misrepresent them. To Keith Skinner and Causeway Resources for the absolutely invaluable collection of cuttings, photocopies, books and videos which comes up whenever their services are sought. To Richard Whittington-Egan for generous advice on the Edalji case and time spent looking up possible references to the Jack the Ripper case.

To Miss Catherine Cooke, curator of the Sherlock Holmes Collection in Marylebone Public Library, and the staffs of the British Library, the Guildhall Library, Kent County Library, and Canterbury, Maidstone and Sheerness Public Libraries. Also, to the libraries and members of Canterbury Christian Spiritualist Church.

To all in Carlton's picture research department for their usual wonderful job of finding things I hoped they could find and things I never dreamed of asking for. And too in design who put together something making my work look so much better than it deserves.

To Richard Jeffs, my agent and Sarah Larer, my editor for constant patience and encouragement; and for sorting out all the sides of setting up book agreements that I can't cope with and leaving me to read and write.

To Paul Savory and Jon Chai for hospitality when researching in London, and to Paul for continued use of his equipment, including time spent exploring the Internet.

CREDITS